Through the years many top notch, professional journalists have approached me about writing articles about my pioneering work, Human BioAcoustics. Invariably we would meet; sometimes, multi-hour interviews were requested. Months would go by until eventually the authors would come back to me explaining that they could not get their mind around the incredible work we were doing. The implications were too vast, the outcomes too extraordinary. The genre had much ancient history; and too much of mankind's future at stake for them to be able to create any meaningful composition. The idea that sounds, without accompanying music, have potential to be an efficient healing modality was more than they could comprehend. The concept that frequency could have created our universe and could be used to allow dominion over our biology and our DNA was a notion far afield from their reality.

I was far less than cautiously hopeful when Jill Mattson approached me to write a book about our work with sound and frequency-based biomarkers. I had read Jill's previous book about healing and knew that she had a depth of knowledge about the history of ancient sound. We met to discuss some ideas but I had little faith that anything would ever come from our exchange.

1

I was astonished, shortly thereafter, when Jill delivered a 400 page manuscript that encompassed my early life and history. It included a narrative of the initial development of the processes of Vocal Profiling right through to our most advanced data and strategies dealing with the effects of sound on human physiology and psychology. I was overwhelmed with appreciation that finally someone understood our efforts. Jill understood our work from an outsider's perspective, and as well as any insider who had been working with us for the last twenty years.

I was stunned at how she had originally woven all of our information into a compelling story about future medicine while simultaneously lacing it with ancient mystery school philosophies.

Jill, as an amateur writer, has brought together a unique awareness of Human BioAcoustics that professionals could not manage. Perhaps, it is her perspective as a violin performance aficionado that provides her with such an uninhibited view of what it takes to allow the soul to perceive sound as both pleasure and wellness. Now through Jill's publication about our work with BioAcoustic Biology, the rest of the world may benefit from what we have known for the past few decades.

*Sharry Edwards*

# Getting started:
# A little bit about the book

I first met Sharry Edwards in the fall of 2008 in Columbus, Ohio. She was soft-spoken and reserved, but the power of her presence and the feeling of quiet strength she radiated immediately struck me. I knew of Sharry's reputation from my years of study on the healing ability of sound. After meeting Sharry in person, I immediately wanted to include a chapter on her in an upcoming book. But after I began to digest the wealth of information I uncovered during my research, it became clear I could write several books on her alone. Since the realities in my life do not permit me the time for several books, I tried to condense the information into this one.

This book is organized into three parts. The book can be read cover to cover in the order it is presented, however that may not be for everyone. Part One: Sharry's Story, is aimed at the general reader. This section gives a brief biography of Sharry and presents her basic work and accomplishments in a nontechnical presentation. We see important events that affected her early development and the foundations of BioAcoustics. Part Two: Technical Details, continues where Part One left off but contains more challenging technical details. This part of the book can be read selectively depending upon the reader's background and interest level (*It could be a reference source for more advanced sound enthusiasts*). Finally, Part Three: Applications, focuses on how one can learn more about Sharry's pioneering work and start to apply her methods. Here I explore free beneficial applications of using sound in your voice that fit compatibly with Sharry's teachings. This section is intended for those interested in immediately starting with their own explorations of the benefits of BioAcoustics,[1] and better health through sound.

Finally, I want to thank Sharry and her gracious colleagues, workers, family and friends for their time, openness and indispensable help in writing this book. Special thanks also go to Steven Flinchbaugh, Rebecca Gonzalez, Robert Schrichte, Barbara Schroeder, Neil Flinchbaugh, Jesse Near and Vamshi Krishna Ghanapathi.

# *Disclaimer*

Please know that this book is not intended to serve as medical advice or make any recommendations or prescriptions for medical treatment. Anyone reading this book should consult a licensed medical doctor before making any decisions regarding their personal health care. Any action taken based on what is presented here is solely, the reader's responsibility.

The book is written for educational and informational purposes only. It is an expression of my opinion and I believe that there is valuable information contained in this volume. I have endeavored to insure, to the best of my ability, that everything in this book is true and accurate. If there are errors they are my responsibility – I did my best.

Thank you. *Jill Mattson*

---

[1] BioAcoustics is the spelling that Sharry uses to describe her knowledge related to the life sounds of humans. In contrast, bioacoustics refers to the life sounds of animals.

# Contents

# PART THREE *Applications*...............268

# Introduction

What do Newton, Shakespeare, Einstein, Lincoln, Mozart, Ghandi and Marx have in common? These extraordinary people, at the most basic level, saw the world differently than anyone before them. True genius is rare. Through their insights and their lives they changed the world forever.

In similar fashion, Sharry Edwards is currently making unparalleled insights into the nature of healing and the role of sound to accomplish near miraculous results. Sharry is making contributions in this world that will have lasting, beneficial impacts on mankind.

It has been my privilege to speak at length with Sharry and to learn firsthand about her groundbreaking achievements and the new science she is exploring, time for which I am deeply grateful. Her vision, dedication and desire to learn more about the powerful sounds contained in our voices inspire me. I appreciate her willingness to share her gifts and ideas; this has expanded my thinking to consider a bigger reality than the one that I see and hear with only my eyes and ears.

Sharry is the recognized leader in the emerging field of human BioAcoustics, literally meaning "life sounds." This field encompasses the study of sound and its effects on living organisms. She pioneered sound-based therapies for health care professionals and created self-discovery tools with astounding results. Sharry received the New Scientist of the Year Award from the International Association of New Science in 2001 and was also a recipient of the prestigious O.

Spurgeon English Humanitarian Award from the city of Philadelphia at Temple University in 2002.

Sharry devised a Vocal Profiling system based on the analysis of patterns hidden within the tones of a person's voice. Our brain combines thousands of different frequencies to create our speaking voice with the net result that we perceive the human voice as one "soundtrack." Fast Fourier Transformers graph the frequencies and volume of the voice. These graphs reflect complicated frequency interactions within the body, yielding simple and unique shapes. Sharry calls the resulting characteristic shapes the voice's "architecture."

This voice architecture holds critical information about the speaker. When we are ill individual pitches in our voice stretch outside of our normal architecture. The nature of these anomalous frequencies holds important clues to the underlying causes. So much information can be found within our voices, a holographic representation of ourselves.

Sharry reads and interprets "vocal codes." Balancing tones harmonize the "stressed" frequencies, returning them to healthy coherence that result in tangible improvements to our well-being. These discoveries rock our belief systems regarding health and wellness. Sharry has often shown remarkable results in helping people who have exhausted conventional remedies. She has established a new approach that offers exciting information and hope for people with a wide array of health issues.

Sharry's methods have shown many documented results, and much of this book attempts to explain her theories and observations and encourage others to conduct research to explore and verify them. My objectives include discussing elemental principals of how the body uses frequencies, vibrations and mathematics, and to present some applications of musical principals within the body's daily operations. I relate Sharry's profound discoveries to other modalities such as color healing and astrology, and conclude by suggesting new creative applications for using Sharry's profound discoveries for wellness and deep personal transformation.

# PART ONE
# SHARRY'S STORY

## Chapter One

# How it Began

I got up extra early on a cold Saturday morning and dressed quickly. That in itself is quite an event - I normally hate getting out of bed. The reason for my uncharacteristic behavior was excitement over what I had learned during a recent visit to southeast Ohio. I had just returned home after a few days spent at Sharry Edwards' Sound Health facility in Albany, Ohio. At Sharry's special invitation, I attended the opening portion of her week-long introductory training course.

I enjoyed a few hours of one-on-one time with Sharry to better get to know her and to ask intimate questions on her work and her life. The new opportunities to learn about the power of sound to heal the human body, mind and spirit and the power of Sharry Edwards' personality and presence had me floating. My mind was buzzing.

Upon arriving home late from Sharry's offices, I had learned so many new concepts that my thoughts were overflowing like a flooded stream. I sat down at my computer in my loft office and I worked furiously for over two hours. About this time, my bored German shorthair tried to climb into my lap. This may seem like an innocent matter to dog lovers – but Danke weighs over 90 pounds. She wanted attention and she wanted to go outside – NOW.

I took my coat and my notebook to the backyard with the dog. After the mandatory short walk, I settled into my usual spot next to a grand old oak tree. Back to work.

Sharry is discovering things about sound and healing that seem miraculous. She is practicing a new science! I wondered how she ever got so far.

Pondering on Sharry's work, I slumped back, leaning against the tree. My vision blurred and I drifted into a state of deep relaxation – like falling asleep. In my mind's eye I perceived a giant, clear, rubbery bubble. Next thing, I was floating inside the bubble. It was like being inside a dream. I felt safe, secure, loved and cherished. I never wanted to wake up or leave that bubble.

The bubble transported me up into the sky – my own "magic carpet," but more like a magic balloon. I found I could go wherever I wanted, whenever I wanted. I traveled into the past and hovered in front of a humble farmhouse where I spied Sharry Edwards as a young child, living in a pristine Appalachian setting. I could look into Sharry's being from my bubble perch. She was born with extraordinary gifts, particularly her hearing.

As I got closer I saw that it was not a farmhouse but an out building that looked like a corncrib. A corncrib has spaces in between the boards to let the corn breathe. Sharry's family had lined the siding slots with cardboard to protect themselves from the elements.

**The outbuilding where Sharry lived as a young child.**

The bubble glistened as it turned and I saw Sharry as a child of about three. In the front of the corncrib, there were little steps and a few boards were aligned to create a loft. The only window in the corncrib was in the front, near the loft. This was where Sharry and her brother slept. Boards were attached to the walls and served as shelves for canned goods. Sharry's mother used old cotton feedbags as curtains in front of these

12

shelves. I saw little Sharry pull aside the curtain to get something to eat. Coming eye to eye with a large snake which must have looking for food, she let out a huge scream!

Sharry's environment was not contaminated with electromagnetic radiation and frequencies that are prevalent in the air today. The space was more acoustically pure without TVs, microwaves, cell phones, electric, radio and computer energies. It is speculated that this setting contributed to Sharry's remarkable hearing abilities. It was clear Sharry's family thrived on this farm eating only fresh, natural whole foods – without toxins and food additives tainting their bodies.

My bubble moved me ahead in time to a deep stream on the same farm. I glimpsed a five-year-old Sharry lying on the ground, soaking wet and exhausted. I somehow knew that she had almost drowned in that nearby creek. I have heard documented reports of people spontaneously acquiring extraordinary abilities or senses after experiencing a near-death encounter. This event greatly enhanced Sharry's already remarkable hearing abilities. After this incident she began to hear many "extrasensory" sounds – from unusual sources – that most do not hear.

Human ears have a nearly dormant mechanism called the sacculus.[2] This organ was used in our evolutionary past. The

---

[2] The saccule is a bed of sensory cells situated in the inner ear. The saccule translates head movements into neural impulses, which the brain can interpret. The saccule is sensitive to movements of up and down (think about moving on an elevator). When the head moves vertically, the sensory cells of the saccule are disturbed and the neurons connected to them begin transmitting impulses to the brain. The vestibular system, which includes the saccule, is important in maintaining balance, or equilibrium. http://en.wikipedia.org/wiki/Saccule

sacculus is a sonar-sensing device that is highly developed in dolphins, but humans do not use it in this manner. We use the sacculus to help our equilibrium and to tell us which way is up or down when underwater. Sharry's sacculus was affected by the near drowning experience and she gained sonar-like sensing capabilities to complement her acute hearing. Sharry did pay the price of having her sense of equilibrium distorted with the changes.

Dolphins have highly evolved sonar-sensing capabilities. They transmit sonar waves, which reflect off of objects in their path. They can interpret the returned waves just as a ship's sonar does. This gives them another sense, another window-on-the-world to receive additional information.

Dolphins also have an extraordinary hearing range compared to humans. While the average adult hears sounds that vibrate at 20 cycles per second to about 20,000 cycles per second, dolphins hear and utilize sounds that vibrate up to 180,000 cycles per second. They hear and understand more frequencies than we do. These mammals can also voice numerous complex and haunting sounds that can travel impressive distances underwater. It is interesting that Sharry shares many of the remarkable abilities to use sound similar to a dolphin.

My clear bubble rolled forward in time and I observed a young Sharry, who now lived with her family in a small farmhouse. She heard specific sounds from her grandmother, who had diabetes. When her aunt started emitting the same sounds, Sharry told the aunt that she might have diabetes.

When the aunt heard this, she yelled at Sharry, calling her a "little witch." What a disturbing event for a young girl. Perhaps the aunt felt that her privacy was invaded or did not want to hear such a diagnosis. Later the aunt tested positive for diabetes.

As a child, Sharry believed everyone heard things as she did. I observed Sharry repeating what one of her aunts had said. The aunt replied that she did not say what Sharry attributed to her. She only *thought* the comment. Rather than marvel at this, the aunt branded Sharry's perceptions as something paranormal. The event would be confusing on its own, but add in the negative reaction from family and difficulties in Sharry's childhood become apparent.

I witnessed a young Sharry becoming reticent to share what she heard to avoid painful situations of being singled out for her hearing abilities. It was as if she tried to ignore her gift so that she would fit in with others and be more "normal."

I understood that Sharry had many painful moments, because she was different. At an early age she did not know that she possessed a beautiful gift. After all, many people distance themselves from those who are "different."

When Sharry was still quite young, she played in the woods with her cousin. The two little girls found a shiny tall tube with a pattern of three interlocking triangles on its side. Sharry and her cousin had never seen anything like this. The event influenced Sharry and she believed it helped shape her outlook on life. The symbol retained special meaning throughout her life and now serves as a logo that grace CD covers and booklets for her company.

Sharry had the shape of the three triangles made into a sculpture. From one view, it resembles the three interlocking triangles which create a tiny triangle in the middle. From another view it resembles this picture which has likeness to the Templar cross. Sharry now uses this design in one of her logos, see below.

**The shadow of the replica of the design that Sharry found**

Although there were many painful moments in Sharry's childhood, several people foreshadowed the contributions that Sharry would make to the human race. A palm reader noted a shape of a beehive on Sharry's palm, relaying that this meant she had extraordinary musical ability and would heal others with her voice. Sharry sent a postcard to Ruth Montgomery, an intuitive, prophet and author. She asked her a question regarding a book that Ruth had published. Ruth wrote back and referenced the "cigar" shaped object with the three triangles that the girls had found in the woods and the unique energy that came from it. The object did have a cigar shape, but Sharry had not shared that information with her. Ruth's writing to her about the shiny object they found in the woods shook Sharry up and scared her. Ruth explained that Sharry's life's purpose was to use sound to heal people. These fortune-telling incidents confirmed what Sharry already knew deep down - for better or worse, she possessed abilities far exceeding those possessed by the average person.

To accept our differences as gifts and pursue the understanding and perfection of them amidst innumerable obstacles is the test of true character. Sharry had many such tests, each making her grow stronger and ever more resolved in her purpose.

Sharry's remarkable hearing abilities proved to be the catalyst for her lifelong journey of sound healing discoveries. With her unique hearing abilities she has identified common sounds that signal physical maladies. She also hears thoughts, emotions and even information from people's subconscious minds. Sharry hears sounds coming from both living and inanimate objects. She sometimes hears tones from the ground, rocks, trees and plants, shapes, medicines and more. She uses this information to come up with unconventional conclusions holding an astonishing number of varied uses.

Giving voice to the sounds she hears, Sharry produces tones to affect blood pressure, eliminate headaches, scramble recorded information on tapes, affect the preservation of foods and endless diverse and amazing applications.

From my bubble, I wondered what the special sounds that Sharry produced were like. Looking down, I saw her get very still and then make a ringing sound with her voice, like someone rubbing their finger on a crystal glass to produce a high pitch that was rich with harmonics. It was as if she heard my thought and produced my sound. The sounds that she hears are often above our hearing range. When she sings them, she is taking then down octaves into her vocal range. I had never heard a person make a sound like that before!

The act of hearing plays a crucial role in developing our ability to speak or verbalize sounds. Deaf people struggle in learning to speak mainly because they cannot hear and learn by imitation. Dr. Alfred Tomatis[3] discovered that we must hear a sound in order to accurately duplicate the same sound with our voices. Not surprisingly, Sharry hears sounds that are beyond the abilities of other people and she can similarly voice sounds that others cannot.

I watched while Sharry continued to make my "sound." She can hear the pitch as well as the rhythm of the sound. Next she drew a picture on a piece of paper - she was drawing my sound. The drawing looked like the edge of a circular saw blade. The notches in the saw represented the periodic changes in volume, representing the rhythm. Often sounds

---

[3] Dr. Alfred A. Tomatis (1920–2001) was an internationally known otolaryngologist and inventor. His alternative medicine theories of hearing and listening are known as the Tomatis method. His approach began as an effort to help professional singers based on his idea that hearing is the root cause of a variety of ailments. His Listening Test and later his Electronic Ear therapy were designed to alleviate these problems.

have a periodic rhythm pattern. I wondered about the mystery of what this shape, rhythm and sound meant.

I wished that I could have been given this gift like Sharry had. She deciphered many mysteries from the unique sounds that only she heard. With this information she created a seemingly miraculous system to benefit people. Miracles can be science that we do not yet understand.

Sharry's hearing gift presented her with opportunities to explore and uncover secrets about sound healing that are beginning to be verified by science and are what she calls the "sonistry" of tomorrow. In the book, The Sleeping Prophet, Edgar Casey predicted that the medicine of the future would utilize frequencies. When he made the prediction it sounded crazy but today, this seems like destiny.

My bubble wobbled, jarring me. The interruption caused me to drop these thoughts. I looked in on Sharry listening to the sounds emanating from trees, rocks, flowers and the ground. Sharry can even hear sounds that she perceives stemming from the side of people's heads, near their ears. With this magical bubble I was able to hear a *rock sound* as Sharry heard it. What Sharry heard was a low rumbling noise. Pythagoras called a stone's sound "frozen music." Pythagoras also heard sounds of harmonics coming from objects, much like the sounds that Sharry describes. I listened to Sharry whispering that rocks have consciousness. Perhaps consciousness makes some sort of sound and that is what she is hearing.

Moving on, I saw Sharry listening to a crowd of people. Some people had screeches in their voices while others made pleasant sounds. Some of the sounds were pleasing, blending together, while others stuck out like a screeching chalk on a blackboard. The noises from a crowd are overwhelming and chaotic. There is so much more going on acoustically than most of us realize.

I thought about the shrieks and jarring sounds that Sharry perceived coming from people. What do these discordant sounds mean? Sharry's gets information about a person's physical, mental and emotional states from her special hearing. She can ascertain when a person is being untruthful, based only on their voice.

**Sharry Edwards**

People inevitably like the comfort of their "secrets" and resent another who can expose their lies. This made me think about how much I value my privacy. How much would our lives change if we knew people's thoughts, feelings and real opinions? If our lies were immediately exposed, what effect would that have on our governments? Divorce rate? The sales industry? Stock market exchange? Business? Many people hide self-serving interests and fears behind dishonesty. I concluded that as a population we do not want complete honesty. Instead of envying Sharry's gift I felt compassion for her; having such a gift wasn't easy.

Peering out of the bubble, I saw Sharry doing chores on the family farm and as a result she missed school frequently. She was the only adopted child of this farming couple and was teased about being their "son" because of the heavy manual labor she performed. Farming requires many laborious hours and her parents needed help. She was a good daughter and worked hard. I saw her dreaming of going to college but not, believing that she would ever have the chance.

My bubble moved on forward in time. She was shopping with her husband and he asked her to pick out a good grapefruit. She chose one, mentioning that it sounded good. He responded that she may not want to let everyone know that she listens to grapefruits. She had long been aware of how unique her hearing was: her awareness that other people were not ready to accept it concerned her greatly.

As this scene faded out, I saw Sharry deep in thought, her fingers dancing at the typewriter. She was typing a paper about tinnitus[4] and becoming excited – could this concept explain the sounds that she heard? She scheduled a hearing test at a free clinic.

I moved out of that scene and into the audiologist's office. When the tests for tinnitus were normal, the audiologist asked Sharry to make sounds like the ones that she heard. When she did, he nearly collapsed. He had high blood pressure and her vocalizations drastically and quickly seemed to lower his blood pressure. This sudden change - which was brought on with her voice - caused his near lapse of consciousness.

The audiologist was a martial arts student and he recalled that sounds similar to Sharry's were used by the ancient Samurai to disable their opponents. This man was beginning to understand Sharry's hearing gifts! Research results later revealed that the sounds she voiced could alter one's blood pressure as much as 30 points. A drop in blood pressure of this magnitude is significant; in fact, a sudden fall of 30 points is enough to severely disable a person. Sharry learned that not only could she hear more than other people but, her voice could make significant changes in a key aspect of a person's physiology.

After this experience Sharry began an earnest, thirty-year exploration of the unique sounds that she could hear and reproduce. She was destined to be a pioneer in BioAcoustics which, is defined as a branch of science concerned with the production of sound and its effects on living systems. She participated in a double blind experimental study with Ohio

---

[4] Tinnitus is the perception of sound within the human ear in the absence of corresponding external sound.

University's school of nursing in a scientific investigation that examined her ability to alter people's blood pressure. The results were astounding and showed that she possessed the ability to alter blood pressure with high statistical significance. So much so, that it made some scientists raise their eyebrows and muse if the results were contrived. The study could not be replicated with any other person because Sharry was the only known person at that time to possess such hearing and vocal talents. Since then, sound has been shown to influence blood pressure.

I watched Sharry undergo two more hearing evaluations that also validated her unique abilities. It was speculated that the cochlea in her ear was wound tighter than most, enabling her to hear sounds that others could not. In addition, she had the ability to voice extraordinary sounds; including, a perfect sine wave.

I did not know what a simple sine wave sounded like but from my bubble, I saw Sharry's audiologist explain that our voices have a complex wave structure.[5] If graphed, it looks like a ragged, highly irregular shape. A sine wave in contrast looks like a textbook picture of a sound wave - symmetrical - and absolutely perfect. Her sine wave sound reminded me of a something made by a machine.

---

[5] Sine waves, when graphed by frequency over time have a curved shape. The sine wave has a pattern that repeats. All waves are made by adding up sine waves. The length of one pattern of the sine wave is called the wavelength. The wavelength is measured by the length or distance between one peak of a sine wave to the next peak. The wavelength can be found in many other ways, too. The sine wave is important in physics because it retains it's a wave shape when added to another sine wave of the same frequency and arbitrary phase. It is the only periodic waveform that has this property. This property leads to its importance in Fourier analysis and makes it acoustically unique. http://en.wikipedia.org/wiki/Sine_wave

Sharry's curiosity drove her to scientifically investigate what she perceived with her extrasensory hearing. There was no research in this area to review. Rather than start with a theory and then attempt to prove it, Sharry observed the effects of sounds and then took a causal, trial-and-error approach to learning. She knew that her sounds had the ability to influence physical issues. Why did this work? What was she hearing and how did these sounds affect people? Sharry observed incredible results regarding the impact of frequencies on people. In her relentless process of answering these questions, a whole new field of healing and deeper understanding of the body was unveiled.

## A World of Frequencies

Some thinkers have long held a fundamental model of the universe that is based on frequencies. Our world is in a state of constant oscillation at many levels. Our cells, organs, DNA, heartbeats, thoughts, feelings and environments all vibrate, creating their own waves.

Dr. William Tiller, Ph.D.,[6] Chairman of Stanford's Materials Science Department, conducted extensive research to understand the vibrational signals of the body. He writes, "Each atom and molecule, cell and gland in our body has a characteristic frequency at which it will both absorb and emit radiation. Each cell generates its own minute vibrational signals from within that must stay in resonance with every other cell for the body to remain healthy."[7]

---

[6] Tiller, W. A. Science and Human Transformation: Subtle Energies, Intentionality and Consciousness, Walnut Creek, CA., 1997.
[7] Fellow to the American Academy for the Advancement of Science, Professor Emeritus William A. Tiller, of Stanford University's Department of Materials Science, spent 34 years in academia after 9 years as an advisory physicist with the

James Oschman offers this explanation about the vibrations of hormones: "At an atomic scale, physical contact between two molecules has less meaning than the way they interact energetically. As a hormone approaches the receptor, the electronic structures of both molecules begin to change. Bonds bend, twist and stretch: parts rotate and wiggle. The orientation and shape of the molecules change so that the active site of the hormone can approach the active site of the receptor. The recognition of a specific hormone by a receptor depends on resonant vibratory interactions, comparable to the interactions of tuning forks."[8]

Waves interact and change each other. For example, when the crests of two sound waves overlap or interfere constructively they combine into a new wave that is the sum of the heights of both waves. When the trough of one wave and the crest of another wave coincide, they combine and cancel each other out. Therefore, any sound wave can be affected by another sound wave.

Although we do not understand all of the details of the science of sound interactions in our complex bodies, Sharry is definitely onto something significant. Using sound as her medicine, she is harnessing a great power for our advantage. Being open to a world of unimagined new ideas, Sharry

Westinghouse Research Laboratories. He has published over 250 conventional scientific papers, 3 books and several patents. In parallel, for over 30 years, he has been a vocationally pursuing serious experimental and theoretical study of The Field, The Quest for the Secret Force of the Universe, the Quest for the Secret Force of the Universe of psycho-energetics, which will very likely become an integral part of "tomorrow's" physics. In this new area, he has published additional 100 scientific papers and four books.

[8] Edwards, Sharry. Vocal Profiling for the Professional, Sound Health: Albany, Ohio, 2002. pg. M1.53.

learns from watching sound transform people's bodies and observing sound in her world.

Sounds have the ability to prickle our skin, make our knees weak, increase perspiration, stimulate irregular heartbeats, create loss of bladder control or cause emotional reactions. Sounds can accelerate bones healing and break up kidney stones. Sounds can be used as weapons and they can influence people's brainwaves. In trained hands, sound is a powerful force.

This relationship also works in reverse. Changing body chemistry creates different sounds. For example, a young man's hormonal change during puberty affects his voice, lowering his voice tones. In another example, our voice changes when we get sick.

When the eye perceives vibrations of light, it converts these signals into electrical-chemical energy. These impulses are passed to the brain where they are interpreted as visual data. When we hear sound, the frequencies are translated into electrical-chemical impulses and interpreted in another region of the brain. The same sequence of events takes place when we are exposed to aromas, tactile stimulation, emotional situations, and so on. We interpret these vibrations after they reach the appropriate area of the brain.

The body does more than just interpret frequencies. Frequencies are also sent to various parts of our body via our neural network - another "body energy transport" system. The importance of processing frequencies goes beyond the sensual aspects such as hearing, seeing and feeling. We incorporate our sound environment and other vibrations into our total body energy. Sharry believes this is one reason why she gets impressive results by utilizing sounds that positively influence the body.

As we continue to gain greater understanding of the relationships between sound and our bodies, we can use sound as an effective alternative to expensive medicine modalities that often bring negative side effects. Perhaps vocal analysis could be used in conjunction with conventional treatments by our medical professionals, giving them better information about what is going on within the body, but at a significantly reduced cost. There is enormous potential for the creative applications of the power of sound, if properly harnessed.

## Our Signature Sounds

Our body has two sound receivers: our ears. They are about four to five inches apart yet, we do not hear separate sounds coming into each ear. If we did, it would be very distracting. We hear one uniform sound when a person talks. Our brain automatically combines sounds coming into our right and left ears. Similarly, all of the pitches in our voice are combined into the one tone that we hear.

Each pitch component has its own volume and phase relationships with other sounds.[9] Our overall signature sound is more like a signature chord.

---

[9] Davis, Dorinne. <u>Sound Bodies through Sound Therapy</u>. Kalco Publishing: Landing, New Jersey, 2004. pg. 244.

Some people increase their intellectual capacities by utilizing their brain's ability to combine tones. When the brain hears a different frequency in each ear at close proximity and below 30 hertz, it averages the two frequencies so we only hear one averaged frequency, which is called a "binaural beat." This is purposely done to engage both the right and left hemisphere of our brain, producing whole brain functioning, rather than operating in either right or left-brain mode. In this way, we can use the strengths of both brain hemispheres simultaneously, a powerful mental place to operate from.

*http://en.wikipedia.org/wiki/Binaural_beats*

Using special software, Sharry can isolate and identify the pitches present in our voice. Through careful observation and trial and error testing, Sharry has been able to isolate and assign the frequencies correlated to each muscle and organ.

An analogy can be made between the voice and white light. White light is the combination of all colors of light. When white light is passed through a prism, we can see the breakout of the component frequencies as the colors of the rainbow. The human voice is like a musical orchestra – all the instruments combine to produce one sound that can be beautiful and uplifting –we know that every instrument has contributed to the overall effect. The voice can even mimic the sound of an orchestra with the amazing abilities of our body's instruments. The vocal chords, the larynx, the diaphragm, the throat, the tongue, the mouth and teeth - together play the song that is the human voice.

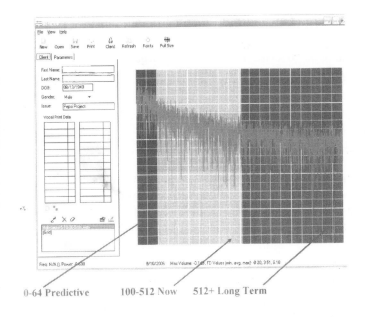

0-64 Predictive    100-512 Now    512+ Long Term

## A sample voiceprint
The vertical axis measures energy in decibels.
The horizontal axis measures frequency in hertz.[10]

Sharrry uses many analogies to understand the depth and complexities of information contained in our voice. She has likened our voice to an aura, which is perceived by some as only one thing although it contains many complex types and

---

[10] The hertz *(symbol: Hz)* is a unit of frequency. It is defined as the number of cycles per second. It is the basic unit of frequency in the International System of Units *(SI)*, and is used worldwide in both general-purpose and scientific contexts. Hertz can be used to measure any periodic event; the most common uses for hertz are to describe radio and audio frequencies, a frequency of 1 Hz is equal to one cycle per second.

categories of information. Like our aura, our voice has different layers. There are frequencies representing layers of brain waves as well as bioelectrical, bio-magnetic, and bio-chemical frequencies from other functions in our body. All the frequencies generated by our thoughts, emotions and bodies interact with the "vocal system" to create our unique voice which is literally - a reflection of all that we are.

Energies and frequencies in the voice reflect the effects of emotions from our past, future, negative thinking and feelings, such as guilt or worries. Another source of dissonance in our voice is created when we are untruthful. Negative emotions in our voice distort the normal frequencies which many believe can result in health issues.

Dorinne Davis, author of Sound Bodies through Sound Therapy, advances this idea even further. She says that, not only do negative emotions alter other tones in our voices but they also create vibrations of their own. Fear and negative emotions produce harmful sounds. "A breakdown in the mind's vibrational energy occurs when the mind creates its own noise or disturbances or when fear is introduced. Fear changes the mind's responses and it also affects auditory processing."[11]

Listening to the right pattern of frequencies can repair the dissonance that we create with our negative thinking and emotions. This can reverse the impact of negative emotions and "dis-ease." It can dissipate undesirable developments, while stimulating new growth.

---

[11] Davis, Dorinne. Sound Bodies through Sound Therapy, Kalco Publishing: Landing, New Jersey; 2004. pg. 231.

Some parts of our bodies have universal frequencies but each person's overall combination of sounds, their voice, is unique. Our universal notes *(such as the frequencies of the muscles)* are combined with our own unique thoughts, actions and feelings which have their own vibrations. There are many dazzling sounds coming from our bodies and they all interact in a unique way, creating a cellular tango - a complex sound matrix. Just as individual singers of a chorus create beautiful harmony, cells in our bodies and other vibrational influences can create intricate and elegant harmonies that affect each other in the dance of life. As a result, our composite frequencies are as unique as our fingerprints.

## Otoacoustic Emissions

People attributed Sharry's gift as clairaudience, a spiritual gift of extraordinary hearing, but gave no credence to it being a measurable physical phenomenon. Sharry wanted objective, concrete knowledge regarding her extraordinary ability. Yet, she found no scientific explanations. Finally, Sharry learned a partial explanation for the sounds that she heard in close proximity to people's heads. In 1978 Dr. David Kemp,[12] who wrote Understanding Otoacoustic Emissions, reported that the ear emits sounds entitled otoacoustic emissions *(OEs),* "which are small sounds caused by the motion of the eardrum in response to vibrations deep within the cochlea." The cochlea does more than receive sound. It also produces low intensity sounds called otoacoustic emissions. Dr. Kemp confirmed the existence of these tiny sounds when ultralow-noise microphones were developed. Sharry picks up these tiny sounds with her unaided ear.

---

[12] Dr. David T. Kemp. Professor of Auditory Biophysics, University College in London.

Researchers have documented that otoacoustic emission sounds are created by various mechanisms within the inner ear. These sounds are related to the amplification function of the cochlea, within the ear. With no external stimulation, the cochlear mechanism amplifies and produces sound.

Several lines of evidence suggest that outer hair cells enhance cochlear sensitivity allowing frequency selectivity and acting as the energy sources for this amplification. Another explanation is, that the sounds are produced by the cochlear outer hair cells as they expand and contract. Yet, another idea suggests that increased inner cochlea fluid motion excites inner ear hair cells, which then vibrate and produce the tiny sounds.[13]

Some believe that healthy ears produce sounds spontaneously when internal sounds are processed and amplified.[14] "Hearing is an active process – the ear actually puts energy into the incoming sound waves to replace energy lost as sound is absorbed by the ear's structure", says Stephen Beeby, an engineer at the University of Southhampton, United Kingdom. "This process helps us hear things we otherwise would not, but as a result some of the energy added by the hair cells escapes, as otoacoustic emissions."[15]

The study of otoacoustic emissions has expanded to include how selective pitches are formed within the ear. Johns Hopkins University research reveals that one of the

---

[13] http://emedicine.medscape.com/article/835943-overview
[14] Kempt, David. Understanding and Using Otoacoustic Emissions, Otodynamics Ltd.: Herts, UK. 1997. pg. 3.
[15] Imfefector – a newsletter featuring innovative steps in technology from around the world. pg. 3.

otoacoustic emissions is produced by the pineal gland and is amplified by the stapedius muscle of the inner ear.

James Cowan[16], in his book <u>Environmental Acoustics: Industrial Health and Safety,</u> says that due to its shape, the ear canal can only create the pitches of the notes F, F#, G, G#, and A. Cowan writes, "The ear canal is, on average, a tube about 1.2 inches in length depending on age and physiology. The ear canal, which is open on one end and closed by the ear drum on the other, actually resembles a pipe organ and can resonate between 2700 and 3500 hertz *(equating to the notes F through A)*."[17]

Additional otoacoustic pitches *(other than the notes F through A)* are recorded coming from the ear. Sharry hypothesizes that the brain creates these frequencies, which are then amplified through the brain fluids *(liquids are a highly efficient conductor of sounds)*, causing the otoacoustic pitches.

Renato Nobili, an Italian physicist who proved that electromagnetic frequencies occur in animal tissues, concurs that currents and wave patterns are found in body fluids. Nobili "found that the fluid in cells holds currents and wave patterns and that these correspond with wave patterns picked up by electroencephalogram *(EEC)* readings in the brain and scalp."[18]

---

[16] Cowan, James. <u>Handbook of Environmental Acoustics,</u> Van Nostrand Reinhold: N.Y., N.Y., 1994.
[17] Edwards, Sharry. <u>Vocal Profiling for the Professional.</u> Sound Health: Albany, Ohio, 2002. pg. M1.52. Quoting from Cowan, James.
[18] McTaggart, Lynne. <u>The Field, The Quest for the Secret Force of the Universe,</u> Harper Collins Publishers: N.Y., 2002. pg. 49.

Scientists have hints about how these additional otoacoustic tones are relayed to the ear, but no one knows for sure how they are transmitted. Since we can record them outside of the ear, we know they get there somehow.

Dr. Tomatis, a French ear, nose and throat specialist, documents the flow of information from the ear to the brain. He states, "the cochlea of the ear breaks sound into its various elements and sends its analysis to the brain... The brain begins its process of differentiating frequencies and sending them to pitch receptors. Then after gathering in the temporal cortex of the brain they are distributed throughout the brain."[19] Dr. Tomatis confirms that information goes from the ear to the brain.

Dr. Tomatis studied the path of the voice within our bodies and its travels along a skeleton. Tomatis believed that the bones of the skull conduct sound waves. To offer a simplistic proof, he suggested that if one hums and allows the sound to reverberate throughout his body, rather than project the humming sound in front of his face, he will feel the voice vibrating his skull.[20]

It has been postulated that through bone conduction via the skull, the ear receives brain wave frequencies and amplifies them. This may be why some otoacoustic emissions are different frequencies than the ones our ear hairs produce.

---

[19] Dr. Tomatis. The Ear and the Voice, The Scarecrow Press: Maryland, Toronto, Oxford, 1987. Translated into English in 2005. pg. 85.
[20] Dr. Tomatis. The Ear and the Voice, The Scarecrow Press: Maryland, Toronto, Oxford, 1987. Translated into English in 2005. pg. 93.

Otoacoustic emissions are produced even while we are comatose or asleep. Testing otoacoustic emissions is a standard method to determine hearing functions in newborn infants. "Anecdotally, audiologists say they can tell different people apart – men, women, even people of different ethnic origins – by the profile of widely varying types of otoacoustic emissions."[21] Scientists are attempting to figure out if otoacoutics emissions can be used like biometry, iris scans or finger prints."[22]

Dorinne Davis, audiologist from the Davis Center, concluded after an experiment that 100% of subjects had an otoacoustic emission that matched a BioAcoustic frequency in their voice that was stressed or inharmonious.[23]

"A myriad of publications on PubMed indicate that disease states can be verified through evaluation of otoacoustic emissions."[24] A John Hopkins University's researcher, Wendell Brown, substantiated that the ear emits sounds that can be used to diagnose disease. There are numerous studies now relating otoacoustic emissions to specific diseases. This link between otoacoustic emissions and disease may help explain why Sharry can "hear" that an individual may be prone to a certain disease.

Guy Berard, MD, reported that "the ear has a full range of frequencies, which can be monitored, recorded and retrained:

---

[21] *Imefector* – a newsletter featuring innovative steps in technology from around the world. pg. 3.
[22] *Imfefector* – a newsletter featuring innovative steps in technology from around the world. pg. 3.
[23] Edwards, Sharry. Vocal Profiling for the Professional, Sound Health: Albany, Ohio, 2002. pg. M1. 52.
[24] Edwards, Sharry. Vocal Profiling for the Professional, Sound Health: Albany, Ohio, 2002. pg. M1.53.

with the effect being the reversal of diseases such as autistic disorder. According to the research reports, the idea is simple and effective: Change the frequency and the body responds by eliminating the disease."[25]

The body has a feedback loop to diagnose and provide a set of healing and prescriptive frequencies. The loop consists of our voice, which produces sound and our ear that perceives it. The voice emits the composite sounds of our physical, emotional and mental health, signaling when help is needed. This immediately alerts our body to specific health problems. Our bodies instinctively know how to fight an infection, heal a wound or release negative emotion *(crying, for example)*. Perhaps part of the inter-body communication includes otoacoutic emissions.

Sharry believes that our ears transmit otoacoustic emissions as stabilizing sounds, which constantly provides healing and stabilizes frequencies to the body. This subtle sound energy playing in the background could be part of the body's self-diagnosis and self-repair mechanisms. Together hearing and voicing of sound create an intra-body communication system on a deeper level. The voice reflects what frequencies are in our bodies and the ears radiate what frequencies we need.

Dr. Tomatis's work demonstrates that the sound based communication system in the body affects more than our health. Correcting people's hearing also results in improvements in their learning and emotional problems.[26]

---

[25] Edwards, Sharry. Vocal Profiling for the Professional, Sound Health: Albany, Ohio, 2002. pg. M1.52.
[26] www.Tomatis.com

Sharry hears frequencies near the sides of people's heads that she correlates to emotions, thoughts and health. Not surprisingly, Sharry suspects a link between otoacoustic emissions and our psychological makeup. If our body is aware of otoacoustic emissions on a subconscious level, this could offer an explanation of how people intuitively "sense" other's emotions and thoughts. At times people sense a strong feeling, without an outward explanation for it. For example, we go into a room and feel that we can "cut the air with a knife." Our eyes tell us that everything is fine, but we sense something else. At times we accurately feel people's underlying emotions and thoughts. Are people's emotions and thoughts reflected in tiny sounds emitted from their ears? Can we, on a deep level receive this communication and interpret it?

The human mind has the ability to select what information it processes consciously. We can focus on one thing, and block out attention paid to something else. For example, we can listen to the teacher lecturing in the classroom or the whispers of the girl sitting next to us. We choose which information is more important and push the other information into the background. We constantly make choices about what is important to us, and the body focuses on the information we deem to be important.

Dr. Tomatis categorizes focusing on sound as "listening," while he classifies "hearing" as the absence of paying attention to sound. "Hearing is a superficial use of one's ear, while listening implies an act of will to connect with the sonic environment and learn what must be known. Listening is paying attention to sound and becoming actively involved in it… The psyche and openness to the outside world interact through the ear. In truth this phenomenon applies to all the sensory organs, but with audition the impact is most remarkable."[27] Tomatis sums up the process of listening, "The mind impacts audition and the ear impacts the mind."[28] What sounds we focus on are affected by our psyche and hence affect us mentally, emotionally and physically.

The human mind regularly gives dominance to information coming from our sense of sight, dismissing our feelings and sounds. The cliché is that "seeing is believing." People agree that if we all look at a red dress, that it is unquestionably red. In truth, red is the only thing it isn't. The dye in the dress does not absorb the color wavelengths of red, and hence the red color wavelengths are reflected back to our eyes. Information from our eyesight does not reveal all the available information, but we think it does.

As we develop our visual sense becomes increasingly dominant. If we think about where the essence of "ourselves" is, most people say "it" is behind their eye as opposed to their ears, heart or brain. This reflects our priority of believing visual information rather than other sensory data. It is normal that humans assign less credibility to their feelings and intuition as information from these sources seem fleeting. We can see something and verify its permanence, but sounds and feelings are here then gone. The more we believe only what we see, the more we diminish our intuitive and hearing abilities. Sharry is a living example that the sense of hearing can lead to a highly evolved ability to understand the world

---

[27] Dr. Tomatis. The Ear and the Voice, The Scarecrow Press: Maryland, Toronto, Oxford, 1987. Translated into English in 2005. pg. 87.
[28] Dr. Tomatis. The Ear and the Voice, The Scarecrow Press: Maryland, Toronto, Oxford, 1987. Translated into English in 2005. pg. 87.

around us. The sense of hearing adds depth and dimension to our reality.

## Back to the Bubble

This image blurred. From my bubble I saw that Sharry received her undergraduate degree over a twelve year period while she raised three children and then she pursued her master's degree. She was the first person in her family to get a high school degree, much less, a college degree.

Gently, the bubble pulled me back from learning about signature sounds and otoacoustic emissions then rolled forward in time again. On this occasion, I saw Sharry working as an administrative assistant in a local college, which offered free college courses as a fringe benefit. This arrangement enabled Sharry to get her degree in communications with emphasis on dietetics, communication styles and learning modalities. She wrote a book on learning styles and hand analysis.[29] She also obtained her master's degree in curriculum development and instruction, and progressed toward her doctorate in the same field. At the time, the Internet was yet to be invented and Sharry knew of no other sound researchers except, Robert Monroe, who wrote Journey Out of the Body and several other books. Monroe experienced out-of-body travel and associated this consciousness with specific frequencies.[30] Sharry journeyed to visit Robert Monroe, but he flatly refused to collaborate with her. This impacted Sharry in several ways. First, she gathered her discoveries and made them available to others

---

[29] Sharry created a system of hand analysis, which she calls amanimology. She related the size and shapes of hands, including fingernails, and related them to personality and learning styles.

[30] Read more about Robert Monroe in Ancient Sounds Modern Healing by Jill Mattson at www.jillswingsoflight.com.

on her own. Second, this impeded her attainment of a doctorate degree. She could not put together a required committee of experts regarding sound and health, as there were none available due to the novelty of her discoveries. The college refused to make accommodations for Sharry to earn her doctorate by being flexible or creative with this requirement.

From the bubble I often noticed people at work telling Sharry to hide her hearing and healing abilities lest others perceive her unfavorably. Once again, her gift appeared as a burden. Despite discouragement Sharry continued her explorations into why certain sounds affected the body in specific ways.

During her work as an administrative assistant, Sharry experimented by creating healing sounds. For example, as she could hear the exact pitch of a headache, she learned that if she replicated the sound of the headache, the headache got worse. She sang a series of increasing pitches, which sounded like a fire siren. This created a glissando sound with all tiny pitches that are in between the smallest notes of our pianos. As she explored the range of notes, she found one pitch that made the sound of the person's headache go away. She was not sure exactly why or how this worked. Sharry reflected that a mother instinctively sings a lullaby to help her baby sleep. The mother intuitively finds the needed pitch. Likewise, she knew what pitch got rid of a specific headache. Sharry also suggested that when people moan they instinctively use a related pitch that aids their own healing.

From her experience Sharry knew some tones heal and others exacerbate problems. If the headache's sound was that of G, singing more G made it worse for some people. However, another pitch such as a C# would mitigate it. Furthermore, there was something about the quality of her voice that others were unable to produce that enabled her to have a positive impact on their complaints.

One of Sharry's first discoveries was that a headache in a specific area of the head always sounded exactly the same in all people. For example a headache involving the temporal lobe was always a G#. A headache in the back of the head would be a different pitch. Sharry believed that the secret to finding the healing pitch was related to a frequency of the specific muscle in the head.

As Sharry conducted her personal research into the correlation between specific sounds that she could hear *(coming from people and underlying conditions such as headaches),* she thought that there must exist universal frequencies for each muscle when it is in the normal, healthy and balanced state. This was an important milestone in her development of the foundational concepts of human BioAcoustics.

Sharry noticed a correlation between the sound of someone's headache and the onset of slight changes in the person's voice. When the muscle of the head was out of balance for quite some time, then the person's voice became discordant or thin *(with missing or weak frequencies).* Therefore, chronic health conditions are readily apparent to her, even though it takes a while for the sound of pain to impact the voice.

A personal experience expanded Sharry's comprehension of the value of her hearing gift. She and her daughter, Ronna, were enjoying a swimming outing at Raccoon Creek near

Moonville, Ohio. Ronna was swinging on a rope. Ten feet below a rocky ledge, the water became deep enough to dive into. Ronna lost her grasp of the rope and smashed into the rocky ledge into a few inches of water. Her lower leg muscle was nearly severed and she was bleeding profusely. It took 25 minutes for emergency professionals to arrive at this remote summer retreat. Sharry was frightened that her child would bleed to death or lose her leg. Sharry administered conventional first aid to stop the bleeding. She heard the distressed signals coming from her daughter's body. Sharry began to sing tones, which you and I could not make. She toned up and down and found pitches that lessened the distress sounds emanating from her daughter. The bleeding slowed. At the hospital Sharry continued to make her sounds, but when she stopped, her daughter screamed in pain again. After a seven-week hospitalization Ronna was told that she would not walk again. However, with the aid of Sharry's frequencies she eventually enjoyed a full recovery. She still has a scar like a "shark bite" to remember her incident at Raccoon Creek.

Each of our body's organs, body systems and bio-chemicals *(such as cortisol, serotonin, histamine, niacin, magnesium, amino acids, hormones, vitamins, minerals, viruses, enzymes, nerves, muscles)* have their own frequency and are reflected in pitches within our voices. Each element in our body has its own signature frequency. A BioAcoustic "frequency-equivalent" ™ can be defined as a frequency representation of a nutrient, muscle, biochemical, genome, pathogen, toxin, gene, or other items in our environment and can represent structural, emotional, metabolic or environmental issues.

> "Just as there is a system of elemental chemical pathways *(chemistry)* there is a fundamental frequency-based organization to our universe, using mathematical based mathways. I call this '*sonistry!*'" S. Edwards

These universal frequency biomarkers serve as benchmarks for optimal health. When we have too much or too little of a vitamin, mineral or body substance, the corresponding frequency will be out of the normal range of our voice's architecture. BioAcoustics can pinpoint the exact nutrient or vitamin that is causing a health issue and whether we need less or more of it.

Sharry experimented with her friends, family and herself, using the "tone de jour" to heal aches and pains. She bought several instrument tuners to identify the healing tones associated with the health problems of those around her. As she catalogued these frequencies she analyzed the data to figure out the relationship between a specific health problem and a healing frequency. Sharry constantly asked herself, "Why did this frequency influence this problem?" If she could figure this out, she could calculate appropriate frequencies to address a wide range of maladies.

Sharry heard environmental sounds that became incorporated into people's signature sounds. Frequencies in our mind, body and feelings interact with environmental sounds. This is healthy when we are in a peaceful and beautiful location. However, there are many external influences that are inharmonious to our bodies. Our bodies need balance. There are many ways to get out of balance, such as:

- Consuming man-made chemical additives in food
- Being exposed to environmental toxins and pollution
- Being near too many free-floating frequencies from cell phones, microwaves computers, TVs, power plants, radio waves…

Dr. Robert Becker, a scientist, author and physician, studied the impact of external frequencies and their impact on our health. "All abnormal man-made electromagnetic fields, regardless of their frequencies, produce the same biological effects. These effects, which deviate from normal functions and are actually or potentially harmful, are the following:

- Effects on growing cells, such as increases in the rate of cancer-cell division
- Increases in the incidence of certain cancers
- Developmental abnormalities in embryos
- Alterations in neuro-chemicals, resulting in behavioral abnormalities
- Alterations in biological cycles
- Stress responses in exposed animals that if prolonged, lead to declines in immune-system efficiency
- Alterations in learning ability

Being exposed to any abnormal field… affects a number of stress-related diseases and cancers… If prolonged, this decreases the efficiency of the immune system, resulting in an increased incidence of infectious diseases and cancers."[31]

Our internal harmony is constantly challenged, stretched and attacked from external sources. Sharry was learning how to

---

[31] Becker, Robert, Dr. Cross Currents, The Perils of Electropollution, The Promise of Electromedicine, Penguin Group: New York, 1990, pg. 214.

harmonize out of balance frequencies, whether or not they originated from within us or came from our environment.

My bubble took me forward in time. I watched Sharry enrolling in a parapsychology course at Ohio University's "Communiversity;" Sharry quickly became a co-teacher of the course. Sharry often demonstrated the phenomena that the professor discussed. She taught this class for ten years. At that time, it became apparent to her that there were no places to buy parapsychology items, such as dowsing rods, books, and other items. In 1976 Sharry started Esoteric Unlimited, a store that offered such products locally.

As Sharry's reputation grew in parapsychology, she gave an interview on a radio talk show regarding reincarnation. People who deemed that reincarnation was sinful picketed the radio station. Sharry watched the picketing from the radio office; she snuck out the rear door and joined the picket line. She identified the picketers' leader and promptly started a friendly conversation. This opened the lines of communication and the disagreement dissipated! This person would later refer to Sharry as a friend. This episode showed Sharry's tenacious, yet winning, nature. Anyone who is introducing a new paradigm counter to the entrenched medical system needs determination and perseverance.

In another example of tenacity, a man fired a shot near Sharry's house "as a warning" after hearing about her parapsychology endeavors. Sharry discovered who this man was and scheduled a meeting with him. She directly confronted him regarding the alleged shooting at her house. During this conversation Sharry addressed and answered the rumors that he had heard about her. Direct communication mitigated this man's anxieties and stopped his threatening behavior. Once again, this incident shows Sharry's courage and resolve. Few people, indeed, would follow up with a face-to-face meeting with someone who was shooting at them.

Sharry's husband, Bill, favored a business model that integrated Sharry's discoveries into the mainstream health care world to avoid being categorized with "alternative" health care services. He believed that piggybacking on the medical field would yield quicker acceptance of this accurate, inexpensive and non-invasive analytical and treatment tool.

The bubble rolled forward and I saw Sharry in the 1980s changing her business's name to Dimensional Resources, which sounded more conventional. By 1995 Sharry had developed the basic foundations of her BioAcoustic system. Furthermore, she had formulated frequency databases and proven methods to enable others to support optimal wellness with sounds, just as she did. A new vision for the business was coming into focus. Sharry's business would record and interpret people's energies to determine ways to balance them in the body, enabling it to heal itself. Most importantly, she developed a system to train others to do vocal profiling using tools and instruments that she developed. The new corporation was called Signature Sound Works. The new corporation did not last long as an office manager embezzled a large sum of money that forced Sharry and her family to make sacrifices, restructure, re-plan and rebuild the business. After this setback in 1996 the title of the corporation was changed to Sound Health Alternatives.

From my bubble I saw similar scenes fly by, one after another. I saw a lamp burning steadily in Sharry's window as the clock struck 4:00 am. Sharry, a night owl, spent night after night digging through research and new scientific discoveries to expand her theories, draw comparisons and discover another set of healing frequencies for the next software package release.

A related nonprofit corporation entitled Sound Health Research was also created to enable the organization to receive tax-free donations and services. A board of directors was established, creating an organization capable of spearheading efforts to establish the methods of sound healing - accelerating success in reaching and helping greater numbers of people.

The concepts that Sharry unveiled created the foundation for a new medicine. Big changes can be difficult and threatening to people. Traditional medicine, the paradigm of the human body and how it works are core beliefs of Western thought.

Sharry's mother-in-law had macular degeneration. Sharry exposed her to balancing frequency-equivalents, as revealed by her voiceprint. Almost immediately her mother-in-law's macular degeneration significantly improved and her sight returned to normal. Sharry's brother-in-law also had macular degeneration. He refused to listen to frequency-equivalents even though they helped his mother. His reasoning was that his doctor had not heard of BioAcoustics. He would not try anything that his doctor did not recommend. Many people will not sway from conventional approaches to health care.

Sharry's BioAcoustic tones positively impact people, but they are reticent to credit their success to the sounds. Sharry described giving a doctor a tone box for an ailment. He quickly recovered. Sharry did not hear from him until he lost his tone box. He explained that when he got better, he assumed that he got better naturally and did not attribute his recovery to her sound box. It was only when he stopped listening to the tone box and his symptoms returned, that he credited the sounds as his source of help.

Why is a change in thinking so difficult especially when there are so many benefits for people? We have created personal databanks from the information we have received throughout life. We form conclusions and base perceptions on this accumulated information. It is our own way of looking at the world. When we receive new information we subconsciously filter and format it to fit our existing model. When we receive information that doesn't "fit" our view of the world, we experience stress. We feel as though a part of our reality is falling apart. It feels like our foundations are collapsing, which, in a subtle sense, they are. When our beliefs are challenged our "fight or flight" mode becomes operational. We don't give up our way of thinking without a fight.

To make a paradigm shift we must make a fundamental change in how we understand our world. This involves reorganizing much of our "data" and the ways that we observe and react to information and events. This is a major change in thinking, affecting our structures of consciousness. It is no easy task to make a paradigm shift!

Some enlightened thinkers have presented a possible reason as to why a major shift in one's thinking is consistently challenging beyond obvious inertia. "Scientists acknowledge that weak electromagnetic fields surround every living biological organism, and indeed are given off by every component, down to the smallest atomic structure."[32] Rupert Sheldrake uses this point to conclude why it is energetically difficult to change an ingrained perception or belief system. People have energy fields – their thoughts and beliefs get integrated into this field, creating an energy barrier that is resistant to change.

Sheldrake points out that if we chop up a magnet into little pieces, each piece generates its own magnetic energy field. Each organ, tissue and cell also has its own field. Sheldrake believes that each person's beliefs and perceptions create an energetic field in which similar thoughts are attracted and collected. He draws a comparison between this idea and Carl Jung's theory of the collective subconscious, which he distinguishes from the personal subconscious particular to each human being. The collective subconscious reflects the consensus of the majority of people like "a reservoir of the experiences of our species."[33]

Sheldrake proposes that these morphic energy fields influence everything from the migratory patterns of birds to plant growth, people's common beliefs and the collective subconscious.

Sheldrake believes that this energy defines and characterizes individuals, more so than DNA. He likens DNA to hardware

[32]Sheldrake, Rupert. *Psychological Perspectives*, Spring 1987: "Mind Memory Archetype: Morphic Resonance and the Collective Unconscious." Quoted from Bartlett, Richard. Matrix Energetics, Atria Books: N.Y., N.Y., 2007. pg. 30.
[33] http://en.wikipedia.org/wiki/Collective_unconscious

that we inherit from our parents, but we download our traits from the collective subconscious of the human race. He believes that these collected subtle energy fields create a powerful force on individuals to "follow the crowd," while thinking differently than the mainstream of thought is like swimming against the tide.

A German biophysicist, Pfritz Popp, helped form the International Institute of Biophysicists, which researches the possibility of a complex network of resonances and frequencies as the body's communication system.[34] He wrote, "In quantum physics, quantum coherence means that subatomic particles not only know about each other, but also are highly interlinked by bands of common electromagnetic fields, so that they can communicate with each other. They are like, 'a multitude of tuning forks' that all begin resonating together. As the waves get into phases of sync, they begin acting like one giant wave and one giant subatomic particle. It becomes difficult to tell them apart. Many of the weird quantum effects seen in a single wave apply to the whole. Something done to one of them will affect all the others."[35] Popp confirmed inter-body vibratory communication.

Popp continued, "Coherence establishes communication. It's like a subatomic telephone network. The better the coherence, the finer the telephone network and the more that refined wave patterns have a telephone. The end result is a bit like a

---

[34] McTaggart, Lynne. The Field, The Quest for the Secret Force of the Universe, Harper Collins Publisher: New York, 2002, pg. 53.
[35] McTaggart, Lynne. The Field, The Quest for the Secret Force of the Universe, Harper Collins Publisher: New York, 2002, pg. 53.

large orchestra. All the photons are playing together, but as individual instruments…"[36]

Sheldrake suggests that systems of thoughts have their own collective fields of energy. Sheldrake comments that, professionals refer to The Field, The Quest for the Secret Force of the Universe of medicine, The Field, The Quest for the Secret Force of the Universe of law, or The Field, The Quest for the Secret Force of the Universe of engineering.[37] Given the solidarity of people's respect surrounding our medical profession, any new idea that could be perceived as threatening to the medical community is met with a strong field of resistance. He believes that long-established belief systems represent an energy that is highly resistant to change. Individuals unknowingly draw on supportive energy when they agree with the majority of people in a field of thought. Sheldrake believes this explains why endorsing an opposing belief is such a daunting task.

Whether one believes Sheldrake's ideas or not, history undisputedly shows the struggle creative people experience when introducing new ideas. Innovative thinkers have always been harassed by society.

Novel and unconventional ways to treat disease do not negate the great accomplishments of the medical field. Parallel concepts, such as frequency or Vibrational Medicine, The Number One Handbook of Subtle-Energy Therapiescan complement traditional medicine and assist doctors. Sharry

---

[36] McTaggart, Lynne. The Field, The Quest for the Secret Force of the Universe, Harper Collins Publisher: New York, 2002, pg. 43.
[37] Sheldrake, Rupert. *Psychological Perspectives*, Spring 1987: "Mind, Memory, Archetype: Morphic Resonance and the Collective Unconscious." Quoted from Bartlett, Richard. Matrix Energetics, Atria Books: N.Y., N.Y., 2007. pg. 31.

works hand-in-hand with many physicians. The revelation of frequency and energy medicine can move humanity light speed ahead, propelling traditional medicine as well!

It is no surprise that Sharry encountered a great number of obstacles. An anonymous caller insisted that she "just lie down and die," and Federal officials instructed, "Do not tell anyone that you have found a cure for a disease." She regularly gets threatening phone calls at her yearly conference. Many detractors stole information and set up competitive companies.

Many struggle with opposition from high levels of business and government, but the number of incidences makes one wonder why Sharry is being given such a hard time. Is it because her discoveries and new avenues of medical treatment threaten the financial bottom-line of existing companies? I remember chuckling when Sharry told me, "Expect someone to emulate, stop or circumvent you, if you have something of value that might be of a threat to his theories or pocketbook."

Sharry does not want any corporation to use her protocols to control the health of the general population. One of her mottos is, "whoever controls people's health, controls the people." She does not want her discoveries exploiting people or destroying the common good. She has not sold her information to pharmaceutical or medical companies, or foreign countries, though she has had offers to do so.

A heroes are often least appreciated in their hometown. People stereotype and resist any change in their existing beliefs and perceptions. For example, "my neighbor's wife can't cure a new disease, she is just a housewife!" Being ordinary and extraordinary at the same time can cause negative reactions from friends and acquaintances - familiarity can breed contempt.

Even Sharry's own family did not initially believe that her unusual tones could produce such incredible results. Her husband was not a firm believer until he experienced them himself; since then he has became a solid and ardent supporter. Sharry's mother only opened herself to hearing Sharry's sounds after learning that her mother had but a brief time to live. Sharry then set up a sound machine under her mother's hospital bed and, much to the doctor's surprise, her mother made a complete recovery as her body created its own heart bypass.

Often it takes a life-changing experience, such as the one Sharry's mother had, to make a lasting shift in perspectives. People are intimidated by solutions that are fundamentally different than the status quo. In order to accept these solutions, most people must experience a significant incident to alter their energy, eliminate resistance to change and allow them to accept a new way.

The flipside of this phenomenon is that once someone has stretched his or her mind to include a new way of believing, it does not go back to its previous narrow-minded state. One by one, people incorporate new ideas about healing into their thinking. This is how social change occurs: one by one, people create a new, expanded model of ideas with which to view their world.

There is a school of thought which holds that only a small percentage of people need to divert their thinking from an established belief in order for others to easily shift their thinking. Proponents of this theory point to a research study published by *The Journal of Conflict Resolution* showing that when a group of people meditated on peace, local violent activities decreased. They believe this demonstrates that a small group of people's thoughts can create an energy that affects a larger group of people.

Jonathan Goldman, sound healing author and composer, advocates that research on the power of group meditations has shown that in order to affect a large group of people there only needs to be the square root of one percent of the population, or about 8,000 people, taking part in a meditation to influence the earth's population.[38]

Slowly but surely, more people are accepting the benefits of sound healing. One by one, people are accepting that the correct frequencies and rhythms can heal and balance stressed frequencies in the body, helping them to achieve total wellness.

Sharry wants her findings to benefit all people. She has dedicated herself to this noble goal, but she faces constraints due to limited funding. Specifically, Sharry is operating a facility and paying all associated expenses and staff as she educates the public and carries on her research.

I visited Sharry's Sound Health facility, located in an old school building in Albany, Ohio. When I last spoke to

---

[38] Goldman, Jonathan. Quoted in the book by Mattson, Jill. Ancient Sounds Modern Healing, Wings of Light: Pa. 2006. pg. 137.

Sharry, she had not written herself a paycheck in over five months. She lives modestly, putting much of any income back into her work. She is not interested in personal gain, but rather she is intent on getting her message out   and that costs money!

To accomplish these larger goals Sharry maintains some trade secrets so people will purchase her informational products and services. Specifically, she retains detailed proprietary information of vocal rhythm patterns and the associated frequency codes. She trains practitioners who use her techniques and database information. She discloses her discoveries and frequency protocols to her trained practitioners. She has a comprehensive library and students who come to Sound Health get the latest and most innovative techniques.

Many people have copied Sharry's work without crediting her. While some use the information to create excellent services, a few provide slipshod work that could be potentially harmful to the credibility of the sound-healing field. Sharry has sued a few people who have blatantly stolen and pirated her work. Lawsuits are expensive, emotionally draining and often unsatisfying. If she were to protect her discoveries all of the time, she would have little time and energy remaining to advance this new field.

I tried to get the bubble to move forward into the future.  I wished to see how this story ends. Does Sharry succeed in overcoming the resistance she faces? Do we step forth and help educate others so that people can realize the incredible promises of improved health benefits? Do HMO's embrace this medicine of the future? Do a few companies steal these ideas and get rich, or does Sharry prevail and take the BioAcoustic system mainstream, so that large groups of people can benefit inexpensively? The bubble would not move. I realized that you and I determine the future!

A dog's wet nose woke me up from my nap at the old oak tree. The bubble was gone. The air was cold. I smiled, thinking of all the history I had seen. What a treat! I could not wait to get back to work with Sharry. I had learned a great deal. I had exciting new technical information on sound healing and I was eager to delve into why Sharry's methods work.

# Chapter Two

# Transferring Sharry's Gifts to You

As we saw in chapter one, Sharry was born into and grew up in a world where sound played a much larger role than it does for most people. The full scientific basis for Sharry's capabilities is beyond our current understanding, but this situation will change. Progress has been made and will accelerate as research and emphasis on the emerging frontier of sound healing continues.

Sharry could naturally hear subtle sounds in people's voices far beyond their spoken words. These extrasensory sounds held incredible variety. As Sharry grew, she thoroughly learned this hidden language and discovered characteristic and unbalanced sounds in the voices of people with underlying health problems. She concurrently generated powerful sounds far exceeding the range and power of the normal human voice. It seemed Sharry could instinctively play with tones that would correct the unharmonious tones emanating from people around her. It may have been instinct or perhaps she learned to hear and communicate on a higher plane. What is clear is that Sharry could associate frequencies with specific illness and create tones that enabled the body to heal itself.

As Sharry matured, she took the pioneering step of understanding her gift and making her new modality widely available to humanity. She grasped the implications of creating effective, low cost, highly selective health care. These efforts will make a lasting impact on mankind and permanently write Sharry's name in history.

Sharry still conducts research and she steadily builds her understanding of this emerging science. She is limited by financial and human constraints, but she plows on tirelessly with the overriding goal of making her discoveries as widely available as possible. She could have been rich if she exploited her personal talents – instead, she has spent her life building a system that she can leave behind to benefit mankind.

Sharry formulated a two-pronged objective:

- To enable others to duplicate what she hears using software she developed *(and understand the implications of what the sounds mean)*
- To devise a method whereby people can provide the tones that she vocalizes through programmable analog tone box.

While working with an audiologist, Sharry learned that a fast Fourier transform *(FFT)*[39] converts recorded vocal sounds into numeric data. This technique measures frequency in cycles per second *(hertz)* and volume *(decibels)*. A visual graph is created showing the size and phase relationships between pitches. With trial and error testing, Sharry confirmed that the information in the voiceprint produced by the FFT was indeed similar to what she was hearing. She spent years working with the FFT, making it more accurate for her purposes. Use of the FFTs provided a method to enable others to see what she could hear.

Next came years of working with voiceprint data to discover what specific pitches, shapes, "architecture" and rhythm patterns meant. In Part Two, Technical Details, there is an entire chapter dealing with discoveries related to the information contained within the voiceprint.

---

[39] In 1822, Joseph Fourier, a French mathematician, discovered that sinusoidal waves can be used as simple building blocks to "make up" and describe nearly any periodic waveform, even irregular sound waves made by human speech. The process is named Fourier analysis. In mathematics, the Fourier transform is an operation that transforms one complex function of a variable into another. The new function...describes which frequencies are present in the original function. This is similar to the way a chord of music described harmony that we hear. The Fourier transform decomposes a function into oscillatory functions. FFTs are computationally efficient algorithms commonly used to convert analog vocal data to digital numeric data for rapid spectral analysis.

When Sharry began this work, the Internet was not yet popular and computer usage was in its infancy. As computers became a widely available tool, Sharry's ability to analyze voice data grew exponentially, so did her corresponding understanding of sounds in the voice. These experiences spawned the idea of including FFTs in computer software programs. Sharry then worked with computer programmers to use her analytical, frequency data to enable others to interpret the sounds that she had spent her life's work identifying.

The logical next step crystallized as she searched for reasonably priced microphones, sound cards and free sound programs for computers to enable large numbers of people to access BioAcoustic information.

People can collect voice samples with a unidirectional condenser microphone[40] that was linked to a computer with a sound card. The one-directional microphone could filter out background extraneous sounds, like those from the cat's meow or a car door slamming. Now, even more effective noise-filtering programs are used.

## Sound Boxes

Sharry simultaneously worked toward solving the riddle of how to enable students to select the appropriate engaging frequencies and how to deliver them to people.

---

[40] Condenser microphones span the range from inexpensive karaoke mics to high-fidelity recording mics. They generally produce a high-quality audio signal and are now the popular choice in laboratory and studio recording applications. They require a power source. Power is necessary for establishing the capacitor plate voltage and amplification of the signal.

At first, Sharry rigged stereo equipment with subwoofers capable of replicating rich lower tones. When instructing others to recreate this sound system, they often made critical shortcuts, which impeded their success. Sharry worked with manufacturers to provide portable, small tone boxes that delivered the high quality sounds that she needed.

One of the first choices faced when creating tone boxes was to choose a digital or analog format of recording the initial sounds.

When we talk to each other in person, we hear analog sounds. When we talk on newer phones, we hear digitally reproduced sounds. The sound has been converted to digital data and transferred over transmission lines to the phone.

Sharry believes that greater expressive information is encoded in analog sound as opposed to digital reproductions. Analog sounds replicate a refined conversion of sound data that approximates the original sound as closely as possible. A digital sound takes a range of tones. This information is averaged and called a bit. This advantage allows for faster data transfer.

Digital cameras have pixels. The quality of a digital camera is measured in part by the number of pixels it uses in making digital photos. The more pixels it employs, the more the digital photograph approximates a picture captured on chemical emulsion photo film. Digital sound recordings work the same way. They capture sample bits of sound.

Sharry believes that the decision to use digital or analog recording styles is critical. She relentlessly pursues the studies, theories and information released by leading scientists regarding the transfer of waves, energy and information in the human body. Her research led her to the conclusion that analog tone boxes should be used. There is more detail on how the body communicates in Part Two, Technical Details. For now we will briefly review how information is transferred via the perineural system in the body.

Audiologist, Dorrine Davis summarizes, "The perineural tissue cells surround each neuron in the brain, accounting for more than half of the brain's cells. They follow every perineural nerve to its endpoint. The information in the perineural system is spread throughout the entire body via the central nervous system that cooperates to send information to specific places."[41]

The central nervous system allows for control of body sensations and movement, and feedback of various activities within the body. In contrast, the perineural connective system integrates and regulates the body processes *(such as wound healing).*[42]

The central nervous system sends information in digital form, while the perineural connective system sends information from the brain in analog form.[43]

---

[41] Davis, Dorinne. Sound Bodies through Sound Therapy, Kalco Publishing: Landing, New Jersey, 2004. pg. 262.
[42] Guzzetta, CE. Adolf, ER, Supplement. Footnote 141 in Dorinne Davis's Sound Bodies through Sound Therapy, pg. 261.
[43] Davis, Dorinne. Sound Bodies through Sound Therapy, Kalco Publishing: Landing, New Jersey, 2004. pg. 261.

Dr. Becker, who was twice nominated for a Nobel Prize,[44] has substantiated a DC analog current system found hidden within the central nervous system.[45]

Becker explains, "We commonly think of the brain as being packed with billions of nerve cells. While there *are* billions of nerve cells in the brain, there are as many, if not more perineural cells. In fact these cells are found wherever nerve cells and nerve fibers are found."[46] The perineural system is activated prior to the nerve impulses; it appears to make actual decisions and regulate consciousness.[47]

Dr. Becker also writes that too much energy overloads the system, producing bodily damage. The body energy systems use subtle, electrical control systems; the idea that more energy is better is outright dangerous.[48]

Based on this research, Sharry uses analog tones for her work.

Sharry experimented with various octave levels of sound and discovered that the body responds best to lower frequency sounds. Lower frequencies were usually more potent for

---

[44] Dr. Robert Becker is a pioneering researcher of electricity and regeneration. He is an orthopedic surgeon and a professor at N.Y. State University, Upstate Medical Center and at the Louisiana Sate University Medical Center. He has authored The Body Electric and Cross Currents, The Perils of Electropollution, The Promise of Electromedicine,

[45] Becker, Robert, Dr. Cross Currents, The Perils of Electropollution, The Promise of Electromedicine, Penguin Group: New York, 1990, pg. 62.

[46] Becker, Robert, Dr. Cross Currents, The Perils of Electropollution, The Promise of Electromedicine, Penguin Group: New York, 1990, pg. 63.

[47] Becker, Robert, Dr. Cross Currents, The Perils of Electropollution, The Promise of Electromedicine, Penguin Group: New York, 1990, pg. 65.

[48] Becker, Robert, Dr. Cross Currents, The Perils of Electropollution, The Promise of Electromedicine, Penguin Group: New York, 1990, pg. 169.

healing and this practice is consistent with Dr. Becker's advice. Sharry lowered her healing pitches by octaves so that the sounds were in the lower end of our hearing range, below 64 hertz. Humans begin hearing at about 14 hertz. Her responsive sounds are in the ranges of brain wave frequencies and can entrain them. Brainwave entrainment is a process in which brainwave frequencies fall into step with a stronger frequency in close proximity. This may be done, for example, to induce sleep.

The earlier versions of sound boxes were the size of two laptop computers. Now, individually designed frequency formulations are programmed into a small box less than five inches tall, called a "Square Two-Tonebox" that is a small analog frequency generator. The box typically has a headphone and subwoofer capacities for clarity of deep tones.

Sharry developed another device to deliver sounds called a SMAD *(Self-Management Auditory Device)*. The SMAD has a dual frequency generator that produces individual tones. This machine is used to test tones before they are programmed into the tone boxes.

Sharry uses a dual frequency generator to pan sound in different directions. Sharry related that earlier in her research a company hired her to use her voice to scramble information stored on iron oxide magnetic tape[49] recordings. This company duplicated the sounds that she made because her voice could scramble stored information on tapes. They could not duplicate her sounds without duel frequency generators.

---

[49] ferric oxide tapes (*cassette tapes*)

Additional sound delivery systems are being implemented, including a "sound bed" vibratory system.

# Chapter Three

## Sharry's Legend Grows

In interviewing Sharry and a number of close colleagues, family and friends, it became apparent that some early episodes greatly affected Sharry and shaped her ensuing career with BioAcoustics. There are many accounts of Sharry's amazing deeds; some have grown to be near legends in the area where she grew up.

Sharry's husband is an extremely practical, down-to-earth, and a soft spoken man. Bill carefully tells stories with minute detail and is reluctant to jump to hasty conclusions. Bill related his own personal experiences and what convinced him to believe that Sharry's discoveries can work as well or better than conventional medicine.

Bill has been physically fit his entire life and always worked outside doing rigorous, physically demanding jobs. He was a serious tennis player and enjoyed other sports. Due to his active life style Bill developed synovitus - an inflammation of a membrane which lines joints such as the knee. The condition is usually painful, particularly, when the joint is moved frequently. The joint usually swells due to fluid collection.

Sharry was in the early stages of her career at this time and as was Bill's habit, he turned to his long time family physician for care. He received a strong anti-inflammatory drug, naproxen, for his knee. Fortunately, he did not experience any side effects and in six weeks the pain was gone, although he still needed to wear a supportive bandage on his knee. Over the years, the synovitus occasionally flared up again. The medicine was expensive, so Bill avoided using it. Within four years, the pain and inflammation were back in full force. He could not bend or fully extend his leg.

In the time since Bill's initial bout with synovitus, Sharry had made systematic progress with her research. She had honed the process of identifying and cataloguing frequencies that alleviated muscle problems. This time, Bill used Sharry's process for the treatment of synovitus rather than taking his customary trip to the doctor's office. His recovery took the same amount of time, but there were no expensive drugs or trips to the doctor. Bill believes that his brain had already learned the frequency of the naproxen when he previously took the medication and that Sharry's sounds enabled the brain to stimulate the same response that the body had when he took naproxen.

Bill recalled two other near miracles he had with sound healing. On one occasion, a torn hamstring muscle was bleeding internally, preventing him from walking. Normal recovery time is a year, but he was back on the tennis courts in about five weeks with frequency-based muscle repairs. He recalled another injury in which his recovery was even more remarkable. He tore his abdominal muscles in a nasty work-related accident. Weeks went by with no healing. Finally, he asked Sharry for help. She created tones with her voice and within two days he was much better and able to resume his active lifestyle.

One day Bill noticed a man in the grocery store wearing a shirt with a tennis logo; the man suffered from a terrible limp. For some reason the usually introverted Bill approached the man. After a brief introduction they found that they shared many interests. Their common passion was tennis. A few days later Bill's new friend, Bob, decided to hit a few tennis balls. Bill was reluctant, given how severely Bob dragged his foot, but Bob was determined to play.

On the tennis courts, Bill took it easy on Bob, hitting the ball directly to him. Bob gamely tried to play, but he painfully limped around the tennis court. Bob could not run and it was obvious that he was struggling badly.

Bob went to Bill's house for a snack and to relax after playing tennis. Bob began to tell his story of how he injured his leg and acquired the disabling limp. He explained that he had suffered a traumatic injury on a motorcycle. A truck pulled in front of him while he was riding at high speed and he plowed into the back of the truck. His leg was nearly severed just below the knee. Fortunately, a medical team was on the scene within minutes and his life was saved. After several months of rehabilitation Bob still had a severe limp and used a cane.

Bob was an accomplished athlete before the accident and he worked exhaustively to regain his mobility and strength. He was relentless in his efforts to get his leg back to normal and as a result he tried a number of experimental surgeries. In one procedure, muscles from his back were transplanted to his leg to reconstruct the damaged areas. After exhaustive treatment and physical therapies Bob was somewhat better, but still walked with a pronounced limp and terrible pain. His foot twisted to the right when he walked, making his gait slow and unsteady.

Bill suggested that Sharry could help him, but Bob's former hopes of recovery had proved to be so disappointing that he refused Sharry's help. During another visit, Sharry listened to Bob's voice as he was talking to Bill during a match. Without Bob's knowledge of what she was doing Sharry played tones in the background when they returned to the house. After about an hour, she asked him about his leg pain. To Bob's surprise it had faded considerably and he was able to walk down the stairs without pain. After he personally experienced the pain relief of the sounds, Bob was excited and hopeful about Sharry's sounds.

Within a few months of regularly listening to Sharry's sound therapy, Bob was much better. After only a few initial sound sessions Bob experienced greatly reduced pain and even stopped taking his daily pain pills. After a few months of the program Bob had no pain and he had gained strength in the leg; amazingly the leg had reshaped and had a much improved appearance. Although he still walked with a limp, he was virtually pain free and had greatly improved his overall mobility. After two years, he had no pain or limp. Bob no longer considered himself to be handicapped, as he immersed himself into an athletic lifestyle again.

Bill believes that Sharry's frequency formulas affect the brain as much as the body. He speculated that the frequencies activated Bob's brain, enabling it to send signals to the back muscles that were now in Bob's leg, establishing a connection and directing them to function in their new location. Sometimes, due to faulty genetics, injury or illness, the brain is unable to create the necessary signals to repair a situation. Bill believes that it is not only the sounds that influence the body to heal, but that they activate the brain, providing necessary signals and reestablishing connections as in Bob's case. The brain's delicate operations are not entirely understood and the study of BioAcoustics may allow scientists to gain breakthrough knowledge that will greatly extend our understanding of how the brain works.

At the moment these ideas are not thoroughly explained scientifically, but the visible and tangible results of BioAcoustics speak loud and clear. These results provide evidence that this process can change our medical world.

Early in her career, Sharry encountered a retired military officer who asked for her help. The retired soldier suffered from emphysema so badly that he could not breathe when he lay down in a bed. He was forced to live a life of inactivity – he could only dream of his former hobby of playing golf.

Sharry prepared a "frequency cocktail" and after listening to his sounds for a few days, the man was soon out of bed, puttering in the garage. A month after his amazing progress, he suffered a sudden relapse. Sharry visited the man to reassess his frequencies. While she was there she discovered that a television set had been placed in the room where he listened to Sharry's frequencies – the TV countered the beneficial sounds. With the removal of the TV his recovery was back on track, resulting in his return to the golf course. This incident made a significant impression on Sharry and afterwards her interest in sound healing grew to new heights; she committed her life to understanding and sharing her healing gifts.

Another friend of Bill's also had emphysema. He had heard of Sharry's successes. This man was unable to speak an entire sentence without halting, and resorted to pulling his arms behind his head to get enough air into his lungs and utter a soft phrase. As he started his treatment with Sharry, he stopped taking his medicine to see if the frequencies alone would improve his condition. Bill describes the day that Sharry tested the frequencies and how he watched his friend's breathing improve in a short time. Sharry asked that the TV be turned off as the TV waves would interfere and alter the beneficial influence of the frequencies. Unable to resist the temptation of watching Chris Evert's tennis match, he ignored those directions. In spite of his limited cooperation, he dropped his hands from behind his head, started telling stories and speaking in full sentences.

Rickii, Sharry's daughter, described a demobilizing back sprain and then walking away from the first sound treatment pain free. With continued sound healing her back was completely better within days. She also related stories about violent allergic reactions to wheat and dairy products. Now, she carries a small tone box that eliminates allergy symptoms in minutes, as she savors anything on the menu while eating out. The last story was that of Rickii's daughter, who was diagnosed with severe autistic disorder at four years of age. Joselyn was unable to communicate normally even though she had learned to read at an unusually young age. Within days after listening to sonic-medicine provided by Sharry, Joselyn spoke clearly using full sentences. She interacted with her world in an entirely new way! Today she leads a near normal life with minimal autistic symptoms.

Jesse, Sharry's son, was eighteen when he shattered his knee on a parking meter in a motorcycle accident. Sharry used her own voice to supply healing tones. To the amazement of the medical community, his knee rebuilt itself and he grew a new kneecap. His damaged leg connected to a new nerve supply and his broken bones healed without any scarring.

June is a volunteer at Sound Health. She is a former law enforcement officer and, as such, she was skeptical of anything that she did not see firsthand. She received a frequency formula from Sharry that in just two days healed a serious and painful foot injury, which had badly hobbled her. She became a BioAcoustic believer and volunteer at Sound Health.

June enthusiastically described a woman who clung to her husband for support in order to walk. The poor man also lugged her oxygen tank into Sharry's office. After her initial auditory experience, she walked to her car on her own. Barely stopping to take a breath, June continued with an amazing account describing a man with an eye problem who regained enough sight to read in just one day!

Terrance Bugno, MD, and Jonathan Murphy, MD, confirmed that listening to low frequency sounds could alleviate painful symptoms for gout sufferers within minutes. "For gout sufferers, like myself, this is like a miracle!" stated Dr. Murphy. "Normally when I have a flare up, it takes two to three days for symptoms to subside and then I am left with the unpleasant side effects from the medication. It's hard to believe that with BioAcoustics you can actually watch the swelling and redness disappear before your eyes."

There is no end to these types of stories that people close to Sharry can recite. It is interesting that Sharry's methods have worked on a wide variety of drastically different physical ailments –emphysema, gout, autistic disorder and muscular problems. Many case studies have videotaped testimonies with before and after shots, bringing hope to the hearts of many. These results plead for further studies and investigations of the effects of frequencies within the body.

### Benefits of BioAcoustics

Below are a list of some conditions that benefit from BioAcoustic sounds:

- Arthritis
- Heart disease
- Diabetes
- Emphysema
- Gout
- Hypertension
- Trauma injury
- Sprains and strains
- Osteoporosis
- Fibromyalgia

- Learning disorders
- Multiple sclerosis
- Temporomandibular joint disorder *(TMJ)*
- Neurological disorders such as anxiety & psychosis
- Learning disabilities such as ADHD and others
- Chronic fatigue
- Senility/Alzheimer's Disease
- Yeast and Epstein-Barr virus
- Allergies
- Insulin resistance
- Seizure Disorders
- Post traumatic Stress Disorder *(PTSD)*
- Traumatic Brain Injury *(TBI)*

Muscular disorders that BioAcoustics has shown outstanding promise for
- Muscle pain and weakness
- Back pain
- Recovery time from sports injuries
- Muscle deterioration for people in nursing homes
- Cerebral palsy
- Fibromyalgia
- Exercise in space *(difficult with weightlessness)*
- Muscle trauma and recovery

Regenerate nerve tissue and related conditions
- Macular degeneration
- Nerve and tissue regrowth and regeneration
- Parkinson's disease
- Multiple sclerosis

## Effective, efficient and noninvasive methods to identify body issues

- Quantitative analysis of head injuries
- Remote monitoring and analysis of traumatic brain injured soldiers on the battle field
- Nutritional analysis *(testing for the frequency-equivalent supplements that a body needs)*
- Trace-body-chemistry analysis

## Other practical applications

- Saves millions of dollars and time in invasive medical tests
- Prevents disease and illness by identifying tonal patterns before a problem becomes physically manifested
- Predict susceptibility to diseases such as cancer, Alzheimer's, heart disease…

## Overcoming specific conditions

- High blood pressure
- Irregular heart rhythm
- Bird flu and swine flu
- Pain management

## Giving aid and insight into emotional and subtle body energy systems

- Aids emotional balance
- Supports the elimination of anxiety disorders
- Documents subconscious emotions
- Identifies personality disorders
- Shows compatibility of people for dating or job placement tasks

<u>Offering a versatile array of environmental improvement and
plant growth enhancements</u>

- Stimulates plant growth and health
- Controls pests – without pesticides that damage the environment
- Offers food preservation
- Offers alternatives to environmental pollution

## Software

Below is a list of many of Sharry's software programs, each
designed to enable people to benefit from her auditory gift.
Her life long quest of deciphering the body frequency
mechanisms and processes has resulted in this impressive
collection of benefits for people using BioAcoustics. All
issues are reported in terms of numeric representations of
frequency-equivalents.

| Software Program | Benefit |
| --- | --- |
| Nanovoice | Freeware to identify personality issues in the voice and reveal one's authentic self |
| Heart Tracker | To evaluate heart stress, damage, circulation, heart beat and overall wellness |
| Vocal Profiler | To ascertain general conditions associated with genes, pathogens, toxins, muscles, amino acids, nutrients, fatty acids, enzymes, antioxidants |
| The New Woman | To identify women's issues associated with pregnancy, child birth, menses, fertility, |

| | |
|---|---|
| | menopause, cancer, thyroid, pituitary and hormone issues |
| Sex Factors | To identify issues with and enhance desire/sexual performance |
| Re-Voice | To determine areas of speaking difficulties caused by trauma or stroke |
| nVoice | To ascertain emotional status via vocal frequencies, showing internal conflicts, interpersonal compatibility and challenges |
| Eye Watcher | To establish issues with vision, color discrimination, cataracts, macular degeneration, color blindness, eye related nutrients and glaucoma |
| Rejuvenation *(anti-aging)* | To delineate aspects of the aging process, levels of anti-oxygents and to relieve stained teeth, gray hair and wrinkles |
| Bio-Diet | To support weight management by identifying and countering FEs associated with inability to manage weight |
| Post-Traumatic Stress Disorder | Designed to be used with U.S. army troops on the battle field to assess and support traumatic brain injured soldiers |
| Pre-Vac | To predict reactions to vaccinations, decrease health issues related to vaccinations and provide information for autistic disorders and ADHD |
| BioAcoustic Toxins | To identify and harmonize stressed toxic FEs in our bodies |
| Nutrition | Identify specific nutritional needs such |

| | |
|---|---|
| Consultant | as vitamins, fatty acids, enzymes, minerals, amino acids, cell salts, antioxidants - to direct ingesting appropriate supplements and food |
| BioAcoustic Muscle Program | To identify weak or strong muscles and predict which ones are likely to be injured |
| BioAcoustic Pathogens | To identify FEs of pathogens, bird flu and viruses in your voice |
| Muscle Factors | To support normal form and function of the muscles related to fibromyalgia and other muscle related issues |
| Swine Outlook | FEs for proteins, genes and activators associated with Swine Flu. |
| Connection Reflections | Data to evaluate potential inflammation and pathogenic associations of joint and muscle pain, and tightness with tendons, ligaments and connective tissues |
| Seizure Perspectives | Assessment information associated with the brain functions that require an organized and coordinated discharge of electrical impulses |
| Golf Swing | FEs for proper conditioning of muscles to increase muscle coordination and control |
| Insulin Resistance | FEs for receptors, proteins, and genes to support optimal blood sugars |
| Mapping Methylation | The methyl cycle determines our resistance or susceptibility to environmental toxins and microbes and our ability to measure resources. If methyl cycle abnormalities are not addressed, chronic illness remains |

| | |
|---|---|
| Immune Rise | FEs of your own unique genetic code in terms of maintaining a healthy immune system |
| Parkinson's Influence | FEs for predicting Parkinson's and FEs to support wellness |
| BioHazard | FEs to alleviate symptoms associated with manmade hazards that are resistant to antibiotics |
| Hair Apparent | FEs to facilitate hair growth and healthy hair. |
| The Gray Matter of Alzheimer's | May help predict, prevent and repair FEs for Alzheimer's disease. |
| Inflammation | FEs to evaluate long-term inflammation associated with joint/muscle pain, loss of structural function and mobility, organ and vascular insufficiency |
| Cholesterol | FEs to manage cholesterol |
| Blood Clotting, Factors and Controls | FEs for warning factors associated with strokes, and controls to maintain healthy blood supply in the brain |
| HcG | Identifies HcG diet biochemicals and proteins, and HCG's relationship to glucose and leptin metabolism plus DNA replication |

| | |
|---|---|
| Sleep Purrfect | Indentifies various processes and vitamins that are essential for sleep, and reviews aspects of medications and other sleep related factors. |
| Exploring Arthritus | Identifies types of arthritis, mitigating causal factors and indicates which therapies are helpful. |
| Nerve Degeneration | An extensive list of brain components are evaluated as well as toxins, biochemicals, medications, vitamins and pathogens that are in the body that may affect nerve degeneration. Nerve degeneration is hard to identify but early detection is beneficial. |
| Anxiety | Anxiety can lead to many severe life incapacitating syndromes, affecting decision making capacities and health. This program evaluates causes as well as therapies related to anxiety. |
| Cancer Crusade | Aids in detection, monitors treatment, both medication and radiation. |

| | |
|---|---|
| Allergies | Evaluates levels of substances that can affect allergies and asthma, including medications, biochemicals, vitamins, minerals, herbs, toxins, and immune system components. |
| Ye Gads | The health of two neurotransmitters, GAD 65 and GAD 67 are crucial because they are at the root of nearly all incurable diseases. Examines their status and relationship with other body processes in your body. Helps identify the potential problems/sensitivities relating to GAD. |
| Kidney | Evaluates filtration of blood, homeostatic functions, removal of wastes, reabsorption of vital nutrients and water, production of the hormones calcitriol, renin and erythropoietin. |
| Adrenal Burnout | In our fast paced world, adrenal burnout is approaching epic proportions. This software reviews genetic and biochemical issues affecting adrenal burnout. |
| Spasticity and Dystonia | Investigates causal factors such as genetic, biochemical, toxin and other factors. Evaluates the impact of medications and suggests which treatments may be at the root of these nerve/muscles issues. |

| | |
|---|---|
| Sines of Life | Identifies indicators associated with fertility, reproduction and labor. |
| Osteoporosis | Evaluates genetic susceptibility, preventative measures and recommends therapies that will address your unique issues. |

More programs are released every year!

**Designated Tone Boxes**
*(Available through trained BioAcoustic Providers)*

| | |
|---|---|
| Little Back Box | To support normal form and function of back muscles |
| Charlie Chaser | To support the alleviation of cramps |
| G - Out | To support the alleviation of gout |
| Fab Abs | To tune and tighten abdominal muscles |
| Face Time Continuum | To tune and tighten face and neck muscles |
| Overture | DNA and RNA repairs the body and maintains stasis. It is possible that the frequency of |

| | these vital body components can become stressed and later re-tuned with the frequency that correlates to healthy DNA and RNA. This box contains sounds to support the body's normal form and function; particularly from the DNA/RNA levels. |
|---|---|
| Bio Body | To tune and tighten overall body muscles, from the shoulders down |
| Muscle Box | To support normal form and function of the muscles related to fibromyalgia and other muscle related issues |

The names of many of these data bases have been found in the Bible Code.[50]

## Summary of Part One

Hopefully you have gained an appreciation of the major influences Sharry faced growing up and how she set out on the course that led to the creation of BioAcoustics.

To recapitulate:
1.  Sharry Edwards was born with "extrasensory hearing" – the ability to hear frequencies outside the range of the normal human ear.

---

[50] Bible codes are words, phrases, word clusters and phrases that some people believe are intentionally in coded form in the Bible. These codes were made famous by the book The Bible Code, by Michael Drosnin, which suggests that these codes give information for the future. The names of some of Sharry's databases such as "Abacus,"[50] "Brain Wave Multiple," "Mathway," "Pre-Vac," "Svani," "Anuba,"

2. She hears sounds emanating from a wide range of sources like inanimate objects such as rocks and the environment to people's bodies.

3. Factors that may have played a part in Sharry's gift of "extrasensory hearing" where being raised in a natural environment without manmade electro - magnetic "pollution;" a healthy lifestyle of hard work, fresh air, pure food and water and a near-drowning incident.

4. From an early age, Sharry was able to develop the ability to vocally produce extraordinary sounds.

5. She learned the sounds for specific illnesses by making connections between sounds she perceived emanating from some people and their illnesses as well as, observed the link between discordant sounds and specific emotional stress.

6. Sharry's vocalizations altered people's health in a positive manner and through time, she has developed a library of healing sounds that support optimal health.

7. She induced a state of openness in moving away from conventional methods, seeking reasons to explain her auditory world by looking for scientific explanations for her experiences and ultimately, creating BioAcoustics.

Sharry's natural curiosity has provided her with opportunities to understand the underpinnings of what she could hear and

---

"BARA," "AHEA," "Biofrequency," and "Svani" are found encoded many times in the Bible Code.

voice. When the experts told Sharry that it was impossible to hear what she did, it only deepened her resolve to understand more about sound.

Sharry's auditory experiences shaped her view of the world, creating a link between sound and health. Most people do not consider the impact of sound on their bodies. By deciphering the meaning of the ever-changing chorus of sounds that she lives in, Sharry builds a different perspective regarding auditory cause and effect linking our environment and us.

It is not a question of whether sound can affect our health. From Sharry's viewpoint, why does sound work? Through her research she has been able to refine and repeat processes, document and validate her procedures and create networks of BioAcoustic practitioners that send in case studies adding to the BioAcoustic knowledge-base.

Sharry has labored long and hard to overcome the difficulties associated with the challenges of creating a comprehensive methodology and a business that flies in the face of conventional thinking and medical practice. Thanks to her tenacious nature, she continues to build useful data.

History teaches that fortuitous combinations are usually required to produce breakthroughs—so it was with Sharry. With her unique gifts, thirst for knowledge, dogged persistence and determination—the ingredients were in place for some extraordinary discoveries resulting in a new science, BioAcoustics.

# PART TWO
# TECHNICAL DETAILS

## Introduction

Part Two of this book features challenging technical details of
BioAcoustics. It not only contains fascinating information for
advanced sound enthusiasts but also attainable knowledge for
the determined beginner.

It is not necessary to read this information to take advantage
of the sound healing benefits. The reader uninterested in the
working theories of BioAcoustics or not prepared to delve
into more technical details can just skip to Part Three,
Applications.

In a closer investigation of Part Two, you will find many of
Sharry's theories about how sound affects us. By observing
thousands of voiceprints and combining this information with
scientific research that corroborates with her results, she
teaches us about sound in terms of science, the mathematical
language of the brain, brain dominance and its effects on
processing frequencies, the applications of color theories
interlaced with frequency tonics and more unsuspected
connections.

Based on years of observing tiny, subtle musical components
that are combined in our voices, Sharry formulates and tests
her hypotheses. Steadily growing audiences listen to Sharry's
sound presentations, giving her numerous opportunities to

perfect her practices and ensure that they work time after time. A large group of practitioners regularly feed data and ideas into her growing knowledge base. Sharry often jokes that she wants data to further her research and if you eliminate your problems when she conducts her research that is your business.

Sharry's practice is very much on the cutting edge of science. Her theories and methods stretch the imagination of conventional thinkers, opening up new vistas. Sharry knows that her methods work; it is only a matter of time before they are fully explained by science. Part Two reviews numerous scientific findings that confirm segments of BioAcoustics. Her ideas beg for more study, modification and explanation.

This section continues with a novel view on how vibratory waves communicate information throughout the body and not exclusively for the purpose of hearing. Some related scientific studies validate many of these ideas.

The BioAcoustic story pursues the significance of pitch, shape, and graphic pattern that can be found when we analyze our voice components. We can see the shapes created by many pitches in a voiceprint and a graphic representation of patterns hidden in the spoken voice. Specific shapes, pitches and patterns convey meaning regarding our mental and emotional health.

After analyzing sound in our body, Part Two describes Sharry's experiences regarding environmental sound and its influence on us. Sharry hears sounds from astonishing sources, yielding insights that clarify physical, mental and emotional influences that we receive from unexpected sources. Understanding these relationships enables us to balance and harmonize our energies with the ever-changing array of environmental frequencies.

Environmental and vibrational influences have surprising effects on us. The curious person interested in music, healing, medicine, color therapy, astrology, math or science will have to hold on to their seats, and get ready for some ideas that change their view of reality!

Sharry retains many sound secrets in hopes that you might come to Sound Health for software, evaluations and education. Obviously not all her secrets are revealed in this book, but many are explained in Part Two which are bound to give you a new view of the world from a sound perspective. These ideas and concepts are useful in alternative healing therapies and give us valuable information to make better decisions on music selections. Finally, this information enables us to use sound to achieve inner harmony and balance amidst a world of frequencies that can assault our harmony.

# Chapter One

# The Frequency Transport System

Sharry observes and experiments with frequencies to determine which patterns of sounds support the body, while easing discomfort and problematic symptoms. After observing countless voiceprints she has constructed theories to explain the pitches displayed in the voiceprints. Sharry refines her practices through trial and error and devises reproducible methods and processes. These methods are based on novel, yet ancient, foundational concepts.

Two concepts are widely used as foundational building blocks in Sharry's work. The first is that energy can be expressed as a frequency or wavelength. It does not matter if the frequency or wave is audible. The second premise is that energy and information are exchanged on waves, which then can be studied through the looking glass of sound.

### First Building Block:
### Energy can be Expressed as Frequencies

"Frequency encompasses more than audible sound. If we enlarge our perspective to take in the fullest possible view of our vibrational world, then frequency can be just about anything...an angle, electromagnetic energy, thoughts and feelings, shapes, or language. If we have a number for the 'frequency,' such as an angle of 45 degrees, we can start to build data."[51]

Let's delve into greater detail about this broader perspective of frequency. Whenever an electric charge oscillates or is accelerated, a disturbance of electric and magnetic fields propagates outward. This disturbance is called an electromagnetic wave.[52]

Electromagnetic radiation is classified according to the frequency of the wave. Types of waves include *(in order of increasing frequency)*: radio waves, microwaves, infrared radiation, visible light, ultraviolet radiation, X-rays and gamma rays. Of these, radio waves have the longest wavelengths and Gamma rays have the shortest. The eye senses a small window of frequencies, called the visible spectrum of light. In theory, any electromagnetic radiation can be detected by its heating effect. This method has been used to detect radiation from x-rays to radio.

As a wave gets wider and longer, its frequency drops and sounds lower in pitch. As the wave becomes smaller, the frequency increases and sounds higher in pitch.

The scientist, doctor and author, Dr. Robert Becker, writes in Cross Currents, "All of the possible frequencies of electromagnetic waves or fields can be put onto an electromagnetic spectrum, starting with the slowest frequency and going to the highest. The electromagnetic spectrum is usually pictured as a line that increases from zero on the left - to trillions of cycles per second on the right. About three-

---

[51] Alexjander, Susan. www.oursounduniverse.com
[52] www.answers.com/topic/electromagnetic-radiation

fourths across the frequency spectrum is something that we are familiar with - light."[53] The spectrum ranging from electric lights to magnetic fields can be mapped along a frequency continuum.

Dr. Becker continues, "This vibrational spectrum is produced by the movement of electrons and has the same characteristics as the Earth's magnetic field, radio waves and X-rays…In summary, magnetic and electromagnetic fields have energy, carry information and are produced by electrical currents. When we talk about electrical currents flowing in living organisms, we also imply that they are producing magnetic fields that extend outside of the body and can be influenced by external magnetic fields as well."[54]

Electromagnetic energy falls into categories, just like elements on the Periodic Chart are grouped into categories. Sound healers group the categories into octaves. An octave is an interval of two musical notes, in which one frequency is half the cycles per second of the other.

This is how octaves are created - starting with 100 cycles per second:
- A tone that is an octave below, is created by dividing the frequency in half and is now 50 cycles per second.
- A tone another octave below has a frequency of 25 cycles per second.
- A tone, another octave lower, vibrates at 12.5 cycles per second.

[53] Becker, Robert, Dr. Cross Currents, The Perils of Electropollution, The Promise of Electromedicine, Penguin Group: New York, 1990, pg. 69
[54] Becker, Robert, Dr. Cross Currents, The Perils of Electropollution, The Promise of Electromedicine, Penguin Group: New York, 1990, pg. 69.

- A tone, yet another octave lower, creates a frequency of 6.25 cycles per second.

Usually the human ear cannot hear below approximately 20 cycles a second. However, a frequency below 20 cycles per second is in the frequency range associated with brain waves, which has been associated with various states of consciousness.

Let's go the other way and raise the initial frequency by octaves. Let's start at 20,000 cycles per second *(the highest sound that people hear)* and raise this pitch by octaves. Each new octave is above our hearing range. As we increase the frequency by octaves the speed of the wave increases and eventually matches the speed of radio waves, TV waves, microwaves and X - rays. After we increase the frequency 40 octaves, frequencies are now measured in angstroms, or millions of cycles per second. These high octaves are measured as light!

Energies can be aligned on a spectrum, going from the slowest cycles per second to the fastest. Categories of frequencies are grouped by octaves. Frequencies that correspond to brain waves can be increased. Each octave serves a specific function in the body.

Physicists sometimes object to combining these energies in one spectrum, because some energy exhibits wave qualities and other energy has characteristics of both waves and particles.[55] This argument dates back to the 1600s when Christiaan Huygens and Isaac Newton proposed competing theories of light. Light was thought either to consist of waves

*(Huygens)* or particles *(Newton)*. Through the work of Albert Einstein, Louis de Broglie and many others, current scientific theory suggests that all particles have a wave nature *(and vice versa)*. In different contexts, because of mass, energy or frequency, some matter seems more particle-like than wave-like. In other contexts such as reduced energy, the same matter demonstrates more wave-like than particle-like qualities.[56]

Author David Tame documents that when ultrasonic sound vibrates a glass rod it causes the rod to produce both heat and light. This infers that sound energy is capable of becoming both heat and light.[57] To further demonstrate the relationship of vibrations on the electromagnetic spectrum Tame cites the work of scientist, Maxwell, who demonstrated that "magnetism and electricity were really aspects of the same force."[58] He hints that we should be able to convert of forms of energy into any other.

---

[56] At the close of the 19th century, the case that matter was made of particulate objects or atoms, was well established. Electricity was understood to consist of particles called electrons. It was understood that much of nature was made of particles. At the same time, waves were well understood, together with wave phenomena such as diffraction and interference. Light was believed to be a wave. By the turn of the 20th century, problems emerged. Albert Einstein's analysis of the photoelectric effect in 1905 demonstrated that light also possessed particle-like properties. Later on, the diffraction of electrons would be confirmed, thus showing that electrons must have wave-like properties in addition to particle properties. This confusion over particle versus wave properties was eventually resolved with quantum mechanics in the first half of the 20th century, which ultimately explained wave–particle duality. It provided a single unified theoretical framework for understanding that all matter may have characteristics associated with particles and waves. *Wikipedia*

[57] Tame, David. <u>The Secret Power of Music: The Transformation of Self and Society Through Musical Energy</u>, Destiny Books: Vermont, 1984. Pg. 231.

[58] Tame, David. <u>The Secret Power of Music: The Transformation of Self and Society Through Musical Energy</u>, Destiny Books: Vermont, 1984. Pg. 231.

Sound healers simply organize energies according to the frequencies, regardless of characteristics of waves and particles. Sharry groups octaves into biomagnetic frequencies, bioelectrical frequencies, neurotransmissions, biochemicals *(amino acids, hormones, enzymes, vitamins, minerals)*, emotional frequencies, structural frequencies *(bones, muscles and ligaments)*, and neurophysical frequencies *(nervous system).*

## Second Building Block
## Energy and Information are exchanged via Wave Frequency Interactions

All subatomic particles vibrate. Lynne McTaggart, author of The Field, The Quest for the Secret Force of the Universe, describes these vibrations. "Much like the undulations of the sea or ripples on a pond, the waves on a subatomic level are represented by periodic oscillations, moving through a medium. A classic sideways S – sine curve, like a jump rope being held at both ends and being wiggled around, represents them."[59] The vibrations of subatomic particles resemble sound waves.

James Oschman,[60] a "vibratory medicine" author, writes that physical contact *(between two molecules)* is not as significant

---

[59] McTaggart, Lynne. The Field, The Quest for the Secret Force of the Universe, Harpers Collins Publishers: New York, 2002. pg. 25.
[60] James Oschman is the author a book, Energy Medicine: The Scientific Basis. This book gives the most skeptical academic scientists a theoretical basis for exploring the physiology and biophysics of energy medicines. He also wrote Energy Medicine in Therapeutics and Human Performance. Jim has degrees in Biophysics and Biology from the University of Pittsburgh. He has worked in major research labs around the world, including Cambridge University in England, Case-Western Reserve University, the University of Copenhagen, Northwestern University, and the Marine

as wave and vibrational interactions. Molecular communications can be compared to the interactions of tuning fork frequencies. "At an atomic scale, physical contact between two molecules has less meaning than the ways that they interact energetically. For example, as a hormone approaches a receptor, the electronic structures of both molecules begin to change. Bonds blend, twist and stretch; parts rotate and wiggle. The orientation and shape of the molecules change so that the active site of the hormone can approach the active site of the receptor. This recognition of a specific hormone by a receptor depends on resonant vibratory interactions, comparable to the interactions of tuning forks."[61] Oschman says that the interaction of cells is characterized by the vibratory influences that they share.

Waves carry energy and information. A TV remote controller, radio waves and telephones utilize waves to carry information. Like Oschman, many sound healers believe that waves or frequencies carry information within our bodies. Information is exchanged through wave interactions.

McTaggart postulates, "One of the most important aspects of waves is that they are encoders and carriers of information. When two waves are in phase, and overlap each other, technically called 'interference' – the combined amplitude of the waves is greater than each individual's amplitude. The signal gets stronger. This amounts to an imprinting or exchange of information – called 'constructive interference.' Interference patterns amount to a constant accumulation of

Biological Laboratory in Woods Hole. His many scientific papers have been published in the world's leading journals.
[61] Edwards, Sharry quoting James Oschman. Vocal Profiling for the Professional, Sound Health: Albany, OH., 2002 pg. MI 53.

information... and waves have a virtually infinite capacity for storage."[62] These experiments verify an important piece of Sharry's process - information to bring the body back into harmony can be carried via bio frequencies.

Sharry's discoveries rely on sound. Sound waves within the human hearing range are only a segment of possible electro-magnetic wavelengths. Since we can hear sound waves, they prove to be a powerful way to study wave phenomena. By listening we observe harmonies and musical properties of sound. These observations teach us not only about sound but other ranges of waves that behave in the same manner.

McTaggart proposes that studies of waves have a broader impact than first meets the eye. "Everything that has ever happened in our world is through wave interference encoding."[63] She adds, "The real currency of the universe - the very reason for its stability - is an exchange of energy."[64]

In summary, two concepts are foundational premises for BioAcoustics:
1. Energy can be expressed as frequency on the electromagnetic scale.
2. Energy and information are exchanged via wave interactions.

### Brain waves

---

[62] McTaggart, Lynne. The Field, The Quest for the Secret Force of the Universe, Harpers Collins Publishers: N.Y., 2002. pg. 26.
[63] McTaggart, Lynne. The Field, The Quest for the Secret Force of the Universe, Harpers Collins Publishers: N.Y,, 2002. pg. 35.
[64] McTaggart, Lynne. The Field, The Quest for the Secret Force of the Universe, Harpers Collins Publishers: N.Y., 2002. pg. 36.

According to the traditional view, people associate sounds with their ears and limit the exclusive realm of sound to hearing. Sharry believes the influence of sound has far greater impact. To understand the complexity of how sound has such a potent effect on us, we will explore different methods whereby sound *(such as the frequencies of our voice)* is transported throughout the body. We will begin this exploration in the brain.

Brian Butterworth combines his expertise in cognitive neuroscience and his broad knowledge of mathematics in his book What Counts, How Every Brain is Hardwired for Math. He likens the brain to an intricate calculator which sends and receives information throughout the body. He determined that our biology and brain are hardwired for math.[65] The body's math is expressed as frequency. Frequency is said to be the language of the body because it easily converts to math. Jeffrey Thompson, a sound healing scientist, said, "The brain's internal communication system, its language, is based on frequency." [66] Our body knows how to interpret frequencies as easily as we understand the meaning of words.

All frequencies can be correlated to brainwaves, by cutting the cycles per second *(creating octaves)* in half until it is in the range of brain waves. The brain translates frequencies that are in the range of brain waves and appropriately reroutes the vibratory information to the rest of our bodies.

In the 1940s, Karl Pribram *(a neurosurgeon and researcher)* theorized about the language of the brain and body. "Our

---

[65] Butterworth, Brian. What Counts, How Every Brain is Hardwired for Math. Free Press: N.Y., 1999.
[66] "Research Behind Acoustic Brain Entrainment," pg. 8. www.neuroacoustic.org.

brain primarily talks to itself and to the rest of the body - not with words or images or even bits or chemical impulses, but in the language of wave interference; the language of phase, amplitude and frequency - the spectral domain. We perceive the world by resonating with it, getting in sync with it. To know the world is to literally be on its wavelength."[67]

## Collective Energy Fields

Not only is our brain wired to use the language of frequencies, but also the entire body, down to the very molecules. Every molecule vibrates in a characteristic way, expressing its own unique energy. This is proven with spectroscopy[68] which records and measures resonant emissions and absorption of waves in molecules. Different movements within the molecule emit different frequencies.[69] According to James Gimzewski, a chemist from UCLA with an extensive background in nanotechnology, "Every cell has a frequency."[70] He calculated the pitch of a cell by measuring the distance the cell wall raises and falls, and its speed or

---

[67] Lynne. The Field, The Quest for the Secret Force of the Universe, Harper Collins Publishing: N.Y., 2002. pg. 84.

[68] Spectroscopy is historically referred to the use of visible light dispersed according to its wavelength, e.g. by a prism. Later the concept was expanded to include any measurement of wavelength or frequency. Spectroscopy is used in physical and analytical chemistry to identify substances through the spectrum emitted from or absorbed by them. *Wikipedia*

[69]"Spectroscopy demonstrates that the relationships between organisms and coherent vibrations in all living systems are as basic as their chemical bonds. There are two ways of altering the body's functions – by adding molecules to a system and by changing the fingerprint of the molecule. Many of the current energy therapies change the signature of molecules to create balance within the body." Davis, Dorinne. Sound Bodies through Sound Therapy, Kalco Publishing: Landing, New Jersey, 2004. pg. 231.

[70] Jim Gimzewski, a UCLA chemist, a leader in nanotechnology, previously worked at IBM's research laboratory in Zurich, Switzerland, where he and colleagues built a spinning molecular propeller 0.0000015 millimeters in diameter.

oscillation. The distance the cell wall moves determines the amplitude or the volume of the sound wave. The speed of the up-and-down movement determines the pitch. The volume of the sound wave is too low to be audible even though it is theoretically within the range of human hearing. Gimzewski poured alcohol cells which made the pitch rise. When the cell died, it gave off a low rumbling noise.[71]

Molecules vibrate and emit frequencies, impacting other molecules. In her book <u>Sound Bodies through Sound Therapy</u> Dorinne Davis explains how the vibration of one molecule moves throughout the body. "If a molecule is charged, the vibrating interaction between molecules sets up an electromagnetic field that entrains adjacent molecules. Nearby molecules respond by emitting the same electromagnetic field."[72]

Davis explains what happens when the vibrations of molecules impact others. "As a result, the molecular movements and energy fields that are generated form collective energy systems."[73] She adds, "As these energetic pathways intersect, they produce coordinated energy actions, which are the foundation of processes such as thought, reproduction, excretion, and movement, among others."[74] Dorinne describes the vibration of one molecule and how it interacts and shares its vibration with its neighbors, creating energy fields in the body.

---

[71] Wheeler, Mark. *Signal Discovery?*
http://www.smithsonianmag.si.edu/smithsonian/issues04/mar04/phenomena.html
[72] Davis, Dorinne. <u>Sound Bodies through Sound Therapy</u>, Kalco Publishing: Landing, New Jersey, 2004 pg. 253.
[73] Davis, Dorinne. <u>Sound Bodies through Sound Therapy,</u> Kalco Publishing: Landing, New Jersey, 2004. pg. 253.
[74] Davis, Dorinne. <u>Sound Bodies through Sound Therapy,</u> Kalco Publishing: Landing, New Jersey, 2004. pg. 230.

Sharry believes that some collective energy systems have constant frequencies in every person's body which she calls "frequency-equivalents" or FEs. Generally, an organ has a stable stream of energy, a collective frequency.

One by one Sharry discovered and tested each frequency-equivalent for muscles, tissues and organs. All bones are composed of nearly identical chemical elements. She hypothesizes that each element in the "Periodic Chart of Elements" has its own signature frequency. Since the frequencies of the component elements are consistent, each bone has a universal frequency. Continuing with this line of reasoning, if each element has its own signature frequency, then each bio-chemical *(made up of elements),* toxin, pathogen, herb and medicine also has a signature frequency. Individual tones of each organ vary slightly. Sharry has created extensive catalogs of frequency-equivalents for healthy organs, tissues, muscles and body systems.

Valance electrons govern chemical reactions. As they are moving energy perhaps they account for their cell frequency.

## Impact of Frequency-Equivalents

Experiments show that a person who receives the frequency formula for niacin, experiences skin flushing. If he ingests niacin, he has the same reaction.

In an analogous situation, high blood pressure responds positively to traditional medication but research proves that meditation can reduce blood pressure as well. As the reader may well recall, Sharry's earlier work provided evidence to show the reduction of blood pressure using her voice. Clearly the human body is a marvelous, mysterious machine that responds on many levels to different energies or treatments.

French doctor and scientist, Jacques Benveniste conducted experiments with low frequency waves from electromagnetic signals producing changes similar to pharmacological chemicals.[75] The low electromagnetic radiation of these signals effectively took the place of chemicals.[76]

McTaggart writes that, "Benveniste demonstrated that you could transfer specific molecular signals simply by using an amplifier and electromagnetic coils. Four years later, he was able to record and replay these signals using a multimedia computer. Over thousands of experiments, Benveniste and Didier Guillonnet *(an engineer)* recorded the activity of a molecule on a computer and replayed it to a biological system, ordinarily sensitive to that substance. In every instance the biological system has been fooled into thinking that it has an interaction with the substance itself and has acted accordingly, initiating a biological chain reaction just as it would in the actual presence of the genuine molecule."[77] Once again this study demonstrates the power of waves to carry information and impact us significantly.

Negative emotions, toxins and pathogens produce frequencies. They create disharmony and spread disorder through the same process of resonance that spreads harmony. The body becomes stressed when harmonic frequency

---

[75] He recorded the sounds of the cells with a purpose-designed transducer and a computer equipped with a sound card.

[76] Less than 20 kilohertz

[77] McTaggart, Lynne. The Field, The Quest for the Secret Force of the Universe, Harpers Collins Publishers: N.Y., 2002. pg. 68.

patterns are disrupted in body organs and systems. If the collective vibration of an organ slips or escalates, disease can result.

BioAcoustical analysis and sound formulations can support one's health. These methods can enhance the medical field. Forms of today's curative medical solutions at their structural levels affect our bodies' FEs. These are some of the things that affect our internal frequencies: medicine, homeopathic remedies, herbs, vitamins, heating pads and ice packs *(Heat is a form of frequency. Temperature varies in a manner similar to pitches)*. Medical treatments already influence the frequency systems of the body. Medical treatments utilizing vibrating waves include X-rays, sonograms, ultrasounds, MRIs, CAT scans and heart pacemakers. Frequency treatments are already an important part of the medical field, but they are not categorized as sound treatment.

### Energy Transportion Systems

As we have seen, one basic BioAcoustic concept is that wave patterns carry information that is delivered to all parts of the body in various ways. Understanding the different pathways of body communication enhances our comprehension of how Sharry uses sound to impact the body.

Sound therapy works effectively with deaf people, suggesting that sound enters the body through other means than just our ears. It also follows that there are more receptors for sound than hearing alone.

Sound can enter the body via the skin. Neurons[78] process and transmit information in the nervous system by vibrational signaling. Some neurons throughout the body specialize in responding to sound, light, touch and other stimuli and then send these signals to the brain. When music is played near us, sound waves hit our skin. Sound receptors in our skin receive the vibrations of the music and then pass it to the nerves. Dr. Tomatis commented on the effects of sound on our skin. "The skin is richly supplied with sound receptors principally in the face, the anterior part of the thorax, the abdomen, the inside of the arms, the palms of the hands, inside of the thighs and legs, as well as the soles of the feet. These places interpret pressures made on the skin by sound waves, even when they are below the threshold of conscious awareness. It makes sense that when someone does not want to listen to something that he may turn his back or step aside, so that he presents the parts of his body that have fewer sound receptors."[79] The sound impulses enter through the skin and travel on nerve pathways to our brain.

An average human child has approximately one hundred billion neurons by the age of two. The neurons are connected together through a network of dendrites that conduct

---

[78] Neurons are responsive cells in the nervous system that process and transmit information by electrochemical signaling. They are the core components of the brain, the vertebrate spinal cord, the invertebrate ventral nerve cord, and the peripheral nerves. A number of specialized types of neurons exist: sensory neurons respond to touch, sound, light and numerous other stimuli affecting cells of the sensory organs that then send signals to the spinal cord and brain. Motor neurons receive signals from the brain and spinal cord and cause muscle contractions and affect glands. Neurons respond to stimuli and communicate the presence of stimuli to the central nervous system which processes that information and sends responses to other parts of the body for action.

[79] Dr. Tomatis. The Ear and the Voice, The Scarecrow Press: Maryland, Toronto, Oxford, 1987. Translated into English in 2005. Pg. 84.

electrical impulses.[80] An average adult has approximately one trillion dendrites that can total almost 10,000 miles in length. Communication *(of information carried on waves)* in our bodies is clearly important.

A system of pulses and body rhythms creates a communication system. Hazrat Inayat Khan, a Sufi teacher who teaches about the impact of music, says, "A person not only hears sounds through his ears, but through every pore of his body. Sound permeates his entire being, and according to its particular influence, it either slows down or quickens the rhythms of the blood circulation; it either wakens the nervous system or soothes it. It arouses the listener to greater passions or it calms him by bringing peace."[81] The frequencies and rhythms that surround us affect our nerves and interact with the rhythm of our heartbeat.

Our heartbeat and pulse can be likened to rhythmic music from a loud speaker that encourages everyone to sway and dance in a unified rhythm. Slower music clearly produces a different experience than music with rapid beats. The scientist, Parncutt, presented evidence that people perceive music on felt-pulse patterns and that the perception of rhythm is not an event based process, but an interval period-based process, with pulses simply serving as event markers

---

[80]"A dendrite is a tiny filament of nerve endings wafting back and forth, like shafts of wheat in a slow breeze - communicating with other neurons sending and receiving their own electromagnetic impulses." McTaggart, Lynne. The Field, The Quest for the Secret Force of the Universe, Harper Collins Publishing: New York, 2002. pg. 88.

[81] Khan, Inayat, Hazrat. The Music of Life, Omega Publishing: New Lebanon, N.Y., 1983. pg. 274.

demarcating rhythmic intervals."[82] We even use pulses to perceive music.

The nervous system is like a two-way highway, communicating information to and from the brain and body. This creates a feedback system that is crucial in the body. If someone cuts a finger, the brain knows and immediately the proper bio-chemical arrives on the scene to clot and repair the wound. The brain and nervous systems transmit this communication via frequencies.

Sharry believes that otoacoustic emissions are at least one way the brain receives information encoded in frequencies and rhythm regarding body maintenance and repair. Her reasoning is simple - she has been able to listen to sounds that seem to be coming from the side of a person's head. If she can tell what a person's health issues are from these sounds, surely the brain can too. At http://www.otoemissions.org or http://www.oae.it there are over 3000 research articles on otoacoustic emissions ranging from the science of hearing to clinical applications of these tiny frequencies.

The brain understands what body repairs are needed, whether it is from otoacoustic emissions, the nervous system or another method. In addition to being able to self diagnose, the body reorganizes according to internal information. We see the results of a system when we watch a cut heal.

Once the brain has diagnosed a problem, how does it insure that repairs are carried out? Sharry believes that the brain uses frequency signals to orchestrate repairs. Our brain

---

[82] 1994 study by Parncutt, quoted by: Thaut, Michael. Rhythm, Music and the Brain: Scientific Foundations and Clinical Application, Routledge, N.Y., 2005. pg. 7.

constantly sends impulse patterns, measured as brain-wave frequencies, to the body by way of nerve pathways. A brainwave is like a passenger on the nerve's subway system. Dorinne Davis adds, "Nerve impulses transmit energy from one part of the body to another. The energy created can be measured through electrical fields generated during the transmission of nerve impulses."[83]

Later in Chapter Four, Processing Frequencies, methods are described in which the brain creates harmonic frequencies to balance and correct body frequencies that are not in tune, otherwise known as disease or stress. For now, we will continue to explore the pathways that frequencies use to travel throughout the body.

The body has numerous methods of sending energy messages other than utilizing the nervous system:

- Energy travels in the circulatory system through arteries and is delivered to the far reaches of our bodies.
- Neurotransmitters are chemicals that relay, amplify and modulate signals between a neuron and another cell.
- Individual cells of the body vibrate, influencing each other's movement and create a continuous vibratory network.
- Waves from our breath, pulse and heartbeat exhibit frequency, rhythm and volume in many parts of the body.
- When we speak, our vocal cavity vibrates, setting up a resonance that can be felt in many structures of the body.
- The body has subtle energy channels, called meridians, which connect body systems, organs and glands.

---

[83] Davis, Dorinne. Sound Bodies through Sound Therapy, Kalco Publishing: Landing, New Jersey, 2004. pg. 260.

Acupuncture and many other healing modalities utilize this energy transportation system.

- There are points on the body called acupressure points, which support the flow of subtle energy. For example, there are acupressure points on our feet, hands and ears that connect with each meridian. Energy from meridians connects to our organs and glands.[84]
- Bone conduction of sound occurs between the inner ear and the bones of the skull. This is why a person's voice sounds different when it is recorded and played back. Bone conduction amplifies lower frequencies, so most people hear their own voice in a lower pitch than it actually is.[85]

Every organ in our body is exposed to a constant stream of vibrations, pitches, rhythms and energy information. Various types of energy that correlate to frequencies and rhythms from our body constantly interact. From these observations a new science reveals itself and is just waiting to be explored.

In summary, frequency, volume of frequency and rhythm can be transported through the body in a variety of means via:

- Ears
- Nerves
- Circulatory System

---

[84]Paul Nogiers, a French neurologist became involved with ear acupuncture in the early 1950's when a woman said she had back pain for years that was cured by a woman who burnt her ear and the pain has been gone since. Dr. Nogiers' scientific curiosity was aroused. He searched for other areas on the ear that might relieve ailments and discovered that the ear has points communicating with the rest of the body. After listening to his lecture, the Chinese pursued the subject, using the Red army as subjects. They developed a map of the ear, with points that connect to other parts of the body to provide pain relief.

[85] http://en.wikipedia.org/wiki/Bone_conduction

- Neurotransmitters
- Breathing
- Pulse/Heart Beat
- Brain waves
- Cellular networks - the vibration of one cell affecting neighbors
- Meridians
- Our voice
- Skin
- Bones

All of these frequencies and rhythms can affect each other. What a complex, dazzling matrix of music and information!

## The Nervous System

The nervous system is an important frequency transport system. It is a network of specialized cells that communicate information about a person's surroundings and internal information. This vibratory information is processed and causes reactions in other parts of the body.[86] When one traces the nervous system, it is easy to understand its connections to frequencies and our voices.

---

[86] "The nervous system is divided broadly into two categories: the peripheral nervous system and the central nervous system. Neurons generate and conduct impulses between and within the two systems. The peripheral nervous system is composed of sensory neurons and the neurons that connect them to the nerve cord, spinal cord and brain, which make up the central nervous system. In response to stimuli, sensory neurons generate and propagate signals to the central nervous system, which then processes and conducts signals back to the muscles and glands. The interaction of different neurons form neural circuits that regulate an organism's perception of the world and what is going on with its body, thus regulating its behavior." http://en.wikipedia.org/wiki/Nervous_system

The Central Nervous System is exactly what the name implies. It is the central system with all of the other peripheral nerves feeding off it. The peripheral nerves are part of the peripheral nervous system.[87]

The Central Nervous System is composed of the brain, spinal cord and associated nerves that control voluntary and involuntary acts. In other words the Central Nervous System controls physical body processes that you do on your own *(moving your arm)* and those you do without having to tell your body to do it *(like breathing)*.

The peripheral nervous system sends information to the central nervous system. It senses signals from the external environment *(sensory-somatic nervous system)* and from the internal environment *(autonomic nervous system)*.

The autonomic nervous system is divided into the parasympathetic *(conserves energy and repairs the body during rest)* and sympathetic nervous systems *(mobilizes the body during activity and "fight or flight" responses)*.

The parasympathetic nervous system is regulated by the vagus nerve that runs along side of the spinal cord. The vocal cords lie within the vagus nerve bundle. The vibrations of the vagus nerve and the recurrent laryngeal nerve, which controls the vocal chords, interact due to their close proximity. When the vagus nerve sends impulses that interact with our vocal chords it may regulate our voices. The voice can access and entrain to the frequencies traveling through the nervous system via the vagus nerve. It is logical that our vocal chords

---

[87] Dr. Standly.com

can reflect the vibrational status of many body functions, reflecting health issues.

Frequency information contained in the voice could impact the vagus nerve which sends waves with information to the brain.

In summary, information in the body travels to the brain through the twelve cranial nerves. The vagus nerve, the recurrent laryngeal nerve and the vocal chords play a major role. The central nervous system is like our body's Internet, allowing information from millions of body processes to collaborate. Frequencies interact, like colors combine in a kaleidoscope. The brain's response to incoming information goes back via the same nerve network to organs and tissues to trigger appropriate action.

### The Perineural Connective System

The perineural connective tissue system *(perineural meaning around a nerve)* is another information-transportation system in the body. With further exploration we learn that, "The perineural tissue cells surround each neuron in the brain, accounting for more than half of the brain's cells. There are more than twice as many perineural cells in the brain as there are neurons. These perineural cells follow every nerve to its endpoint. Until recently, scientists thought that these cells only had a supportive structure. Now, it is known that they conduct information. The individual cells vibrate and affect each other's movement. Resembling a ripple effect, a vibration is passed, cell-to-cell in a continuous vibratory network."[88]Dr. Becker gives us an imaginary picture to see how the vibrations of the cells affect each other, "in the brain nerves cells can be likened to raisins in a pudding of perineural cells."[89]

The central nervous system controls body sensations and provides feedback regarding various activities within the body. It responds quickly to stimulus. The perineural cells form the protective layer surrounding the peripheral nerves.[90] In contrast, the perineural cells responds slowly and more globally.

Scientists are discovering other pathways of cell-to-cell communication. Stuart Hameroff, an anesthesiologist from the University of Arizona, discovered that microtubules, the scaffolding of cells, are exceptional conductors of pulses. A vibration in one microtubule affects its neighbors and resonates in unison. [91]

In summary, the structures of the perineural and central nervous systems are markedly different. The central nervous system is a fast method of transferring information, while the perineural is a slower but very accurate transmission. The information from the perineural system and other cell-to-cell vibratory networks spreads slower throughout the entire body

---

[88] McTaggart, Lynne. The Field, The Quest for the Secret Force of the Universe, Harper Collins Publishing: N.Y., 2002, pg. 92.

[89] Becker, Robert. Cross Currents, The Perils of Electropollution, The Promise of Electromedicine: the Perils of Electropollution, Penguin Group: N.Y., N.Y., 1990, pg. 63.

[90]http://www.copewithcytokines.de/cope.cgi?key=perineurial%20cells

[91] McTaggart, Lynne. The Field, The Quest for the Secret Force of the Universe, Harper Collins Publishing, New York: 2002, pg. 92.

versus the central nervous system, which quickly sends information to specific places.[92]

## Digital and Analog Sounds

Sounds, or data transmissions, can be coded or packaged into electrical signals in two methods: digital or analog.

Analog technology translates audio *(such as the human voice)* into electronic pulses that are continuous waves and correspond in magnitude to the quantities they represent. For example, older analog phones convert sound waves into identical electrical waves that are analogous to electrical signals generated in nature. The analog systems use a continuous range of values to represent information.[93] All frequencies are a wave-like form. The speed of transfer is slower than digital because it is direct current. Audiophiles argue that analog process is more precise than the digital system of sound transfer. Analog data transfer is slow and not capable of transferring large amounts of data, but it is extremely precise.

In the old style of an analog phone, the voice bounces off a membrane in the speaker, which vibrates much like hitting a snare drum with your fingers. This vibration transforms into electrical signals and then travels on copper wires to another phone. A magnet in the receiving speaker converts the energy into sound.

---

[92] Davis, Dorinne. Sound Bodies through Sound Therapy, Kalco Publishing: Landing, New Jersey, 2004. pg. 262.
[93] *http://en.wikipedia.org/wiki/Analog_recording_vs._digital_recording*

Digital, a binary format, breaks a signal into a binary format and audio data is represented by a series of 1s and 0s. These signals carry electronic pulses, where 0 represents pulse-not present and 1 represents pulse-active. The number of pulses per unit creates a signal code. This process has similarities to Morse code. It also resembles the rhythm component of music. Computers operate in a similar way. This method is extremely fast and transfers large amounts of information.[94]

The digital data often represents electro-magnetic signals, such as electricity, radio waves, microwaves, or infrared signals. These signals can be sent on copper wires, optical fibers, wireless communication channels or storage media.

Davis describes the digital system in our bodies. "The central nervous system uses neurons conducting impulses from place to place, as electrical impulses. It employs a digital sound format to provide high-speed, high-volume information."[95]

In another example, the transfer of analog frequencies is similar to sunshine in the early part of the day that gradually increases in brightness then decreases in the same manner in the evening. At any given moment, the sunshine is either more or less bright than the preceding and succeeding moments. In contrast, a room lit by an electric bulb is either dark or light depending on whether the current is switched on or off. This process is similar to digital. Similarly, the shades in a film-photograph merge smoothly into neighboring colors and shades as with analog, whereas a digital photograph

---

[94] Becker, Robert, Dr. Cross Currents, The Perils of Electropollution, The Promise of Electromedicine, Penguin Group: New York, 1990, pg. 59.
[95] Davis, Dorinne. Sound Bodies through Sound Therapy. Kalco Publishing: Landing, New Jersey, 2004. pg. 260.

consists of distinct and separate, tiny dots.[96] In the digital process, sound waves are divided into groups and averaged. This average frequency represents a group. LCD televisions, wireless phones, cell phones, some standard phones and computer screens use this process.

When we talk in person, we exchange analog sound. When sound initially hits the eardrum, the waveform is analog, but the brain sends signals in digital form using the central nervous system. The brain digitizes the analog frequencies that the body hears.

Our world utilizes both analog and digital communications. Sending information using analog methods is less complex and was used earlier in history. Early phones transmitted sounds in an analog format. Today a digital process is used on our phones. Computers initially transferred data in an analog format, but later evolved to digital. Analog TV signals in the USA converted to digital in 2009. Dr. Becker, who was twice nominated for a Nobel Prize, believes that early-evolved body systems evolved in a similar progression, first using analog frequencies and later developing digital formats for communication.[97]

Today, many sophisticated computers are hybrids, containing analog and digital components. Our brain operates in a similar manner as hybrid computers do. The central nervous system sends information in digital form, and the perineural connective cell system sends information from the brain in analog form.

---

[96] Businessdictionary.com
[97] Becker, Robert, Dr. Cross Currents, The Perils of Electropollution, The Promise of Electromedicine, Penguin Group: New York, 1990, pg. 59.

Dr. Becker[98] has substantiated an analog current system found hidden within the central nervous system.[99] The perineural system cells send information in a slow wave formation in an analog format and are unable to transmit large amounts of data. "Although the speed and quantity of wave forms is limited, analog format works best for precise control."[100] The perineural cell system is activated prior to nerve impulses and appears to make actual decisions and regulates one's level of consciousness.[101]

Dr. Becker continues, "Analog data transmission and control system, located in the perineural cells transmits information by means of the flow of a semiconducting DC electrical current that sense injury and controls repair, and it may serve as the morphogenetic field itself."[102]

The determination of the best method to transfer sound is far from complete. There are benefits from using both methods. Many sound healing processes, such as the Tomatis[103] method

---

[98] Dr. Robert Becker is a pioneering researcher in The Field, The Quest for the Secret Force of the Universe, the Quest for the Secret Force of the Universe of electricity and regeneration, an orthopedic surgeon and a professor at NY State University, Upstate Medical Center and at the Louisiana Sate University Medical Center. He authored The Body Electric and Cross Currents, The Perils of Electropollution, The Promise of Electromedicine.

[99] Becker, Robert, Dr. Cross Currents, The Perils of Electropollution, The Promise of Electromedicine, Penguin Group: New York, 1990, pg. 62.

[100] Davis, Dorinne. Sound Bodies through Sound Therapy, Kalco Publishing: Landing, New Jersey, 2004. pg. 261.

[101] Becker, Robert, Dr. Cross Currents, The Perils of Electropollution, The Promise of Electromedicine, Penguin Group: N.Y., 1990, pg. 65.

[102] Becker, Robert Dr.. Cross Currents, The Perils of Electropollution, The Promise of Electromedicine, Penguin Group: N.Y., 1990, pg..65.

[103] Dr. Alfred A. Tomatis (January 1, 1920–December 25, 2001) was an internationally known otolaryngologist, and inventor. He received his Doctorate in Medicine from the Paris School of Medicine. His alternative medicine theories of

use digital sound and work through the central nervous system. Other sound healing systems, including BioAcoustics, utilize analog sound and the perineural connective system to send energy information. Each system offers different strengths that may be explained in part by the digital versus analog transfer process.

Specialties for Tomatis auditory therapy include learning disabilities, problems with speech, language acquisition and development, brain dominance, handedness, singing, hearing and behavioral problems. Specialties for BioAcoustics include improving muscle tone, reversing trauma, stroke rehabilitation, controlling proteins and receptors and absorption of nutrients. BioAcoustics also excels at alleviating symptoms of chronic fatigue, fybromyalgia, stroke, autism and others.

With research more information will become available on the effects of digital versus analog communication in our bodies. As we become more sophisticated, we will better understand which energy transport system is best for specific health problems.

Sharry cautiously refrains from using brainwave frequencies in digital format with the exception of using FE's to kill

---

hearing and listening are known as the Tomatis method. His method began to help professional singers based on his idea that hearing is the root cause of a variety of ailments. His Listening Test and Electronic Ear therapy alleviated auditory processing problems, dyslexia, learning disabilities, attention deficit disorders, autism, sensory integration and motor-skill difficulties. It is also claimed to have helped fight depression, learn foreign languages faster, develop better communication skills and improve creativity and on-the-job performance. Some musicians, singers and actors found it helpful in fine-tuning their skills.

pathogens.[104] A CD uses digital format. Sharry experiences better success with analog and she found a few digital frequencies to be potentially stressful to the body. To illustrate this point Sharry associates a low digital sound as a frequency-equivalent with prostate cancer.

# Chapter Two

## The Voiceprint

Like music, our speaking voice is a measurable arrangement of sounds. Our voices' tonal qualities plus the sounds of our language dance together. Language contains discordant and harsh sounds as well as harmonic sounds. Each word contains individual sound units called phonemes. A phoneme is the most basic unit of an uttered sound.

Fast Fourier transformer devices, abbreviated as FFTs, break the sound of our voices into individual pitches and graph them. An algorithm dissects a sequence of values into different frequencies. It can also count the number of times each pitch occurs during a period of time.

This FFT analysis mathematically organizes the sounds created by phonemes. The FFTs evaluate the pitch of each

---

[104] James Marshall, musician and actor, worked with Sharry using frequencies to counter the swine flu in his piece, *Le Ciel*.

phoneme so they are effective with all languages. Any sound, including moaning, crying, laughing or nonsense syllables can be analyzed.

In the time span of approximately one minute, there may be as many as 100,000 pitches sounded in our voice.

### Types of Voiceprints

There are two variations of voiceprints used in BioAcoustic analysis. One produces time-domain graphs and the other creates frequency-domain graphs.

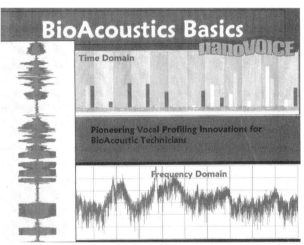

**Frequency and Time Domain Voice Prints**

A frequency-domain vocal graph uses the measurement of cycles per second to record each tiny sound created by our body. All of these minute sounds combine and produce our voice. Each tiny, vertical line on this graph is an individual frequency-equivalent represents vibrations in our body.

Sharry equates elements and compounds with frequency-equivalents similar to molecular weights based on her research. Muscle frequencies are based on nerve interactions, while emotional frequencies are based on brain waves.[105]

Sharry's software equates frequency-equivalents with bio-chemicals, genetics, muscles, genomes, pathogens, nutrients, toxins and processes in the body. For example, one program graphs the frequency-equivalents of muscles, while another software program reports those frequencies associated with our eyesight. These programs relate each graphed line to an identified FE.

In contrast, time-domain vocal prints create bar graphs. Each bar graph represents the number of times each pitch is sounded by phonemes. This information is used for personality profiling, group dynamics, matchmaking and understanding personal actions and reactions. More detail on time-domain vocal prints will be covered in Part Three, Applications, in the nanoVoice description.

## Architecture in the Voiceprint

When a voice is recorded for about two minutes and this data is inserted into a FFT program *(FFTs are included in some of Sharry's software)* a frequency-domain graph is produced with wave-like shapes.

---

[105] Fucetola, Kathy and Ralph. "The Lady who Sings God." pg. 5.

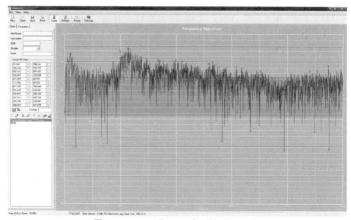

Frequency-Domain Voiceprints

Sharry refers to shapes created by the pitches within one's voiceprint as the voice's "architecture." In general, a balanced, healthy voice pattern resembles a wave, with its own unique shape. After observing thousands of vocal graphs, Sharry deciphered the meaning of certain shapes within the voice's architecture.

Pitches that fall within the larger wave-like shape represent healthy and harmonious frequencies. Frequencies outside this healthy wave represent stressful and inharmonious frequencies in the body.

The scattered shapes of the voiceprint, outside of the larger wave form, represent health problems. In contrast, when one is healthy the frequencies "collect" in the smaller, more unified and solid wave pattern.

Sharry watches the body sing its many songs and notices if any frequencies are missing or low. She then provides the missing FEs to trick the brain into delivering them.

Each person's healthy frequency range can be different. Typically, men have a lower range of frequencies in their voice while the range is higher for women and children.

After extensive research, Sharry categorized specific architectural shapes created from voiceprints and discovered the meaning of each nuance. Certain shapes in the architecture seemed to repeatedly reflect specific health issues. For example, Sharry defines shapes that correlate to the presence of toxins, pathogens, poison, inflammation, infections and more. There is a shape that signifies that a frequency is neither abundant, weak nor balanced, but completely missing. Listening to a missing FE tricks the brain into making the FE and gives it the means to repair itself. Most people would not have the motivation and perseverance to categorize the significance of subtle detail in a voiceprint.

Sharry refers to points on the vocal graph that are above the range of a person's voice as "risers." Risers show frequencies that are over abundant, perhaps to the point of toxicity. Our bodies need balance. For example, if a person ate too many peaches he would not want any more. Similarly, too much or too little of a frequency creates unbalance in the system. In another example, when the frequency-equivalent of a muscle is too high, it can be tight or inflamed.

Points on the graph that are low, called "stringers," indicate deficient frequencies. Using BioAcoustic parameters risers and stringers identify toxins, pathogens and detect hidden stresses that may lead to disease. Fewer risers and/or stringers are indicative of better health. In fact, it is ideal that the voice gathers in a limited bandwidth of pitches, which resembles a waveform created by closely drawn vertical lines.

When we crave a certain food, the voiceprint reflects a food's FE *(or an octave of the FE)* as out of balance. Do we crave sugar because its FE helps the body to balance low adrenal energy? Do we desire soda pop because it is a FE that substitutes for fat digestion or do we desire a food because it has a nutrient or an FE that our body needs?

A balanced voiceprint does not look like a straight line, which would sound mechanical and monotonous. A person with this variation of a voiceprint would be in denial of the normal range of emotions. Sharry observes that people with breast cancer often have voiceprints with too narrow of a frequency range. The body requires a full range of harmonious pitches, in order to be healthy. Life apparently wants us to experience, balance and master all frequencies. A healthy span of frequencies represents the full range of emotions, thoughts and our physical body operations.

Spiritual growth is the endless expansion of successful experiences, giving a person a wider and deeper mastery of life, increasing one's vibrancy and strength of being. As one's vibratory spectrum is enriched and expanded, the intensity of illumination is raised. As the vibratory spectrum of light becomes richer, it moves towards white light, containing all colors corresponding to all emotions. When we are missing frequencies, we invite lessons and people that help us master situations with the same energy. After success we weave those frequencies into our internal harmony. Sharry tells us,

"Just as a rainbow is incomplete without its full spectrum of colors, the body needs the full spectrum of sounds to establish and maintain the perfect state of health."[106]

## Accurate Analysis

Many in physical pain have undergone extensive testing and receive no clues to the cause of their problem. Others are told their physical ailment is in their head. The voiceprint eliminates the guesswork of interpreting symptoms as it precisely identifies body frequencies that are out of balance and stressed. Once this science is perfected, it should be inexpensive and less invasive than many current medical testing procedures.

One of the many values of a voiceprint is its ability to hone in on the root of one's symptoms. *(The root cause is often the weakest point or FE on the voiceprint.)* In contrast, physical pain can be misleading when one is attempting to find the root of a problem. For example, one may feel back pain, yet the voiceprint reveals that the out-of-balance frequencies are from the back of the stomach. When the stressed muscles from the back of the stomach are harmonized, the back pain disappears. Voiceprints often provide clues for a more accurate identification and location of health issues.

The voiceprint shows numerous issues in the body at one time. For example, it may show a virus, a weakened immune system and toxins in the liver. The complete frequency analysis may clarify the relationships of various health

---

[106] Edwards, Sharry. <u>Vocal Profiling for the Professional</u>, Sound Health: Athens, Ohio, 2002. pg.. MI-29.

imbalances, pointing out when one issue causes or escalates another.

When Sharry prepares sounds to harmonize the body she tweaks one or two percent of a frequency which can make a difference in its potency. For example, the FE that counters the venom of the Brown Recluse Spider must be accurate. If it is tweaked as little as .06 hertz it will not work. A frequency tonic can be molded to reflect tiny frequency variations that are needed on an individual basis.

It is recommended using a trained BioAouctic practitioner to interpret complex data to create your sonic preparations.

### Prevention

Harmonic imbalances are present before chemical imbalances are created in the body. Timely voiceprints predict the onset of physical symptoms. An illness may be predicted as much as 30 days in advance, allowing one to seek preventative action.

Each pitch, as measured by the number of cycles per second, displays whether or not a harmonic imbalance is in the warning stage or is a physical issue. Frequency imbalances in the range of 0 to 64 cycles per second are used as predictive data. These slower vibratory cycles have not solidified into a physical problem in our body. These vibrations are still pliable, easily molded and harmonized. Problematic stringers and risers that range between 65 to 512 cycles per second represent current physical health issues. Stringers and risers with wavelengths from 513 cycles per second and higher reflect long term, chronic physical issues. The highest frequencies are related to long-term physical conditions.

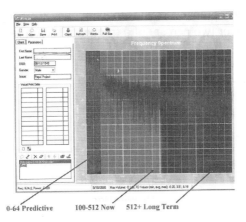

0-64 Predictive    100-512 Now   512+ Long Term

## Predictive, Current and Long-Term Frequency Ranges

In mystic circles "involution" is the process of spirit crystallizing into matter. Evolution is the opposite, the process of spirit releasing out of matter. Frequency-domain voiceprints separate pitches by frequency, reflecting how far disease has manifested into matter, mirroring the process of involution. The stages of illness follow a pattern: we create disharmonious thoughts and feelings; over time the octaves of these disharmonies crystallize into soft tissues and bones *(and become disease). A*s the frequencies increase in speed, the disharmony becomes more permanent.

Evolution, the reverse process, loosens the "spirit" from the disharmonious anchor of matter. Evolution is accomplished by maintaining inner harmony and peaceful feelings. The great psychic, Edgar Casey, believed that matter and energy "involve" and "evolve." He said, "The spirit is life. Mind is the builder. Physical is the result."[107] Cayce believed that our thoughts shape our characteristics, personality, emotional habits and physical health.

## The Mind-Body Link

Traditional medicine views people as sophisticated biological machines. Clearly, the human being is more than flesh and blood. There are deep relationships between the body, mind and spirit - each affects the others. Voiceprints reveal frequencies corresponding to physical, mental and emotional aspects and relationships among these energetic layers.

At every moment we create frequencies. Through resonance, vibrations ripple through every level of our being. To explain how resonance works, picture a string on a violin. Resonance occurs when a passive string vibrates after a different string *(that is the same or an octave)* is vibrated. In a classic example, one tuning fork is mounted is on a wooden box. If another similar tuning fork is struck, placed on the box and then muted, the un-struck mounted fork will be heard. A unison or octave will provoke the largest response as there is maximum likeness in vibratory motion. Other resonance links occur at intervals of three and five notes apart, though with less effect.[108]

The frequencies in our body produce additional "ripple effect" tones, the strongest of these being octaves. Other "ripple effect tones" are intervals of thirds and fifths higher

---

[107] Ritberger, Carol, PHD. <u>What Color is Your Personality?</u> Hay House: Carlsbad, CA., 2000. pg. 23.
[108] http://en.wikipedia.org/wiki/Resonance

than the original frequency. A more detailed description of resonance is presented in chapter three *(Musical Concepts within the Body)* of Part Two.

When we feel an emotion, we create a specific electro-magnetic wave. After testing countless voiceprints, Sharry correlated frequency-equivalents to specific emotions. The frequency-equivalents for emotions are universal.

Our emotions are affected through octave resonance from brainwaves, and frequencies of organs, tissues, muscles and bones. Conversely, our feelings also create vibratory responses on all of these levels and octaves. All frequencies in our physical bodies are connected to our emotions through resonance.

Emotions and thoughts weave in and out of our being all day and interact with our internal harmonic structures. This harmony, or lack of it, impacts our physical bodies. Negative or stressed feelings create disharmony and imbalances in our body.

If a frequency is out of balance, the octaves of this same frequency are not coherent either. Due to the phenomena of resonance, voiceprints can reveal the underlying emotional causes of physical ailments. A voiceprint not only tells us what is amiss in our physical body, but it also gives the specific negative emotion associated with the condition. For example, anger escalates blood pressure.

Sharry recalls a young boy with behavioral problems directed toward his mother. After taking a voiceprint, Sharry detected a frequency denoting his stressed emotion. She created a formula of sounds to counter this frequency imbalance. His behavior improved for a short while and then reverted back with no sustained success. Next Sharry looked for something deeper in his voiceprint to find the root cause of the emotional issue.

An exact octave below the boy's stressed emotion was a frequency associated with a deficiency of vitamin B-12. After listening to appropriate frequency-equivalents, the vitamin B-12 deficiency cleared. His emotional issues with his mother permanently disappeared. Sharry concluded that the root cause of his emotional problem was a nutritional imbalance that triggered his negative emotions.

We are familiar with the adage, "mind over matter," but vocal profiling shows us that "matter over mind" is equally valid. For example, we understand that worry contributes to an ulcer but an ulcer produces a Frequency-Equivalent that supports worry, too. The link between our health and our emotions is a two-way street.

## Voiceprints Change as our Words do

The information contained in a voiceprint changes each time we record a voice sample. As our words, thoughts and emotions shift during various discussions, so does the information revealed in the voiceprint. Numerous voiceprints are taken to get a complete health profile. A problematic frequency may occur only once or it may show up over and over again, signifying that a critical issue is present. Repeated voiceprints document how often problematic frequencies occur.

Often the content discussed in a voice sample affects which frequency-equivalents are displayed in the voice print. Sharry observed that when we talk about our health, frequency information about vitamins, minerals and nutrients is often present in the voiceprint. If we discuss a skin disorder, information about the skin is usually revealed. If we talk about our love life, the voiceprint often reveals associated feelings, as well as information concerning the health of our heart.

Louise Hay[109] has written several books on the connections of feelings and physical bodies. She believes the electromagnetic energy of an emotion accumulates on a subtle level in a specific location in the body. For example, emotions regarding people we love collect around our hearts. When we cannot "stomach" something, these stressed feelings settle around our bellies and influence our digestion and stomach health. When we feel overwhelmed or cannot "shoulder" our responsibility, these feelings impact our upper back muscles, tissues and backbone.

### Research Needed

After watching many successes Sharry achieves breakthrough insights into how our bodies work. Lack of resources has prevented Sharry from scientifically investigating all her discoveries. Many scientific studies could confirm or modify her observations and methods. She has produced consistent results in helping the body to improve issues that the medical field currently offers minimum treatment. Sharry's discoveries may provide solutions to many unsolved riddles

---

[109] Books by Louise Hay: <u>You Can Heal Yourself</u> and <u>Heal Your Body A-Z</u>.

of our time. If even half her discoveries are validated, this could offer hope to millions.

Here are some samples of her fascinating observations:

- Frequencies from environmental toxins, such as formaldehydes used in building construction, are consistent risers in voiceprints of people struggling with learning disabilities. We should study the relationship between certain building materials and learning disabilities.

- People with autism have allergies to a chemical found in vaccinations, preventing absorption of necessary vitamins, particularly vitamin A. If we took certain chemicals out of vaccinations could we reduce autism rates?

- People with multiple sclerosis characteristically lack the musical notes A and D in their voices. Will listening to these sounds improve this insidious disorder?

- Too much high fructose corn syrup *(an ingredient found in many popular foods)* has been shown to diminish mental clarity. A study could reveal the relationship of fructose corn syrup and mental performance. To raise national educational performance, should we improve the school lunch menu?

Who would consider the health implications of building materials or chemicals in vaccinations without a reason? Vocal profiling unveils the health impacts of unsuspected substances. If confirmed, this information could enable us to prevent suffering and costly remedies.

Sharry showed me a fascinating phenomenon. She took a voice sample using a free software recorder, called

Audacity.[110] The paid version of this program can slow down a voice recording and reverse it as well.

Sharry recorded her voice when discussing a picture of a mosque. When Sharry slowed down the recording, a dotted picture emerged, resembling the picture of the mosque. She then described a finding of David Oats, who was a guest on her weekly radio show. David reversed recorded voice samples. He declared that there were hidden vocal messages when the voice sample was reversed and slowed down about 20 percent.

### Summary of Voiceprints

A voiceprint can:

- Reveal an accurate picture of physical and emotional frequencies in the body.
- Reflect imbalances before they physically manifest, enabling the prevention of disease.
- Correlate specific emotions with physical issues providing a precise mind-body link.
- Provide unsuspected links between our environment, nutrition and our health. Further study may enable us to prevent troublesome health issues.

---

[110]http://audio.populardownloads.com/audacity/index.html?utm_source=google&utm_medium=cpa&utm_campaign=audio-audacity&gclid=CMvQ_InnuKICFRRM5Qod0VVb7Q

# Chapter Three

# Music in the Body

Music creates melodies[111] and harmonies.[112] Rhythms, dynamics[113] and tempo[114] animate a song's melody. Instrumentation and the expression of feelings add depth to music. The following musical elements can be heard within the orchestra of our bodies.

## The Melody

When one frequency after another is recorded on a voiceprint, a melody is created. Sharry uses voiceprints to track biochemical processes in the body that express themselves as frequencies. She learned that body-processes create frequencies with a melody and a rhythm - for example, digestion creates a series of musical frequencies, a song.

The French physicist, Joel Sternheimer, identified pitches of amino acids in plants. Amino acids align in a certain order to create a protein. He organized the notes of each amino acid in the same order that they formed a protein. This produced recognizable melodies such as "O Sole Mio" and "Blue Danube." When he played the protein's melody back to the plant, its growth doubled and improved its resistance to

---

[111] a series of notes that creates a recognizable musical phrase
[112] consonant sounding intervals of notes
[113] various volumes of sound
[114] variations of the speed of a rhythm

drought and disease.[115] The plant thrived when it heard its
own song!

## Dynamics

The time-domain voiceprint counts the number of times a
frequency occurs, documenting the distribution *(volume or
loudness)* of each note. Our body is full of notes, each with a
different volume. This parallels dynamics that are essential to
good music. The dynamics of healthy pitches in our bodies
fall in a specific range. When a frequency is too loud or too
soft, health issues can result.

## Glissando

In music, a glissando is a rapid slide of ascending or
descending consecutive tones. Fire sirens often raise and
lower in pitch in a smooth transition, which represents a
glissando. Many ancient sound healing practices, such as
toning, involve people singing and listening to glissandos.

A health frequency-domain voiceprint displays a wave like
pattern comprised of individual tones. A healthy person's
voiceprint creates patterns that represent a glissando.

## Tempo and Rhythm

The frequency-domain voiceprint can show patterns or pulses
in our voice's architecture, reflecting rhythmic patterns.

---

[115] Maman, Fabien. The Role of Music in the Twenty-First Century, Tamado Press:
Boulder Co.,1997. pg. 15.

Our heartbeat and breath establish tempos and rhythms in our bodies. Sharry tells us that internal pitches need to be in the proper rhythm for our bodies to heal itself.

Our pace and musical tempos change as we vary our physical, mental and emotional activities. For example, our tempo speeds up when we exercise and relaxes during meditation.

## Instrumentation

Organs and body systems create sounds that resemble instrument groups. The lungs represent the wind section of an orchestra, our heart mimic a drummer. Each organ is like an instrument playing in our internal symphony.

Different instruments each have their own timbre or quality of sound. Sounds from different organs and body processes also have variations in timbre.

Differences in timbre are produced from varying volumes of harmonics. Most people do not notice harmonics unless they are in a cathedral or a building with excellent acoustics. They perceive an echo after each sound, which includes harmonics. People clearly hear harmonics when they listen to different instruments. When a violin plays a C and a trumpet plays the same note, people can tell the difference. Varying volumes of harmonics create the difference. The harmonics created by the violin *(a wood instrument)* compared with harmonics created by the trumpet *(which is made of metal)* are the same pitch, but the volume of the harmonics varies. The material that the instrument is made out of creates resonance ranges in which certain harmonics are emphasized. Higher harmonics are emphasized in the violin's music, while lower harmonics are louder in the trumpet. The difference in sound quality is called timbre. The untrained human ear typically does not perceive harmonics as separate notes. Instead, harmonics are perceived as the timbre of the tone.

## Intervals

Two or more frequencies expressed at the same time or sequentially create intervals. An abundance of tones in our bodies creates a steady stream of changing intervals. Sharry discovered the effects of each musical interval in the body, but she retains these details as proprietary information. Just as a car with a stereo system blasting deep bass tones that rattle our bones, high notes tickle our skin. Different intervals have a stronger impact on various levels of our bodies.

## Chords

Three or more different notes that sound simultaneously create chords. Chords are the underlying patterns of notes that accompany musical melodies. Many frequencies in the body mirror chords without people realizing that chords sound inside their bodies.

Major chords produce a happy feeling. Minor chords result in a sadder feeling, almost as if one is withdrawing. Other chords create distinctive feelings reminiscent of the Greek tetra chords; each note pattern emulates a type of personality with distinctive emotional qualities. Tiny frequencies in our bodies create all of these variations of chords.

## Expression of Feelings

The master musician moves our hearts as we immerse ourselves into the emotion he creates. Music can make us weep, dance, march or enter a meditative space. The music within our body resonates with our feelings.

Further, each pitch created in our physical bodies is an octave of an emotional frequency-equivalent. Emotions are evoked due to resonance with pitches from other body processes.

The musician's emotions are subtly intertwined within his musical notes. For example, a barbershop quartet is most harmonious when the musicians are harmonious with each other. The relationships between band members can be subtly felt deep within the group's music.

Most things that we do are imbued with emotions, although it may be unconscious. Even something as small as clipping our nails may be accompanied with feelings of caring for ourselves. Emotions create a silent track during many of our daily activities. Music transforms these silent tracks into our hearing range.

## Musical Phrases

Music that lasts, like the classical music of the Renaissance, makes mathematical sense. Classical music employs patterns of similar notes, intervals and rhythms. It is coded with rhythmic and tonal mathematical underpinnings. Many classical composers designed mathematical relationships between notes, creating a musical phrase and then repeating this pattern many times. A musical design is created from repeating patterns of notes. Our bodies like patterns of sound.

Hans Jenny, a Swiss physicist, took videos and photos of sound vibrations impacting sand. The sound caused the sand to vibrate, move and form shapes. Consonant intervals produced pleasing, symmetrical patterns and recognizable shapes in the sound. Harsh and dissonant sounds created lopsided and distorted shapes.[116] Hans Jenny showed that certain intervals, especially the frequency-equivalents of intervals created with whole number ratio, create symmetrical patterns.

The timing of notes also involves mathematical structure. For example the timing of many classical phrases follows the mathematical formula for the golden ratio.[117] The golden ratio is a proportional relationship between segments in a line. Musical phrases have been timed to reflect the mathematics of this revered proportion. Many Renaissance artists and architects also proportion their works to approximate the golden ratio, because it is consistently perceived to be beautiful and pleasing.

---

[116] From Cymatic videos described in: Mattson, Jill. Ancient Sounds Modern Healing, Wings of Light: Oil City, Pa 16301. pg. 45.

[117] In mathematics and the arts, two quantities are in the golden ratio if the ratio between the sum of those quantities and the larger one is the same as the ratio between the larger one and the smaller. The golden ratio is an irrational mathematical constant, approximately 1.6180339887. At least since the Renaissance, many artists and architects have proportioned their works to approximate the golden ratio - especially in the form of the golden rectangle, in which the ratio of the longer side to the shorter is the golden ratio - believing this proportion to be aesthetically pleasing. Mathematicians have studied the golden ratio because of its unique and interesting properties.

# Octaves and Resonance

Harmonic and musical theory incorporated the intrinsic scientific phenomena of wave interactions of octaves and other resonances. The physical body also utilizes the implications of wave interactions and resonances.

Resonance is easily explained with an example: Two violins are tuned exactly the same, as we pluck one string it produces a field of sound energy that triggers the other violin's matching string, the matching string will vibrate and produce the same sound.

Resonance occurs when a system absorbs more energy. "In physics, resonance is the tendency of a system to oscillate at maximum amplitude at certain frequencies. At these frequencies, even small periodic driving forces produce large …vibrations, because the system stores vibrational energy."[118] When an object is exposed to a frequency and this oscillation matches the system's natural oscillation or frequency, the system increases its energy. Further details of this process are, "Resonant systems can generate vibrations of a specific frequency, or pick out specific frequencies from a complex vibration containing many frequencies."[119]

Resonance occurs with all types of vibrations or waves. There are mechanical, acoustic and electromagnetic types of resonance.

Let's pretend that each of us is a wineglass and a certain frequency makes us shake, just like sound can make a

---

[118] *http://en.wikipedia.org/wiki/Resonance*
[119] *http://en.wikipedia.org/wiki/Resonance*

wineglass shake. This is the "fundamental frequency" of our body. Related frequencies will also impact us as follows:

- **Sympathetic resonance** occurs when our fundamental frequency vibrates our body. Our body naturally matches this frequency. This is the strongest resonant vibration in music and our body.

- **Octave resonance** occurs when we hear any octave of our fundamental note. Our body naturally matches this frequency.

- **Harmonic resonance** occurs when an interval of a third *(three notes apart),* or a fifth *(five notes apart)* of our fundamental frequency vibrates our body. Sharry believes there is also a vibratory relationship with the interval of a minor sixth, which directs and influences body maintenance. Harmonic resonances are the weakest of resonance vibrations.

- **No Resonance** is a tone that has no relationship with the fundamental frequencies or its harmonics. A tone with no resonance may cause stress. Our body will not noticeably match a frequency of no resonance.[120]

Sharry observed the sympathetic resonances that her sound formulas produce within people's bodies. For example, when the note B is sounded in your body, one of the natural resonances created is F, five notes away. When B, F, and F# sound together, the resulting vibrations nourish the kidneys, help mineral distribution, alleviate high blood pressure and facilitate the system of fluid distribution throughout the body. Sharry correlates these notes with emotional energy created by doing too much for others. The person who needs these frequencies learns to set his own boundaries. One with a care-

---

[120] Thompson, Jeffrey, as quoted in <u>Ancient Sounds Modern Healing</u> by Jill Mattson. Wings of Light: Oil City, PA, 2006. pg. 183.

taking nature must take care of oneself. There are other emotional lessons associated with these frequencies.

## Harmonics

The scales used in the West approximate the harmonic series although they do not produce these exact frequencies. Given the enormous number *(billions)* of possible ways to divide octaves into intervals, why have only a few scales been so strongly favored? A study by Gill and Purves concluded that civilizations prefer scales similar to the harmonic series.[121]

Harmonics are softer and difficult to distinguish from the root tone. The pitch of any root note and its complex array of harmonics are perceived as only the root note. We do not hear each harmonic as a separate note, but we sense them as the "color" of the root note. For example, the C on a violin sounds different than the same C on a trumpet, reflecting emphasis of different harmonics.

When one drops a pebble into a pond, waves ripple around the pebble and move outwards in larger and larger circles. Similarly when we see graphs of sound waves they look like a wavy line. This is a 2-D representation of them. In 3-D, they resemble a tiny bubble getting progressively larger. As a sound expands, reflected waves interact and create harmonics.

Here is another description of how harmonics are created. Harmonics are shorter and faster waves that are reflected between two ends of the string. When a string is struck, the

---

[121] Gill, Kamraan, Purves, Dale. "A Biological Rationale for Musical Scales," Center for Cognitive Neurobiology: Duke University, N.C., 2009.

resulting frequencies, whose wavelengths do not divide evenly into the length of the string, get suppressed and the vibrations that persist are called harmonics. The harmonic wavelengths are 1, 1/2, 1/3, 1/4, 1/5… of the length of the string. [122]

The following illustration is yet another explanation of how one pitch creates harmonic tones. A string vibrates along its entire length and produces a fundamental note. At the same time softer vibrations are created from segments of the string, from a half, a third, fourth, and fifth of the string…. These segments form a harmonic series of vibrations. [123]

The vibration rate of each segment is a multiple of the frequency of the whole string. Each segment vibrates respectively twice, three times, four times, etc., as fast as the whole string. For example, if the fundamental frequency of the entire string *(the root note)* is $f$, the harmonics have frequencies $f$, $2f$, $3f$, $4f$, etc. The vibration of the whole string produces the fundamental tone, and the segments produce weaker subsidiary tones. [124]

Harmonic frequencies follow this mathematical formula and continue onward and upward - potentially to infinity. Harmonics are frequency components of everything. Jonathan Goldman summarizes, "Since anything that vibrates creates harmonics, and the universe is composed of nothing but vibrations, everything creates fundamental tones and harmonics, ranging from electrons orbiting around atoms to

[122] http://en.wikipedia.org/wiki/Harmonic
[123] *http://en.wikipedia.org/wiki/Harmonic*
[124] Columbia Encyclopedia: Harmonics

the planets orbiting around the sun."[125] Many universal principles of botany, chemistry and other sciences follow principles of the harmonics series.

In many esoteric schools of thought the study of musical harmony was the study of everything because we are hard wired to recognize harmonics and other sounds representing special geometric shapes. To illustrate this point, consider that when a building or a person is considered "beautiful," their proportions follow a certain geometry, suggesting that we are hardwired to enjoy this geometry.

German physicist Ernst Chladni published a book in 1787[126] describing his experiments with visualizing musical tones as auditory geometrics. He sprinkled sand on round and square metal objects, and then vibrated the edge with a violin bow and elaborate shapes formed in the sand. Patterns formed whenever harmonic frequencies were applied to the flat surfaces. Once again, this suggests that there is something special about these harmonic intervals. *(See Appendix B for information about the suppression of harmonics in history.)*

Vibrations in our bodies create pitches, triggering harmonic notes. Inaudible subtle sounds interact with our subtle energy and create harmonics. Harmonics intermingle with the web of sound that envelopes us. We do not hear all of these tiny sounds, but they affect our mind, body and emotions. Also, the voiceprint captures the frequencies of these harmonics.

---

[125] Goldman, Jonathan. Healing Sounds: The Power of Harmonics, Inner Traditions: Vermont, 2002. pg. 31.
[126] Chaldni, Ernst. Entdeckungen uber die Theorie des Klanges.

Harmonics and pitches are both frequencies. Both the originating frequency and the resulting harmonic frequencies impact the body. Harmonics have lower volumes, but low level energy *(low frequencies on the electromagnetic scale)* can be extremely important in our body, according to Dr. Becker in his book <u>Cross Currents, Perils of Electopollution, Promise of Electro Medicine</u>.[127]

Low levels of energy, such as energy from harmonics, radiate from our bodies in analog format. As we described earlier, analog systems use a seamless range of values to represent information, producing continuous tones. Analog sounds are a precise representation of the original sound.

Digital and analog sounds create different patterns of harmonics. Therefore, even though the root pitch may be the same, the harmonics are different in digital and analog sounds.

When drawn, analog harmonics look like a concentric circle around the root frequency. If the first ring *(first harmonic)* represents 10 hertz, then the second ring *(second harmonic)* represents 20 hertz, and the third ring correlates to 30 hertz. Analog sound produces simple predictable waves.

Digital sounds produce what Sharry calls "untrue harmonics." The digital tone is composed of averaged pitches within a range of sounds. Each averaged pitch produces a harmonic series. The resulting pattern of harmonic series varies according to the distance between each averaged sample of sound.

---

[127] Becker, Robert, Dr. <u>Cross Currents, The Perils of Electropollution, The Promise of Electromedicine</u>, Penguin Group: New York, 1990. pg. 71.

When recorded digital harmonic frequencies are drawn, they look like a set of steps. Each step represents a bit of sound information. Each step then produces another harmonic series. A tremendous number of harmonic waves interact, forming a complicated wave. Sharry has found that digital sounds are effective in shattering toxins and pathogens and allowing the body to excrete the pieces.[128]

Another reason that Sharry uses analog sounds in her tone boxes is because of the exacting harmonics created by analog frequencies. The brain readily recognizes harmonics and these frequencies balance and tune multiple systems in our body. The pitches in a harmonic series affect various body parts and processes.

Harmonics create a 16 note "chord" that often mirror recognizable, biological processes.[129] Sharry reports that some analog harmonics follow bio-chemical processes in the body - such as the Kreb's cycle *(a series of steps in the oxidation of carbohydrates)*. Listening to the harmonics of the Kreb's cycle has produced remission in some types of cancer.[130] Harmonic series play a crucial role in the healing of the body.

When different harmonic series interact, a sound matrix is created within the body. Sharry compares the interrelating harmonic groups to Rubik's Cubes. Sharry's advanced

---

[128] Kirilean photography produced by Fabien Maman at www.Tamo-do.com shows that certain pitches are capable of breaking up helia cancer cells. Typically, toxic and pathogen cells are not as pliable and flexible as other cells.

[129] http://www.lifespirit.org/SHRI-string-theory.htm#String%20Theory

[130] Davis, Dorinne. <u>Sound Bodies through Sound Therapy</u>, Kalco Publishing: Landing, New Jersey, 2004. pg. 246.

software analyzes the interaction of different harmonic patterns and how one detuned harmonic affects the entire series.

## Music within the Body

In a broad perspective, from melodies to rhythms to emotional expression, our bodies sing our unique songs, participating in the choir of the uni-verse *(meaning one song)*. An old Chinese saying echoes this theme, "There will be a time when man will not be known by his name, but by his personal melody."[131]

Unlike a musical composition, our bodies have consciousness. Our brain is the orchestra conductor that creates an innate musical system to restore our harmonic imbalances. We consciously choose music to help us express an emotion, but the attraction goes deeper. We are attracted to frequencies that our body needs to maintain its health on many levels. If we need the sound of a D to alleviate a stressed frequency in our body, subconsciously we find ourselves attracted to songs that are in the key of D. Perhaps we will be drawn to a person who emulates this D frequency as his signature tone. Our body subconsciously recruits the singers *(be they people, places, sounds, things, or nutrients)* that emulate the frequencies that our bodies crave to complete internal harmonic balance.

Ancient modal systems of music recognized these marvelous links between music and our well-being. Musical "Feng shui" *(music to harmonize and balance our unique energy)* and healing mantras have been long practiced by many ancient civilizations.

---

[131] Edwards, Sharry. <u>BioAcoustic Biology.</u> Sound Health: Albany. pg. 1-21.

# Chapter Four

# **Processing Frequencies**

Sharry experienced a breakthrough discovery when she associated pitches with colors. Raising pitches many octaves higher to correspond to the frequencies of light illustrated a fascinating link between colors and frequencies. Sharry simplified sound healing by using this process to correlate colors with musical notes. This correlation produces an extremely useful application of sound healing.

Sharry learned to silence the noise of a refrigerator by identifying the frequency of the refrigerator's hum and sounding the inverse proportion *(the reciprocal)* of it. *(F times 1/F equals one).* It was illuminating to discover that sounds have "counter-frequencies" that cancel each other out. This understanding led to the incredible discovery of how to "cancel out" the frequency-equivalents of toxins, pathogens and other undesirable frequency-equivalents! Sharry refers to these counter frequencies as antidotes. Calculating a frequency-equivalent to cancel a pathogen, toxin or a stressed frequency is a foundational core of BioAcoustics.

Thousands of times, Sharry calculated and used "antidote" frequencies and then tested the effects. Sharry simultaneously used her special hearing and voice capabilities to identify antidote frequencies that worked time after time. She used the underlying relationship between the frequency and the counter frequency. The counter frequency *(the reciprocal)* of a note was usually six notes away, creating an interval of a musical minor sixth. When Sharry superimposed the frequencies and counter frequencies onto a color wheel, the two notes that were a musical minor sixth apart were complementary colors! This led her to believe that complementary colors are reciprocals, or inverse proportions of each other. Said another way, a pitch that is an interval of a minor sixth away *(or an octave of a complementary color)* can balance many problematic stringers and risers in our voiceprint.

Sharry made the process of calculating counter frequencies easier by thinking of the body's frequencies in terms of colors. The sounds associated with complementary colors are six musical notes apart on the musical scale. Frequencies associated with complementary colors can cancel each other out. In addition to being an elemental building block in BioAcoustics, this application has other ramifications. Scientists have been absorbed with measuring brain waves in a linear fashion. Beta, alpha, delta and theta brain waves are organized in a linear progression. If scientists superimpose brain waves on a color wheel, they would figure out more of the math of the brain and body.

## Emotions and Pitches

Each frequency has an octave that is in the broad band of emotions. We can temper our emotions by tuning to reciprocal tones of the emotional frequency.

Some of the emotional challenges associated with each note are:

- C - Difficulty self-directing and self-empowerment issues
- C# - Secretly hard on self, hard on others as a cover, and can be defensively sarcastic
- D - Lack of self-approval, complains and likes to fix people/things/issues
- D# - Difficulty sharing emotions
- E - Self sabotages and needs to be needed
- F - Procrastinates or is a workaholic, an inability to integrate perception and action
- F# - Works on unimportant things, avoids important tasks and, at worst, just ignores everything
- G - Have problems prioritizing physical issues and tends to get depressed
- G# - Spreads self too thin, lack of confidence, and sways from egotistical to lack of self-esteem
- A - Has problems prioritizing non-physical issues and tend to rely on what they think you mean
- A# - Others are more important than them, they give a great deal physically and emotionally and are hurt easily
- B - Martyrs, think they deserve things but do not know how to get them without appearing selfish

## Note Correlate Chart

This chart [132] describes some positive associations with pitches and emotions.

| NOTE CORRELATE CHART | | |
|---|---|---|
| **EMOTIONAL** | | **PHYSICAL** |
| self power, ego, self direct, leader, excitement physically motivated | red C | large, thick muscles, heart gross circulation, female reproduction |
| champion of justice, fair play, hard on self, stubborn hard on others as a cover | red/orange C# | tendon, ligaments, tissue linings, circulation of digestion, bowel |
| self approval, expects reciprocation caretaker, likes to organize, examine and fix self and others | orange D | liver, gallbladder, pancreas digestion, appetite, production of enzymes and hormones |
| information brokers, not apt to share "real" self easily, uses narrative examples to teach | or/yellow D# | cellular oxygenation, transport of minerals and oxygen to eyes and muscles |
| self approval issues, uses words first to convey message and meaning, appreciates appreciation | yellow E | wet moist tissues, lungs, eye nose, bronchial structures diaphragm, mouth, gums |
| planner, ability to see flaws in the plan of others, balance between perception and action | yel/green F | kidney, environmental allergies prostate, male reproduction, lower back, cranial balance |
| one who carries out the plans, doer intuitive about the needs of others share and loves wholeheartedly | green F# | blood filtering and screening manages mineral balances flow of fluids, nutrients |
| game player, likes to mix and manage the physical aspects of life motivated by future events | green/blue G | neurotransmitters, balance of minerals and enzymes bone matrix, water balance |
| wants to make a difference, likes to help and satisfy others hands on, time conscious | blue G# | resource maintenance and storage, with C# retrieves nutrients from the bowel |
| spiritual, takes care of the needs of others, interprets/acts from within self | blue/violet A | eye flexibility, electrical issues non-physical issues, resource management, aging |
| highly intuitive, reads between the lines, can put aside self for others likes mental games, hurts easily | violet A# | immune system, adrenal issues with E-allergy related, body detoxification, oxygen regulation |
| link between self and universe needs harmony and balance in personal life and occupation | violet/red B | subtle circulation, body/mind connection, small body mechanics nerves, body magnetics |
| meditative, answers to God's LAW | B/C white | body system integration and communication |

[132] All copyrighted charts have been printed with permission from Sharry Edwards.

## Brain Dominance

Sharry found a fascinating phenomena regarding how each brain hemisphere processes frequencies and this affected her frequency remedies.

The left and right hemispheres of our brains each work differently. The following table illustrates the specialties of left-brain and right-brain thinking:[133]

| Left-Brain Functions | Right-Brain Functions |
|---|---|
| Logical | Random |
| Sequential | Intuitive |
| Rational | Holistic |
| Analytical | Synthesizing |
| Objective | Subjective |
| Looks at parts | Looks at whole |
| Detail oriented | Uses feelings |
| Facts rule | Imagination rules |
| Reality based | Fantasy based |
| Forms strategies | Presents possibilities |
| Practical | Impetuous |
| Likes math/science | Likes philosophy/ religion |
| Uses words and language | Uses symbols and images |
| Likes order/pattern perception | Likes spatial perception |

[133] http://www.funderstanding.com/content/right-brain-vs-left-brain

Most people predominately utilize one brain hemisphere or the other. There are gifted people who use both halves of the brain equally.

As we have said, each brain hemisphere has separate functions and methods of processing information. Many functions of one hemisphere cannot be done in the opposite hemisphere. For example, "the right ear *(and the left-brain)* is involved in coordination of phonation, the all-musical facilities and the left ear cannot replace these functions."[134]

Dr. Tomatis links the right-brain with the left ear, and the left-brain with the right ear. He further describes the pathway of sound from each ear to its associated brain hemisphere. He details, "Stimulus in the left ear has to cross the corpus collosum in the brain and will lose time in conduction of impulses."[135] People habitually process most frequencies with either their right or left ear. We have right or left ear dominance, just as we are right or left handed. Dr. Tomatis reports that those with left-ear-dominance may experience learning disabilities, because the sound information has further to travel, lengthening the time it takes to be processed.[136]

The following experiment will demonstrate right or left ear dominance. If one is right-ear-dominant and he blocks his

---

[134] Dr. Tomatis. The Ear and the Voice, The Scarecrow Press: Maryland, Toronto, Oxford, 1987. Translated into English in 2005. pg. 25.

[135] Dr. Tomatis. The Ear and the Voice, The Scarecrow Press: Maryland, Toronto, Oxford, 1987. Translated into English in 2005. pg. 26.

[136] Dr. Tomatis details how to change ear dominance by short bursts of intense sounds for short periods of time. He calls this auditory saturation and likens it to the same process that happens when your eyes are subjected to a bright flash of light. Dr. Tomatis. The Ear and the Voice, The Scarecrow Press: Maryland, Toronto, Oxford, 1987. Translated into English in 2005. pg. 22.

right ear with his hand, sound is forced to use the longer route of the left ear. Sounds lose some high pitches along the way and it seems lower in pitch.[137] When someone blocks the right ear and if sound appears to drop, then he is right-ear-dominant. If blocking the right ear does not produce a lowering of a pitch, then the person is left-ear-dominant.

When one is left-ear dominant the blocking of the right ear makes no difference, because the sound is primarily processed through the left ear. If one is left ear dominant the blocking of the right ear does not change anything.

Another method of determining brain dominance is to note preferences for doing things with the right or left side of the body. People who habitually use the right side of their body predominantly use their left-brain hemisphere. People, who favor the left side of their body, prefer right-brain usage. Some people are equal in their brain usage.

While working on a project with researchers at an air force base, Sharry found clues that led to her discovery of brain dominance and frequency processing. In this project, Sharry was to select a sound and a flashing colored light to help pilots avoid stress while flying. A sound of eight cycles per second was effective in some cases. Sharry observed that this frequency worked on 40 percent of the pilots when a green light flashed. If the pilots saw a flashing red light, a different 40 percent remained alert. Since Sharry's education included learning modalities and brain dominance, she noted similarities in percentages of effectiveness of the flashing colored lights, their rhythms and the percentage of brain

---

[137] Dr. Tomatis. The Ear and the Voice, The Scarecrow Press: Maryland, Toronto, Oxford, 1987. Translated into English in 2005. pg. 22.

dominance among people. Statistically, 40 percent of the pilots would be right-brained, 40 percent would be left-brained and the remaining 20 percent would use their whole brain.

Sharry concluded that brain dominance altered the impact in the body of color and frequency. In order for the frequency to be effective, those using their right-brain hemisphere needed one color and rhythm combination, and those using their left-brain needed the complementary color. This insight proved to be a keystone breakthrough in her fascinating string of discoveries.

Each brain hemisphere processes information differently *(including pitches and color)* and not surprisingly, calculates frequencies and colors differently. It seems that they process FEs in an opposite manner. Brain dominance determines whether we need to listen to one pitch or another that is a musical minor sixth away in order to balance a problematic stringer in our voice print. Each brain hemisphere we use to process a color that we see or a pitch that we hear, creates a different or opposite effect. Not considering brain dominance is a mistake often made by color therapists. For example, if you give a left-brained color and a left-brained sound to a left brained person, the color and sound cancel each other out.

Sharry came up with formulas on how to select antidote frequencies taking brain dominance into account:

- **Left-brained people process sounds that correspond to opposite *(complementary)* colors**. To balance a problematic frequency for a left brained person, give him the weak or missing pitch.

- **Right-brained people process sounds that correspond to the same color.** To balance a problematic note, the likely solution is listening to more of the problematic frequency. When the same frequency is sounded the body produces the antidote.

Whole-brained people use their right and left brain hemispheres for approximately equal amounts of time. The method of processing colors and sounds with these people varies, depending on which brain hemisphere they are using.

Here is an example illustrating how each brain hemisphere processes colors differently. A right-brained person, who is clairvoyant sees Sharry's aura as violet, but a left-brained person sees the same aura as gold, the complementary color of violet. A whole-brained person sees the color white, the combination of the two. In all cases, Sharry's aura remains the same.

My son and I experienced issues with dyslexia. Initially my son copied letters that he saw upside down and backwards. With training and several years of school, he altered his perception. Now, he copies the letters he sees "correctly" as he has been taught. His brain corrected his interpretation of his vision to conform to what people told him the letters looked like. I doubt that his brain was rewired, but his brain translated the frequencies to satisfy his teachers.

I wonder if right and left brained people actually see colors differently, but our society teaches us to translate the frequency so that we all identify the FE in the same way. In the example of Sharry's aura perhaps we see different colors in the aura because we have not been trained to see the aura as this color or that. Similarly, the frequency for a red pigment color remains the same, but maybe some initially saw it as red and others as green depending on which brain hemisphere they were using. Both have learned to identify the frequency of red with the color of red, regardless of their initial intake of frequency data. Perhaps some see the color green and in a split second subconsciously shift the perception of this frequency to red, the complementary color. If this hypothesis is correct, then it would be difficult to recognize the different ways the brain hemispheres process frequencies.

The process explained below will clarify how to lower and raise problematic frequencies depending on which brain hemisphere a person is using.

The voiceprint's graph reflects the pitch of A#, above the range of the voice's healthy architecture. Our goal is to lower the A# frequency.

---

### Background Information

A# is equivalent to the color violet and E correlates to the color yellow. Violet and yellow are complementary colors.

---

To lower the A# frequency, do we need to listen to A# or listen to more of its reciprocal, E? Logically it should not make a difference, but it does! If we are right-brained we should listen to A#. If we are right-brained, listening to E will not balance the overabundant A#.

In contrast, if we are left-brained we should listen to E to lower and harmonize the problematic frequency. If we are left-brained, we process together colors and sounds that are opposites. Therefore, we need the opposite color, yellow to balance violet, or E to balance the A#.

The differences in approaches to correct a frequency imbalance stem from the opposing methods that each brain hemisphere uses to calculate frequencies and colors.

Each brain hemisphere responds differently to various modalities of medicine for the same reason, because each processes frequencies differently. An analogy occurs with allopathic medicine that refers to the broad category of medical practice, known as Western medicine. The term allopathic, when used by homeopaths, refers to the use of substances that produce different symptoms than a disease. For example, if one had poison ivy an allopathic doctor would give him "anti-poison ivy". An allopathic treatment for fever may use a drug, such as an antibiotic, to attack the cause of the fever - such as a bacterial infection.

A homeopathic remedy can be a tincture of poison ivy which your body builds resistance to and fights it off naturally. A homeopathic treatment for fever is one that can use a diluted dosage of a substance to induce a fever so the body can overcome it and then dissipate an even greater fever.

The FEs of allopathic medicine are more effective with predominately left-brained people who process FEs as opposites. FEs of homeopathic medicine are more effective with those who are predominately right-brained, who process FEs as similar energy.

Ancient civilizations recognized this phenomenon and altered the type of medicine practiced among people depending on their brain dominance and how they used their senses.[138] The methodology of medicine varied according to different brain dominance.[139] Perhaps they used allopathic medicine for left-brained people and homeopathic medicine for right-brained people. Modern knowledge must progress along a similar path to understand the significance of some ancient practices.

People can shift brain dominance throughout the day. The brain hemisphere best suited to a task takes over. An artistic project may trigger the predominant use the right brain hemisphere, while adding a series of numbers may create a shift to left-brain hemisphere dominance. It would seem that the frequency that a body needs can change throughout the day. Sharry was working with a child with seizure disorders. One frequency helped him when he used one brain hemisphere and hurt him when he switched to the other. While Sharry was considering how to stabilize the child's brain usage, his brother recalled being taught during yoga to breathe out of the right nostril by closing his left nostril with his finger. He suggested that Sharry stuff a crayon up his brother's nose so he would use only one nostril while listening to the healing frequencies hence, stabilizing his brain usage. What an idea! Sharry put cotton in one nostril, which caused his baby brother to use the opposite brain hemisphere consistently, so he could benefit consistently from a tonal pattern.

---

[138] Gerber, Richard, MD. The Number One Handbook of Subtle-Energy Therapies, third edition. Bear and Co.: Vermont. 2001. pg. 330.
[139] Gerber, Richard, MD. Vibrational Medicine, The Number One Handbook of Subtle-Energy Therapies, third edition. Bear and Co.: Vermont, 2001. pg. 330.

# Color Healing

If the issue of brain dominance is not complicated enough, a third factor affects the selection of a counter frequency formulation. An examination of colored lights, used for healing purposes, makes it easier to explain this phenomenon.

Many believe that the sole purpose of the eyes is to see and that the main usage of color is to satisfy our personal tastes. In contrast, people who utilize lights for healing believe that colors have a far deeper impact on the health and psyche of a human being.

In antiquity healers used materials to filter sunlight to create the effect of colored lights, which they used to treat people. Ancient writings describe people using colored lights for healing purposes in Heliopolos, Egypt, as well as in early Greece, China and India.[140] Today, there are still healing modalities using colored lights. Two modern pioneers were Edwin Babbitt and Dinshah Ghadiale. The Dinshah Health Society[141] offers a color-spectrum-based health system. This system has been in use since 1920 and was used in a major medical center in Philadelphia for many years. This system utilizes simple, low-powered lamps and color filters to counter particular physical problems.

Many people have difficulty imagining that a colored light causes a physiologic effect inside the human body. Traditional medical research has observed effects of light

---

[140] Gerber, Richard, MD. Vibrational Medicine, The Number One Handbook of Subtle-Energy Therapies, third edition. Bear and Co.: Vermont. 2001. pg. 275.
[141] http://www.dinshahhealth.org

within the body. Blue-light therapy is used for some types of neonatal jaundice. Blue light is applied to the skin to cause a chemical reaction in the blood circulating under the surface of the skin, effectively lessening bilirubin levels.[142] In another case, an ultraviolet light generates the production of vitamin D. The human body produces vitamin D when exposed to sunlight. Additionally, full spectrum light exposure helps those with seasonal affective disorder *(SAD),* a condition believed to be caused by insufficient light exposure through the eyes to the hypothalamus and to the pituitary gland, which controls the endocrine system.[143]

Color healing assumes that chemical elements radiate FEs that have octaves resonating within the color spectrum. For example, the prevailing corresponding color wave of hydrogen is red and that of oxygen is blue.[144] Each organ also has sympathetic resonance with a color wavelength. The liver is believed to radiate energy that is an octave below red; the pituitary, green; the spleen, violet; the circulatory system, magenta and the lymphatic system, yellow.

When a particular organ or body system is underactive, its energy has decreased. An energizing color is projected on the skin near the organ, sometimes the entire body. If a system is overactive *(due to a fever),* the remedy is the opposite. A depressing color is used. Everything on the red side of the spectrum is more or less stimulating while the blue portion is sedating.

---

[142] Bilirubin is the yellow breakdown product of normal heme catabolism. Heme is found in hemoglobin, a principal component of red blood cells. Bilirubin is excreted in bile and urine, and elevated levels may indicate certain diseases. It is responsible for the yellow color of bruises, urine, and the yellow discoloration in jaundice.
[143] http://www.dinshahhealth.org
[144] http://www.dinshahhealth.org

People who use color and sound in combination need to consider the interaction of these energies. It is as if lights and tones speak the same language, but one has a higher pitched voice. A red light and a sound frequency that correlates with red can create an increased amount of "red" energy, depending on one's brain dominance; the combination of the same color and sound can also cancel each other out.

We can apply Sharry's rule of thumb when we combine sounds and colors. As we noted earlier, left-brained people perceive color and sound differently. For these people, the tone and its complementary color cancel each other out. Right-brained people perceive color and sound as the same and more of the problematic frequency has a canceling effect. Whole-brained people adjust the method of processing colors and sounds, depending on which brain hemisphere they are using at the time.

In summary, first we learned that a complementary color (a frequency that is an octave of a complementary color) can balance a stressed frequency. In this way complementary colors are opposites. Second, we discovered that each brain hemisphere processes frequencies and colors in opposite ways so the above formula varies once again based on brain dominance. Third, we learned that colored lights and frequencies affect one another. They interact, even though they are in different octaves. They can complement each, but brain dominance can reverse the impact.

There is another tier of complexity regarding the selection of antidote frequencies. Sharry watched some FEs successfully cancel problematic sounds and then she superimposed them on a color wheel. She observed that sometimes the antidote frequency followed scientific rules for mixing colored pigments. Other times it followed the rules for mixing colored lights. Some people process frequencies as if they were lights and others combine frequencies using the rules of mixing colored pigments.

The reason this happens is unclear and Sharry does not offer an explanation. In a philosophical attempt to grasp why this happens, Sharry divides people into "earth" and "light" categories.[145] Earth people are attracted to nature and have a natural instinct with herbs. Perhaps these people predominately process colors as pigments. Others are abstract thinkers and spiritually interested in the light. Their bodies may prefer to process colors as lights. These innate tendencies may affect the body's color processing preferences.

Sharry developed a primitive way to discern if a person primarily processes colors as lights or pigments. On the Color, Tones and Signs chart on page 260 locate your astrological sign. Your signature tone and color are listed next to your astrological sign.

If your favorite color is the same as your astrological sign, then you are likely left brained. If your favorite color is 180 degrees across the color wheel *(if your favorite color is the complementary color of your astrological sign)*, then you are most likely right brained and are showing a pigment response to color.

---

[145] Sharry got this idea from Auel, Jean. The Clan of the Cave Bear. Random House; 2002.

If your favorite color is across the color wheel and adjacent one shade, then your body process your favorite color as lights combine, not pigments.

Your favorite color is statistically linked to your astrological sign and your body's preferred method of mixing colors as if there were lights or pigments.

I am a Capricorn which corresponds to the color of blue violet and the complementary color of yellow orange. If I processed colors as pigments then my favorite colors would be blue violet and yellow orange. My favorite colors are blue and yellow. Yellow is an adjacent color on the right of yellow orange on a color wheel. Blue is the color adjacent to blue violet on a color wheel. My favorite colors are across the color wheel and adjacent one shade. I process colors as if they are lights.

Colored paints and colored lights combine differently, yielding different hues. When we combine all pigments together *(the colors of the rainbow),* the color black is created. In direct contrast, the presence of all the same frequencies of visible light creates white light. The light and pigment processes are inversely related; in one case, the colors combine to form the color black and in the other, they mix to form white light.

Objects absorb some wavelengths of the rainbow colors and reflect others. The unabsorbed colors are seen by the eye. A red object does not absorb red wave lengths. The pigment-opposite of red is green and all of the green waves are absorbed. Pigment colors are solid. Light bounces off of them or is absorbed. This information is translated by your eyes and brain.

In subtractive mixing of color, pigment absorbs certain wavelengths and they are subtracted from what you see. The subtractive color model starts with white and different pigments subtract *(or absorb)* colors from the reflected light creating its color.

Light colors are in the air, space or gas. When colors combine their frequencies are added. This color system starts without light, the color black. Light is added from a light source. Light wavelengths combine and create color. For example, red and green combine resulting in yellow. Red and blue produce magenta. All additive colors combine to form white.

The selection of a complementary color to lower an abundant frequency varies depending on whether or not the body processes the frequency body as light or pigment. The body may use the pigment process at times and the light process at others.

When mixing colored lights, primary color sets are any three colors of the correct intensity that combine to produce white light. There are a number of primary colors sets. The most common is red, green and blue. One colored light can be composed of two primary colors of light and combine with the third color needed to form white light. Mixing the proper intensity of the right two colors creates white light. For example, the complementary color of red light is cyan light, which is the combination of blue and green light. When cyan light is added to red light, white light is produced. Although it appears that we added two colors to create white light, we actually added three.

Only two complementary pigment colors are required to BioAcoustically cancel each other out, but to create this same effect with light, three colors are needed. When transposing the complementary light-color on a color pigment wheel, the complementary light-color is across the color wheel and adjacent one shade.

When Sharry and I were discussing complexities of how our bodies calculate frequencies, she laughed and told me that science depicts red pigment as the note of C. The Rosicrucians[146] (*a mystic school*) depict red as F#. Dinshah[147] practitioners who use colored lights for healing depict red as the note of G. This appears to be a contradiction, but in a way they are all correct. For the left-brain, physically oriented person, red is processed at the frequency of C; for the right-brained, emotionally oriented person, red is perceived as F#; and for the light oriented person, red may be perceived as a G. People perceive notes and colors differently, depending on how their body calculates frequencies.

Each musical note can impact people differently. Sharry pointed out that she hears a sound coming from the earth. If everyone could hear what she does, people would hear different notes coming from the earth. Those with left-brain dominance would hear an F, and those with right-brain

---

[146] The Rosicrucian system of study provides a foundation that ties together different aspects of metaphysical study and demonstrates their interconnectedness to natural laws that govern all realms. Many Rosicrucian teachings go back to the mystery schools of ancient Egypt and Europe. www.Rosicrucian.org

[147] Dinshah Health Society utilizes safe, specific colored light for particular problems with a simple, low-powered lamp and color filters.

dominance would hear B. The notes B and F correspond to complementary colors. The earth frequency could also be heard as F #, its "light-reciprocal."

## Other Factors affecting Antidotes

The way our bodies process frequencies is intricate: we are a complexity of frequencies that interact not only internally, but also with environmental sounds. There are additional variances that affect how we process lights, colors and frequencies.

"People process color differently depending on eye color, geographic location, atmospheric conditions, time of day and altitude."[148]

The human eye's ability to perceive color according to the amount of light that hits it is called the Purkinje Shift.[149] Dimmer light triggers more of the eye's blue wave length, making blues more vivid. More intense light fires the red wavelengths, making red appear more vivid. This causes mountains in the distance to appear "blueish" and red flowers more vivid when we are close to them.

Atmospheric conditions also affect coloration. "Hot, high, dry and sunny locations such as Jaipur, India show intense coloration. Cool, low, humid and cloudy locations such as the coast of Thailand show a darker and drabber coloration."[150]

---

[148] http://www.khazargems.com/color_and_gemstones.asp
[149] http://www.khazargems.com/color_and_gemstones.asp
[150] http://www.khazargems.com/color_and_gemstones.asp

Color is in the eye of the beholder. Another factor that affects how we see color is our eye coloration *(blue, brown, or hazel)*. Think of the color of our eyes as colored sunglasses. Blue eyes can differentiate up to 30% more color shades than dark colored eyes, because they are a lighter color.[151]

Colors and sound can impact us in many ways and on numerous levels. Imagine a huge pool into which someone drops a dozen pebbles. Each pebble creates rings of waves, which interact with other waves. Waves bounce off the sides of the pool. Reflected waves angle back further changing each other. The science of these intricate interactions is complex.

Numerous people say that there is yet another level to creating a healing antidote and have suggested that one's intent and attitude affect healing. Jonathan Goldman underscores this with his formula: "frequency plus intent equals healing."[152] Many studies on the placebo effect demonstrate that an ill person's belief of recovery impacts their healing. Clearly, attitude and positive intent play a role in effecting healing formulas.

In this complex analysis of discovering what frequencies or colors are needed to harmonize stressed frequencies in our voice, a simplification is welcomed. We are attracted to the frequencies that harmonize us whether it is a balancing frequency, a favorite color, a song we love, a pleasing fragrance, a food we find delicious, or a person, place or thing. We are subconsciously drawn to the pitches, colors and

---

[151] http://www.khazargems.com/color_and_gemstones.asp
[152] Goldman, Jonathan. <u>Shifting Frequencies</u>, Light Technologies Publishing: Az., 1998. pg. 5.

FEs of things that are uniquely healing. What we enjoy heals us!

Due to the maze of complexities involved in deciphering a sonic formula for antidotes, visit a trained Sound Health practitioner to get your healing frequencies.[153] If you see a practitioner trained by Sharry you will be required to test your frequencies in person. Due to all of these complexities testing insures that your final frequencies will accomplish your goals. Alternatively, if you take Sharry's course, you receive software and procedures to navigate through these complexities of sound healing.

# Chapter Five

# **More Body Math**

There are additional considerations in the selection of optimal sound formulas. We will discuss an overview of these concepts; Sharry retains proprietary details regarding the understanding and implementation of advanced sound applications. If you are interested in further education on

---

[153] At www.nutrasounds.com there are sections on "Becoming a Client" and "Finding a Practitioner" for anyone interested in getting a BioAcoustic reading. One can schedule a session from Sharry, but be prepared for a waiting period. To accommodate more people, Sharry trained thousands of practitioners, who use her software, her databases and techniques. These people are located across the United States and also in other countries. Their contact information is listed on the website.

these topics, she teaches a weeklong course that provides additional information.

In 1623, Galileo Galilei is credited with writing, "The great book of nature can be read only by those who know the language in which it was written. And this language is mathematics."[154] The German philosopher, scientist and mathematician, Leibniz *(1646-1716)* reflects on musical frequency patterns, "When engaging in music, the mind is engaging in an unconscious exercise in math."[155]

Present day author and mathematician, Brian Butterworth, postulates that math is the language of the brain. There are no language barriers in math. A mathematical equation such as $1 + 1 = 2$ is the same for every culture. Further, our brain and biology are hardwired to respond to the basic principles of math.[156]

Sharry believes that the numbers associated with the pitches that comprise our voices represent the language of our body. Sharry uses the language of the brain, which is mathematics *(expressed as frequencies or brainwaves)* to "talk" to a body.

Decoding the math of the body is not simple. Body-math is complicated but once mastered, it is predictable. The sonic world within our bodies has mind-boggling interactions and musical complexities; mathematical relationships underline everything.

---

[154] Edwards, Sharry. Vocal Profiling for the Professional. Sound Health: Athens, Ohio, 2002. Module 1.
[155] Thaut, Michael. Rhythm, Music and the Brain: Scientific Foundations and Clinical Applications, Routledge: NY, 2005. pg. 30.
[156] Butterworth, Brian. What Counts, How Every Brain is Hardwired for Math. Free Press: N.Y., 1999.

According to Butterworth, without frequency expressed as electromagnetic energy, our bodies could not be animated.[157] Sharry has unraveled many mathematical formulations. Each nutrient, biochemical, organ and emotion has predictable, mathematic relationships. They communicate through the neurological, nervous, circulatory and other systems.

Since the language of the body is math, numbers correspond to sound frequencies like the letters of our alphabet. The number of the cycles per second *(hertz)* is used as the numbers in this mathematical system. The cycles per second can be used in the same manner as the numbers that we manipulate in math class.

There are many ways that a mathematical equation can yield the same answer. Remember that waves interact, combining and subtracting - depending on how they overlap. There are many combinations of wave interactions that yield the same answer. For example, someone needs a six-cycle frequency to balance a pitch in his voice. He could listen to a frequency of six cycles per second, or two frequencies at the same time: one wave of five cycles and another of one cycle per second. Different sound waves, when in phase, combine energy. In the example above, the two waves can create a six-cycle frequency, because $5 + 1 = 6$. Keep in mind that not all six-cycle frequencies have the same effect on the body. One would think that a $1 + 5$ frequency is the same as a $2 + 4$ frequency, but it is not. The body requires the correct formula for obtaining a certain frequency.

---

[157] Butterworth, Brian. <u>What Counts, How Every Brain is Hardwired for Math.</u> Free Press: N.Y., 1999.

A wave of two cycles per second that is in phase with a three cycles per second wave combines and forms a wave of five cycles per second *(2 + 3 = 5)*. A person can receive the frequency of a five by many means, such as $3 + 2 = 5$, or $1 + 4 = 5$, or $10 - 5 = 5$. Often, only one mathematical way of obtaining a frequency will influence the body to correct itself. So, how do we tell which formula is the appropriate pattern?

Many chemical processes take place within the body. Each chemical process can be expressed with math and the FEs of nutrients can be inserted into mathematical, chemical equations. Many equations of body processes are known and can be found on line at "pub-med" for instance. Each element and nutrient in the chemical formula has a corresponding FE. Using the cycles per second as a numbering system, the frequency of a nutrient can be used as a mathematical number and inserted into equations of chemicals reacting in the body. When these numbers are inserted into the chemical equation the formulas make mathematical sense. The right frequencies in the appropriate mathematical pathway are critical for body processes to function optimally.

For instance, the Krebs cycle is a series of biochemical changes that occur during the metabolism of fats, carbohydrates, and amino acids, which facilitates the storage of energy. It is named after Hans Krebs *(1900–1981)*, the biochemist who identified it. The fundamental process involves oxidizing acetate molecules to carbon dioxide and water to transfer metabolic energy to "high energy" bonds for later use by the body. The Krebs cycle is a specific chemical formula that describes nutrients and how they transform in each stage of the equation. Sharry inserts the FEs of nutrients into the Krebs cycle formula and then creates a series of tones to support the innate metabolism of nutrients.

Calcium and magnesium are used together in the body. When one combines the FEs of calcium and magnesium the result is the FE of the bone matrix protein, phosphorus. The body's chemical processes can be shown mathematically with FEs. BioAcoustically speaking, biochemical relationships are also frequency relationships.[158]

Thousands of mathematical associations of frequencies which follow biochemical processes in the body have been identified. Author, Rita Holl,[159] correctly hypothesized that voiceprints of people with osteoporosis would show calcium FEs out of balance.

The FE of an element or compound allows the body to detect its presence, but the body is adept at compensating, substituting and transmuting frequencies. If biochemicals have similar frequencies, they are nearly interchangeable, performing the same work. Sulfur and palmitic acid have similar FEs. They can substitute for each other in the fight against invading pathogens. If an enzyme is not available to help counter invading pathogens, other biochemicals with similar FEs can compensate.

The note of C strengthens the thumb. The FE of the thumb muscle corresponds to the FE of zinc. The body will accept the zinc FE to support the thumb muscle.

---

[158] Sharry Edwards infers a relationship between electrons and frequency: "The valance electrons govern chemical reactions, and 'valances' are frequency shells around the nucleus of the atom."
[159] Holl, Rita. *Alternative Health Practitioner*. 1996.

When a body needs a nutrient, it shows up as lacking or surprisingly abundant in the voiceprint. Calcium shows up as overabundant for people who have osteoporosis and need calcium but can't assimilate it. This may happen because the nutrient is not in the right form for the body to utilize it or the body needs another nutrient to assimilate the over abundant frequency. We do not need to apply a complementary color because we do not want to cancel out this frequency. It is not problematic like a pathogen or toxin. We want the body to utilize the FE of a nutrient.

Biochemicals must be in balance for the body to utilize them. Every biochemical has another frequency that activates it. For example, we take magnesium with calcium in order for our body to create phosphorus, which enables the body to absorb both calcium and magnesium. When the body is unable to use calcium, deposits collect in the joints, creating the condition called arthritis. When one has attention deficit disorder, one's adrenaline FE is too high because the body cannot use it. Sharry's formulas of FEs mirror biochemical equations that allow the body to balance nutrients and vitamins, enabling them to be utilized.

If niacin's FE is a B and you listen to it, you activate the niacin. An additional frequency, called an energy-equivalent, combines with the frequency of niacin to be used in the body. In the example referring to attention deficit disorder, the sounds of an energy-equivalent pitch can allow the body to absorb and utilize adrenaline, which may help the body to decrease the problematic symptoms of attention deficit disorder.

Sharry discovered a three-step process for the body to utilize vitamins and nutrients. She uses this analogy: to get your car moving, the ignition must be engaged, in gear and someone has to step on the gas. Similarly, three steps are necessary to allow the body to efficiently use FEs of nutrients.

In this analogy, the FE starts up the car, the energy-equivalent puts the car in gear, and stepping on the gas is similar to ensuring that frequencies are in the proper rhythm. These steps are required to package a nutrient's FE in order for the body to use it. These three steps have a mathematical relationship that Sharry does not want to disclose.

We do not want energy-equivalents for all things in our bodies. In fact, it may be good to lessen some energy-equivalent sounds; we want to use the energy-equivalent for a longevity gene, but not a cataract gene!

In summary, in order to use FEs to assist the body to absorb nutrients and vitamins, three components are required:
- A primarily analog frequency comparable to the deficient nutrient or vitamin
- Energy of the nutrient energy-equivalent
- A specific rhythm to engage it

The software that you receive when you take Sharry's course automatically creates the proper rhythm.

# Atomic Mass and Frequency

A friend of Sharry's, Ralph Fucetola, compared the work of physicist Max Plank[160] *(a founding father of quantum theory[161])* with Einstein's famous relativity theory. In the early 1990s, Plank documented the connection between the energy of a particle and the frequency of the associated wave.

Plank's formula says that:[162]

| Plank's Constant | Einstein's Theory of Relativity |
|---|---|
| Energy = H *(Plank's constant)* F *(frequency)* | Energy = m *(mass)* $c^2$ *(speed of light in a vacuum)*$^2$ |

---

[160] Karl Marx Planck, better known as Max Planck *(1858 –1947)* was a German physicist. He is considered to be the founder of the quantum theory.

[161] Max Planck proposes that empty space is bursting with activity. McTaggart, Lynne. The Field, The Quest for the Secret Force of the Universe, Harper Collins Publishers: New York, 2002. pg. 23. McTaggart. "Particles cannot be separated from the empty space around them. Fluctuations in the atomic world amount to a ceaseless back and forth of energy - like a ball in the game of ping pong." pg. 23.

[162] The Planck constant *(denoted h),* called Planck's constant describes the sizes of quanta in quantum mechanics. It is the proportionality constant between energy *(E)* of a photon and the frequency of its associated electromagnetic wave *(v)*. Planck correctly hypothesized that some types of energy could not take on any indiscriminate value: instead, the energy must be some multiple of a very small quantity *(later to be named a "quantum")*. This is counterintuitive in the everyday world, where it is possible to "make things a little bit hotter" or "move things a little bit faster," but the quanta of energy are very, very small. Nevertheless, it is impossible, as Planck found out, to explain some phenomena without accepting that energy is discrete: that is to say like the integers 1, 2, 3… instead of the line of all possible numbers. http://en.wikipedia.org/wiki/Max_Planck; http://en.wikipedia.org/wiki/Planck_constant

Both of these formulas are descriptions of energy. Can they be combined?

$$HF = mc^2$$
or
Plank's constant multiplied by frequency = mass times *(speed of light)*$^2$

Plank's constant and the speed of light are constant, but frequency and mass vary. BioAcoustic enthusiasts believe that frequency is related to atomic mass. Does a relationship exist between frequency and mass? Does one exist between frequency and energy?

Sharry can hear an element and mechanically calculate its frequency using her voice. After conducting experiments with many elements, she concluded that the mass of the element was close to the frequency of the sound that she heard emanating from it. She used the frequencies of atomic weights in her earlier computer programs. Now she uses a more effective system of calculating body frequencies. Not wanting to publicize trade secrets, she declined to describe this new system.

There is an additional consideration when combining frequency formulations. Western society classifies illnesses separately and there is little discussion of the impact of one health problem on the other. With BioAcoustics we can look at one pattern of frequencies and see how a "fault" in one pattern interacts with others patterns, sometimes causing chain reactions with additional negative implications. Fixing a FE in the middle of a harmonic pattern may only create temporary relief if we don't correct the initial frequency fault that creates cascading intonation issues. In these cases symptoms dissipate while listening to certain sounds but will reoccur if the root FE problem is not corrected.

Health problems in the body can interact. Suppose someone has a back problem, temporomandibular joint *(TMJ)* and a liver problem. If these issues are related by octaves or in the same harmonic series, then only the root cause needs to be corrected for all three to improve. After the root problem is identified and corrected, the others correct themselves like cascading dominoes. Unfortunately, if one of the three problems is corrected, and it is not the root cause, this correction will be temporary.

The root issue could be at various levels within the body *(or in the electromagnetic spectrum of frequencies)*, such as:

- **Physical and structural** (*like bones and muscles*)
- **Maintenance** (*such as the heart valves and the replacement of villi in the intestines*)

- **Processing** *(as in kidney filtering and mental and emotional processing)*

Frequencies must be grouped in a specific manner to target levels of the body. I noted that the materials in the above categories vary in density. The denser an object is, the harder it is for a sound to impact it. As a substance becomes denser, higher energy or frequency is required to influence it.

Sharry's software, Svani, available only to advanced practitioners, creates a prototype of many harmonic formulations that allows one to determine root causes of cascading frequency issues.

# Chapter Six

# Pursuit of Scientific Development

## DNA and String Theory

Watching FEs combine and transform in the body gave Sharry insights to an inherent riddle belonging to modern string theory, a developing branch of theoretical physics.[163]

There are different mathematical models explaining string theories, but they all describe the natural forces *(gravitational, electromagnetic, weak and strong interactions)* and matter *(quarks and leptons)* in a mathematical system.

---

[163] String theory is a developing branch of theoretical physics that combines quantum mechanics and general relativity into a quantum theory of gravity. The strings in string theory are one-dimensional oscillating lines, but they are no longer considered fundamental to the theory, which can be formulated with points or surfaces. There are many string theories. String theory itself comes in many different formulations, each one has a different mathematical structure and each best describes different physical circumstances. One shared property of these theories is the holographic principle. Another shared principle is that some include the standard model of particle physics. This leads many physicists to believe that the theory is the correct fundamental description of nature. In particular, string theory is the first candidate for the theory of everything, a way to describe all the known natural forces *(gravitational, electromagnetic, weak and strong interactions)* and matter *(quarks and leptons)* in a mathematically complete system.

In string theory, elementary particles are infinitesimal, one-dimensional, string-like objects rather than dimensionless points in space-time.

Different musical notes can be created on a string belonging to a musical instrument. In string theory, musical notes compare to "excitation modes." The string can vibrate in different excitation modes just as a guitar string can produce different notes.[164] The elementary particles can be thought of as the "excitation modes" of musical strings.[165] Each frequency describes a different elementary particle.

The only difference in this analogy is that the guitar string is two-dimensional. In string theory, the guitar strings would be in every dimension, and the strings could be excited in either direction. Scientists theorize that the particles could move through not only our dimension, but other dimensions as well.[166]

In string theory and in guitar playing, the string must be stretched with tension in order to become excited or vibrated. The strings in string theory are floating in space-time, not tied down to a guitar. Nonetheless, they have tension.[167]

Relativistic quantum field theory *(the quantum-mechanical theories whose changeable variables are space and time)* describes observed behaviors and properties of elementary particles, but current theories only work when gravity is so weak that it is almost nonexistent. Similarly, particle theory

---

[164] *http://en.wikipedia.org/wiki/String_theory*
[165] <u>Britannica</u>. String Theory
[166] <u>Columbia Encyclopedia</u>, String Theory
[167] *Answers.com http://www.answers.com/topic/string-theory*

*(the branch of physics that studies subatomic particles and their interactions)* only works when we pretend gravity does not exist. String theory is believed to close this gap. In the 1980s, string theory became popular when it provided a quantum field theory that could describe gravity and electromagnetic forces.[168] String theory sensibly describes a string excitation that carries the specific gravitational force. This was a great victory for late 20th century physics.[169]

A concern with string theory is that no one knows how these vibrating strings create structure. Sharry's work has repeatedly shown that sound presentations react like RNA functions.

RNA can be likened to workers while DNA is analogous to instructions or blueprints. When a child cuts his finger, the RNA worker cells build scaffolding to maintain cell shape,[170] acting as adhesion for other materials, and bringing in blood. RNA cells insure that the repair process is carried out as the wound heals. DNA contains genetic instructions used in the development and functioning of living organisms. DNA is often compared to a set of blueprints, a recipe, or a code - it contains the instructions for repairs.

---

[168] *Answers .com http://www.answers.com/topic/string-theory*
[169] *http://www.superstringtheory.com/basics/basic3.html*
[170] RNA controls the pattern of frequency and in doing so it regulates protein synthesis and genetic information. A gene is the basic unit of heredity in a living organism. All living things depend on genes to hold the information to build and maintain their cells and to pass on their traits to offspring. Proteins are made of amino acids arranged in a linear chain. The sequence of amino acids in a protein is defined by information encoded in a gene. Many proteins are enzymes that catalyze biochemical reactions that are vital to metabolism. Proteins also have structural or mechanical functions and form a system of scaffolding that maintains cell shape. Other proteins are important in cell signaling, immune responses, cell adhesion and the cell cycles. http://en.wikipedia.org/wiki/RNA

String theory proposes that DNA could be likened to a string and RNA could be an excitation mode on the string that produces a result.

One of the greatest mysteries of biology is how organs and systems evolve in the body. Modern scientists mostly understand how we have blues eyes or grow to be six feet tall. What is rather elusive is how cells know where to place themselves in each stage of the building process so that an arm becomes an arm rather than a leg.

Scientists question how these cells organize and assemble into something resembling a three-dimensional human being.[171] In The Field, The Quest for the Secret Force of the Universe, McTaggart reflects on this idea, "Geneticists appreciate that cell differentiation utterly depends on cells knowing how to differentiate early on and then somehow remembering that they are different and passing on this vital piece of information to subsequent generations of cells. Scientists shrug their shoulders as to how this might all be accomplished, particular at such a rapid pace."[172]

To answer this question, many biologists and physicists have advanced the idea that radiation and oscillating waves are responsible for synchronizing cell division and sending chromosomal instructions around the body.[173] They theorize that frequency or vibration may be involved in the answer.

---

[171]McTaggart, Lynne. The Field, The Quest for the Secret Force of the Universe, Harper Collins Publisher: N.Y., 2002, pg. 44.

[172] McTaggart, Lynne. The Field, The Quest for the Secret Force of the Universe, Harper Collins Publisher: N.Y., 2002, pg. 46.

[173] McTaggart, Lynne. The Field, The Quest for the Secret Force of the Universe, Harper Collins Publisher: N.Y., 2002, pg. 48.

Herbert Frohlich, from the University of Liverpool, who received a Max Plank Medal, introduced the idea that some sort of collective vibration was responsible for getting proteins to cooperate with each other and carry out instructions of DNA and cellular protein.[174]

The physicist, Popp, found that DNA sent out a large range of frequencies and that some frequencies appeared to be linked to certain functions,[175] suggesting that vibrations provide some sort of communication.

Vibrational speeds of the elements vary in the Periodic Table of Elements. "Two Cornell physics graduate students, Barry Stripe and Mohammad Rezaei, reported in the June 1998 issue of *Science* that each atom has a signature energy level that can be used to identify molecules and unknown chemicals by measuring the vibrational signatures."[176]

McTaggart suggests that DNA can be likened to the master tuning fork in the body. It could strike a particular frequency and certain other molecules would carry out its instructions. Does the RNA sonically "read" the DNA blueprint?

Sharry smiles and points to BioAcoustics for more information. If the findings of BioAcoustic math are applied to string theory, they can create a working model or theory explaining how things become structure. As different chemicals in the body combine, so do their frequencies,

[174] McTaggart, Lynne. The Field, The Quest for the Secret Force of the Universe, Harper Collins Publisher: N.Y., 2002, pg. 49.
[175] McTaggart, Lynne. The Field, The Quest for the Secret Force of the Universe, Harper Collins Publisher: N.Y., 2002, pg. 44.
[176] Edwards, Sharry. Vocal Profiling for the Professional, Sound Health: Albany, Ohio, 2002. pg. M155.

transforming their combined FEs. In BioAcoustics, one can observe RNA frequencies combining with other frequencies of substances and watch the waves transform again and again. For example, BioAcoustically speaking, the FE of oxygen and sulfur combine to form the FE of hydrogen, mimicking the creation of our universe. This frequency bumps into other things and continually transforms. After about the tenth round of transformations it becomes a hormone. Using the math of BioAcoustics, one can watch elements and compounds forming. We can observe the structure of things form and watch the underlying mathematical equations of frequencies being displayed. Things become structure by connecting elements to FE's and doing the math. Applying this math to string theory provides answers to string theory's unanswered questions. By likening FE's to execution modes in string theory, we can observe the FE math as it forms structure. As we watch these musical transformations, we realize that the body is a frequency-based universe. Watching frequencies transform and recreate can be like watching the universe being created!

## Research

We can learn about body processes by observing "The Great Mathematician" *(our body)* doing its work and gather potential breakthrough ideas for testing. A scientist can translate a human biological theory into frequencies and observe the process and results of his theory. It is a relatively cost effective and quick method. If the frequencies and math support the theory, it pays the scientist to invest the time and money to conduct a full scientific experiment. Why not stack the deck in your favor?

Here's an example. Autistic children's voiceprints pinpoint the presence of a thermasol which is an ingredient of a DPT vaccination *(for diphtheria, whooping cough and tetanus)*. BioAcoustic observations show that sometimes this chemical appears to destroy the body's ability to utilize vitamin A which can act like a toxin. Collaborating information reveals that in all cases of autistic disorder the person has received a DPT vaccination.[177] It is worth investigating the connection between thermasol and autistic disorder. Could future suffering from autistic disorder be eliminated?

If more BioAcoustics results were studied with the scientific method, veracity would be given to this emerging science and these findings could catapult our progress toward eradicating diseases and help us to understand our emotions, minds and bodies better.

---

**A Sampling of Sharry's Vocal Profiling Observations**
*(to be studied scientifically)*

---

The frequency for high fructose corn syrup is overabundant in voiceprints of children that exhibit poor concentration. Can research connect high fructose corn syrup[178] and a

---

[177] Tenpenny, Dr. Sherri. <u>Saying No to Vaccines</u>. NMA Media Press, Quote from Dr. Mayer Eisenstein MD JD. Back cover.

[178] Rudolf Steiner, a great mystic and scholar in the last century, commented on artificial sugars. "Chemically derived substances are like a 'synthetic mirror image' of their natural counterparts. Their origin lies in the physical world with no relationship to the realm of life forces." Synthetic sugars are cut off from living influences. Some mystics suggest that these "shadow" foods deplete our soul. Steiner reported that there has been a gradual descent of using sugar from the flower of a plant *(honey)* to the stem *(sugar cane)* to the root *(beet sugar)*. According to spiritual science the plant has an inverted affect on people, with the root affecting the head

child's ability to focus? If our country is serious about improving the educational performance of children, should they investigate nutritional guidelines for children, especially the school lunch menus?

Sharry observes that FEs of natural foods and herbs facilitate vocal coherence. The FEs of manmade synthetic medicine does not create vocal coherence, but negative side effects and harmonic imbalances. The impact of manmade substances that we consume can be studied by observing how these FEs alter body processes. For example, fibromyalgia is associated with the FEs of stored drug deposits *(prescription or otherwise)* in muscle tissues. Can this be evaluated? Can we prevent fibromyalgia?

Voiceprints have shown that FEs created by fluorescent lights are associated with prostate cancer. Can research validate this connection?

Sharry observed that when an autistic child with savant genius recovered from autistic disorder, she lost a great deal of her savant genius. Can studies be devised to understand the link between savant genius and autistic disorder?

If two people are both missing the same notes and using the same brain hemisphere, they experience personal friction

forces. When the head is not balanced with the heart, materialism flourishes in a civilization, according to Steiner. Francke, Sylvia. The Tree of Life and the Holy Grail, Temple Lodge: England, 2007. pgs. 106 -107.

and can repel each other like poles of a magnet. They are attracted when they use opposite sides of their brain. Could this information be confirmed and then used in relationship counseling?

Women are known to admire a man with broad shoulders, a strong chin and a flat stomach. The FEs responsible for these traits are octaves of male hormones such as testosterone. These frequencies are the same as Sharry hears emanating from the shape of a man's torso. In contrast, men are attracted to circular shapes that may be found on a woman. Is attraction a science? Can we measure it? Predict it? Change it?

As an adult Sharry created weekly sonic formulas to maintain vocal coherence. Surprisingly, her feet grew two shoe sizes and she also grew two inches in height. What is the relationship between balanced vocal coherence and human growth? The mummies of the ancient Egyptians stand no bigger than four feet tall. My feet would have hung out of the beds made during the American Revolution. My children tower over me and I was taller than my mother. What is the science behind an increased size of populations? Is there a connection between improvements in consciousness *(overall health of thinking, feeling and physical health)* as measured by vocal coherence and the size of the physical body that stores that consciousness?

When sperm combines with an egg, the chemical ATP is produced. The FE of ATP is an octave of the FE of white light. Much of the body's ATP is stored in the eyes. When we die, the ATP breaks down and many people see white lights on their deathbeds. It is interesting that white light FE is created at conception and people often see white light during the dying process. Is this phenomenon at death due to the breakdown of ATP in the eyes at death? Does this chemical process explain the spiritual event of seeing white light during a near death experience?

The addition and subtraction of frequencies sometimes yields unexpected results. Since these equations do not mirror chemical equations, what is the explanation of them? Do these frequency equations prepare the way for discoveries? A few examples are:

- Oxygen + hydrogen = nitrogen
- Nitrogen + hydrogen = nitric oxide *(cell respiration)* and sex hormones
- Oxygen – hydrogen = ATP *(the first chemical created after conception)*
- Carbon – hydrogen = vitamin C *(a vitamin not produced by humans)*
- Water – oxygen = hydrogen
- Oxygen + hydrogen = nitrogen

At a government facility, Sharry "sang" to three vegetables, which quickly dehydrated. Researchers attempted to calculate frequencies to preserve food by dehydration. The researchers produced a sine wave similar to Sharry's voice and then exposed the vegetables to it, but the vegetables eventually decayed. The only known variable between the sounds that Sharry and a machine can create is her pattern of harmonics. *(Ohio University's sound lab verified the unique harmonics in Sharry's voice: intervals 3, 6,and 9 notes apart.)* Could we preserve food by exposing it to this pattern of harmonics?

Could exact birth times be determined by monitoring voiceprints for hormone levels of expectant mothers?

People with Duchenne's muscular dystrophy BioAcoustically show an inability to utilize choline. Could this disorder be treated with energy-equivalent levels of choline?

Certain sounds repel insects. Could we use sounds instead of pesticides that are harmful to our environment?

Sound health discoveries may not be taken seriously without research to confirm the wealth of information being discovered. Even if a sampling of Sharry's observations were tested and proven, the credibility of BioAcoustics could spread and allow more people to reap its benefits.

Once these findings have been verified, the diagnostic feature of BioAcoustics could become widely used. Given the ever-increasing health care costs, which are now two trillion dollars a year in the United States, why overlook BioAcoustic's relatively inexpensive benefits?

# Chapter Seven

# Musical Scales

Most people think that all musical scales use the same notes. This could not be farther from the truth.

Western music only uses the notes that we hear on the piano, so easily we assume that all notes are the same. Other scales assign different frequencies to notes. For example, Hindi music has numerous variations of the note G: G+ and G++. Other scales, which are not used in the Western Hemisphere's musical system, use different frequencies and also varied intervals between notes which affect us differently - physically, mentally and emotionally.

Throughout history many scales were used; in fact, the scales were selected because of the effects that they produced on listeners. Many have even attributed the characteristics of a culture to the scale they listened to. The Western equal-temperament scale is equated to "aural caffeine" as its intervals stimulate activity.[179] These advocates also claim that listening to Western music, which stimulates activity, preceded the industrial advances in countries like the USA, Europe, Japan, China and India.

---

[179] From an article on the Internet *(http://home.earthlink.net/-kgann/tuning/html)* that describes the differences between just intonation and the equal temperament scale.

Earlier scales employed mathematics to create consonant sounding intervals from whole number ratios between notes. The equal-temperament scale modifies intervals so that musicians can conveniently go from one key to another, but this is at the expense of the natural consonance or harmony that other scales can create. Listening to calming musical scales is reputed to support the advanced meditation practices of Eastern cultures.

In addition to using different scales, ancient Eastern music utilizes modes. Modes use many frequencies and scales that are not available on our pianos. The ancient modal system of music selects a group of notes to create a specific mood that impacts a person in a unique way. Often intervals of octaves, fourths and fifths *(with consonant whole number ratios)* are included. A modal song is comprised of these exclusive notes, but the notes can be replicated in any order or rhythm. This method not only creates a special mood but also, pours a good dose of these frequencies into the listener's body.

Ancient and Eastern musical scales have mathematical relationships between notes that Westerners do not experience. Often these scales are derived from mathematical equations reflecting nature's patterns.

Johannes Kepler, a 16th century scientist,[180] formed a musical scale by calculating the ratios of the planets at their furthest

---

[180] Johannas Kepler *(1571-1630)* was the first person to: correctly explain planetary motion, thereby, becoming founder of celestial mechanics; investigate the formation of pictures with a pin hole camera; explain the process of vision by refraction within the eye; to formulate eyeglass designing for nearsightedness and farsightedness; explain the use of both eyes for depth perception; describe real, virtual, upright and inverted images and magnification; explain the principles of how a telescope works; discover the properties of total internal reflection. In addition he: formed the basis of integral calculus, explained that the tides are caused by the moon; used stellar

and nearest distances from the sun. He used these ratios to create notes of a musical scale. He believed that copying mathematical patterns found in the heavens and converting these to musical patterns would be beneficial to listeners.

Sharry hears the frequencies of various chemical elements and has observed a close correlation between atomic mass and frequency. Sylvia Francke tells us that, "A musical scale can be designed using the mass of elements *(and compounds formed from these elements)* that are found in the human body - which closely correlates to the diatonic scale[181] created by the scientist, Kepler, after his research on planetary orbits."[182] Kepler noticed that the ratios between the planets' extreme angular orbits created equating to harmonic intervals. Kepler's measurements of planetary orbits create ratios similar to those found in just intonation. [183]

## The Just Intonation Scale[184]

---

parallax caused by the earth's orbit to measure the distance to the stars *(the same principle as depth perception). (Today this branch of research is called astrometry.)* Kepler suggested that the sun rotates about its axis; derived the birth year of Christ, that is now universally accepted; derived logarithms purely based on mathematics; and coined the word "satellite."

[181] Diatonic most often describes music that uses traditional major and minor scales. Diatonic and chromatic are terms that characterize scales. Often diatonic refers to musical elements derived from the "white note scale," C–D–E–F–G–A–B. The chromatic scale consists of all semitones. http://en.wikipedia.org/wiki/Diatonic_scale
[182] Francke, Sylvia. The Tree of Life and The Holy Grail, Temple Lodge: England, 2007. pg. 201.
[183] http://alternativespirituality.suite101.com/article.cfm/sacred_geometry
[184] In music, just-intonation is any musical tuning in which the frequencies of notes are related by ratios of whole numbers. Justly tuned intervals are usually written either as ratios, with a colon *(for example, 3:2),* or as fractions, with a slash *(3/2).* Although in theory two notes tuned in an arbitrary frequency ratio such as 1024:927 might be said to be justly tuned, in practice only ratios using quite small numbers are given the name; more complex ratios are often considered to be rational intonation but not necessarily just-intonation. Intervals used are then capable of being more consonant. http://en.wikipedia.org/wiki/Just_intonation

Just intonation is any system of tuning in which all of the intervals between notes can be represented by ratios of whole numbers. Intervals in the just intonation system are considered to be acoustically pure.

Just intonation is not a particular scale, nor is it tied to any particular musical style. It is, rather, a set of principles, which can be applied to a limited number of musically significant intervals to generate an enormous variety of scales and chords.[185] This type of process creates a just intonation scale such as:

| Note | C C | D | E | F | G | A | B |
|------|-----|---|---|---|---|---|---|
| Ratio | 1/1 2/1 [186] | 9/8 | 5/4 | 4/3 | 3/2 | 5/3 | 15/8 |

Another way to do it is as follows:

| Note | A A | B | C | D | E | F | G |
|------|-----|---|---|---|---|---|---|
| Ratio | 1/1 2/1 [187] | 9/8 | 6/5 | 4/3 | 3/2 | 8/5 | 9/5 |

The larger number in the ratio represents the greater string length and hence the lower pitch. The ratio for an octave is 2:1; an interval of a fifth 5th is 3:2; an interval of a 4th is 4:3.

In the book, <u>Just Intonation Primer</u>, there is a description of the sounds of these sounds, "A formal definition of just

---

[185] http://www.justintonation.net/primer2.html
[186] The chords F-A-C, C-E-G, and G-B-D are just major triads. A-C-E and E-G-B are just minor triads, but D-F-A is not. [186]
[187] The chords D-F-A, A-C-E, and E-G-B are just minor triads and F-A-C and C-E-G are just major triads, but G-B-D is not.

intonation may be difficult for the novice to grasp, but the experience of listening to intervals is unmistakable. Although it is difficult to describe the special qualities of just intervals to those who have never heard them, words such as clarity, purity, smoothness, and stability come readily to mind. The supposedly consonant intervals and chords of equal temperament, which deviate from simple ratios to varying degrees, sound rough, restless, or muddy in comparison."[188]

These simple-ratio intervals are "special relationships" that the human auditory system is able to detect from a host of complex stimuli. The human auditory system recognizes them as consonant. Musicians around the world have recognized the significance of listening to notes made from whole-number ratios for at least 5,000 years.

## The Equal Temperament Tuning Scale

Early classical pianos used the just-intonation scale. Each piano only played in one key or had numerous pitches for every sharp and flat. The pitch of F# in the key of G was slightly different than the pitch of an F# in the key of D. For example, one piano might have three different F#s and three C#s and be able to create notes for three different scales.

In the equal temperament system of tuning adjacent notes have identical frequency ratios. An octave is divided into 12 equal steps.[189] There is only one pitch for each note, enabling musicians to economically go from one key to another. In the Western Hemisphere, the equal temperament scale is a

[188] Doty, David. The Just Intonation Primer, The Just Intonation Network: San Francisco, CA., 2003. Introduction.
[189] http://en.wikipedia.org/wiki/Equal_temperament

universal musical language. In 1939 it was adopted as a universal musical scale.

The equal temperament scale "tempers" its notes. For example, G and C are five notes apart. This interval is comprised of two notes that create a ratio of 1/5 exactly. Using the equal-temperament system, this interval is slightly less than the 1/5 required for a perfect fifth. This slight reduction *(flattening)* in frequency is referred to as "tempering." It is not possible to tune all intervals of 3rds, 5ths...to their exact ratios *(such as 1/5 for fifths)* and simultaneously have all octaves come out being exactly in the ratio of 2/0. Pythagoras noted that when whole number ratios are used for intervals that the octave is not an exact ratio of 2/0, but 2/0+.[190] In contrast, in equal temperament tuning, the octaves have a ratio of 2/0 and all other notes are tempered.

Mystics have criticized the use of the equal-temperament scale because the difference between each note is obtained from an averaged figure. They describe the equal-temperament scale as "dead rigid" images of notes instead of, scales that reflect mathematical patterns found in nature and our bodies.

## Pythagorean Tuning

Pythagoras believed the musical scale mimicked the movements of the planets, which he believed, were not elliptical but circular.

Pythagorean tuning is a system of musical tuning in which the frequency relationships of all intervals are based on the

---

[190] The discrepancy between twelve justly tuned fifths *(ratio 3:2)* compared with seven octaves *(ratio 2:1)* is referred to the Pythagorean comma.

ratio 3/2, which represents an interval of a fifth.[191] Thus it is not only a mathematically elegant system, but also one of the easiest to tune by ear.

Its name comes from medieval texts that attribute its discovery to Pythagoras, but its use has been documented as long ago as 3500 B.C. in Babylonian texts. It is the oldest way of tuning the 12-note chromatic scale. Since all intervals have integer (whole number) ratios based on the powers of two and three, Pythagorean tuning is also one variety of just intonation.[192]

"Pythagorean tuning is characterized by consonant octaves, perfect fourths and perfect fifths, based on ratios of the numbers one, two, three and four. All other intervals in Pythagorean tuning are dissonant."[193]

To derive a complete chromatic scale of the kind common on keyboards by around 1300, we take a series of 11 perfect fifths: Eb, Bb, F, C, G, D, A, E, B, F#, C# and G#.[194]

---

[191] Pythagorean tuning is based on a stack of perfect fifths, each tuned in the ratio 3:2, the next simplest ratio after 2:1, which is the ratio of an octave. In applying this tuning to the chromatic scale, a problem arises: no number of 3:2s fits exactly into an octave. Because of this, the G, separated by twelve fifths from the A, is about a quarter of a semitone sharper. This is known as the Pythagorean comma. http://en.wikipedia.org/wiki/Pythagorean_comma

[192] http://www.music.sc.edu/fs/bain/atmi02/pst/index.html

[193] http://www.justintonation.net/primer2.html

[194] The one potential flaw of this system is that the fourth or fifth between the extreme notes of the series, Eb-G#, will be out of tune: in the colorful language of intonation, a "wolf" interval. This complication arises because 12 perfect fifths do not round off to precisely an even octave, but exceed it by a small ratio known as a Pythagorean comma (see Section 4). Happily, since Eb and G# rarely get used together in medieval harmony, this is hardly a practical problem. http://www.music.sc.edu/fs/bain/atmi02/pst/index.html

A color represents a range of FEs or, hues of the same shade. For example red can range from red orange to red purple. Musical scales can select from a variety of pitches that fall within a color range. Different octaves within our body and/or different body systems can use various scales and pitch variations.

Different scales are comprised of notes created from a variety of frequencies. One color can encompass a range of frequencies or several notes. When superimposing one just intonation scale on the color wheel, the complementary pigment color is directly across the color wheel. When a Pythagorean scale is overlaid on a color wheel, the note directly across the circle is the not complementary color, but one color adjacent to the complementary color. Likewise, when mixing lights, as opposed to pigments, the complementary colors are also across the pigment color wheel and adjacent one hue. There appears to be a correlation between complementary light colors and Pythagorean tuning.

| Just-intonation Complementary Colors | Pythagorean Tuning Complementary Colors |
|---|---|
| Red and Green | Cyan *(blue/green)* and Red |
| Orange and Blue | Orange and Cyan |
| Blue and Orange | Blue and Red/Orange |
| Purple and Yellow | Purple and Orange/Yellow |

### The Solfeggio Scale

In <u>Healing Codes for Biological Apocalypse</u> Horowitz and Puleo, claim that the ancient Solfeggio tones "vibrate the exact frequencies required to transform spirit to matter or matter to spirit."[195] They also write that the Solfeggio tones are capable of "spiritually inspiring humankind to be more Godlike." [196]

This book unveils a pattern of numbers encoded in the Bible: Numbers 7:12-89, that can be converted into frequencies. The content of this seemingly unimportant text is about mundane activities that occurred on different days. The Pythagorean skein[197] is then applied to the numbers of the verses associated with different days. For example, the text describing the first day is on verse 12, which has a Pythagorean skein of 12, or 1+2 = **3**. The second day starts on verse 18, or 1 +8 = **9**. The third day is located on verse 24, or 2 + 4 = **6**. These three sums, 3, 9, and 6, create the first set of numbers of the Solfeggio scale. When you apply the same process to the rest of the chapter you get the following set of numbers:

**Solfeggio Scale[198]**

$1^{st}$ set = 396 hertz
$2^{nd}$ set = 417 hertz
$3^{rd}$ set = 528 hertz
$4^{th}$ set = 639 hertz
$5^{th}$ set = 741 hertz
$6^{th}$ set = 852 hertz

*(These tones are not in our musical scales or pianos.)*

---

[195] Joseph Puleo and Leonard Horowitz, Healing Codes for a Biological Apocalypse, Tetrahedron Publishing Co.: Idaho, 2001, pg. 59.

[196] Joseph Puleo and Leonard Horowitz, Healing Codes for a Biological Apocalypse, Tetrahedron Publishing Co.: Idaho, 2001, pg. 61.

[197] In the system of the Pythagorean skein, individual numbers are added up and ultimately reduced to the numbers 1 through 9. For example, with the number 245, 2 + 4 + 5 = 11. With the number 11, 1 + 1 = 2. The Pythagorean skein for the number 245 is 2.

[198] Notice the numerical pattern in the ones, tens and hundreds column.

David Hulse from SomaEnergetics[199] developed a teacher certification program using the Solfeggio frequencies for healing benefits. He described the benefits of listening to this scale after researching their benefits in history and confirming the benefits through thousands of sessions.

## The Benefits of the Solfeggio Scale

- **Turn grief into joy** *(396 hertz frequency)*. The first Solfeggio tone liberates energy, eliminating hidden blockages and subconscious negative beliefs.
- **Connect people to the Source** *(417 hertz)*. This tone helps people to change.
- **Repair DNA** *(528 hertz)*. This frequency brings transformation and miracles into our life. This frequency repairs broken DNA, the genetic blueprint upon which life is based.[200]
- **Connect people to spiritual family** *(639 hertz)*. This frequency creates harmony in relationships.
- **Solve problems and increase intuition** *(741 hertz)*. This tone gives us power of self-expression to be who we really are.
- **Return people to spiritual order** *(852 hertz)*. This frequency links the mind, body, insight, consciousness and spiritual evolution.

The sounds of the Solfeggio scale are embedded in my "Paint Your Soul" CD. Tuning forks were made to replicate these

---

[199] SomaEnergetics *(Soma meaning, "body" in the original Greek)* are sound therapies utilizing tuning forks tuned to the frequencies of the Ancient Solfeggio scales. These therapies release blockages in the energy bodies and assist one with connecting with Source.
[200] http://orgoneproducts.org/blog/2008/04/02/ancient-solfeggio-frequencies-528-hz-dna-repair/

pitches and they twinkle in the background of this sonorous music.

Here are a few comments on the "Paint Your Soul" CD with the Solfeggio tones playing softly in the background:

- "As I listen to your music for the very first time, I felt it immediately begin to minister love, peace and well-being to every cell in my body. Frankly, that hasn't happened EVER in my life. I felt every cell coming into perfection as I closed my eyes to breathe in this amazing music." *M. Murphy.*
- "I found in your music a hidden secret, the unconfused part of myself that I know to be the truest, most precious and the most sacred part, which I have steadfastly ignored." *Dr. Michael Lagan*
- "When I listen to your beautiful CD my cares melt away and I feel the illusion of fear dissolve as I experience the truth of light and love." *Anne L*
- "There are many talented people in this world, but few who matches Jill's and whose talent penetrates AND is welcome in the heavenly realm. Know that your gifts are not just benefiting us earthlings..." *Noemia*
- "With your music I feel divine mother energy surround me in a large dose of unconditional love." *Sarah L.*

Listen to the "Paint Your Soul" CD at www.jillswingsoflight.com and receive complementary mp3s at www.jillshealingmusic.com.

# The Body Scales

Each person's body develops its own musical scale either using one described above or, creating its own unique scale or scales. Sharry can hear notes in a person's body, then match tones to the unique musical scale created by each body. Her practitioners are able to prescribe accurate tones that are unique to individuals because the FFTs precisely identify which frequencies a body needs.

Finding the exact scale and individual tones that the body requires is critical. Sharry describes a woman with hyperostosis *(an overgrowth of bone)*. This woman's body could not utilize calcium and she built up calcium deposits. The frequency of calcium her body needed was slightly different than what other people could ingest and utilize as calcium. A voiceprint revealed that the precise frequency of calcium that she uniquely needed was an isotope of calcium.

Isotopes are different types of atoms of the same chemical element, having a different atomic mass. Isotopes have nuclei with the same number of protons, but different numbers of neutrons. Isotopes can be illustrated by the process of making biscuits. When a recipe calls for baking soda, flour and salt and the ingredients are not mixed well, one biscuit may have more salt than the others. This biscuit represents an isotope.

Although the woman in our example had taken over the counter calcium supplements, none of them helped. Only when she was given the appropriate FE for the isotope of calcium that her body needed - was she able to utilize it alleviating her symptoms.

In summary, the scale used in the Western Hemisphere only uses select frequencies. More scales are available that mirror patterns found in nature and reflect a math that underlines our world. In antiquity, different scales and music were created to mimic nature and it was discovered that mathematical patterns affect our consciousness. Special music was the key to developing character, virtue, and spiritual evolvement in ancient Greek and Chinese musical thought.

Pythagoras lived roughly 570 – 500 BC, and believed that the cosmos was governed by numbers.[201] By using the appropriate numbers beneath music one could restore harmonious equilibrium. Kitty Ferguson, who wrote <u>The Music of Pythagoras</u>, tells us, "One Pythagorean theme was to find the underlying mathematical structure of the world and use the power of mathematics to unlock its secrets."[202] In the final analysis, music was a set of numbers.

Our bodies each have their own unique musical scale. Sharry discovered that many of us *(but not all)* use a scale similar to the just intonation scale.

+-

---

[201] Ferguson, Kitty. <u>The Music of Pythagoras</u>, Walker and Co: N.Y., 2008. pg. 151.
[202] Ferguson, Kitty. <u>The Music of Pythagoras</u>, Walker and Co: N.Y., 2008. pg. 130.

# Chapter Eight

# **Rhythm in the Body**

In the womb, our ears are one of the first organs to develop. We hear our first communication from the rhythm of our mother's heartbeat. We receive reassurance through a steady rhythm all throughout our lives. Hearing is one of the last senses that we lose when we die. The human body can be compared to an orchestra, with the heart drumming the constant beat under normal circumstances.

David Burrows reflects on the unconscious modeling of life in music, "Music's movements mime the striding, the leaping, the rocking motion, the twisting and turning of the human organism in its landscape and in its mindscape. In 'musicking' we model sensations of expansion and contraction, intensification, slowing and accelerating, detached from the roots of such sensations in daily living."[203]

Rhythm affects our pulse, heart rate, breath and stress response. It can influence the pace of our voice, stride and activities. A rhythm can increase or decrease our energy. Various beats and pulses strengthen the elasticity of our internal rhythms, helping us gain vitality.

---

[203] Burrows, David. Time and the Warm Body: A Musical Perspective on the Construction of Time, Brill: Boston, 2007. pg. 68.

There is more power in rhythm than we realize. Harmony and frequency are only a portion of the equation that can improve our mind, emotions and bodies. We need the proper rhythm as well. Michael Thaut,[204] in his book about scientific foundations for rhythm, music and the brain, states, "The brain is neurologically superbly sensitive to processing the time elements in music in a rapid, precise and meaningful manner."[205] Rhythm is an extremely important element that orchestrates the body's music!

Thaut describes rhythm as creating the "major syntax and grammar of time in music."[206] He further adds that rhythm translates the perception of time not like pulsing ticks of a stop watch, but as frequency patterns unfolding horizontally in time.[207] One can view this in a voiceprint and observe patterns in pitch and rhythm. Haut continues that, "Rhythm in music translates the perception of time into a sensory language."[208]

Thaut continues, "The recent body of brain research shows impressively that sensory experiences change the brain…developing neuronal architecture – the wiring scheme of the brain – into a more and more diverse and efficient

---

[204] Michael Thaut is vice president of the International Society for Music and Medicine. He received the National Research Award from the American Musical Therapy Association.

[205] Thaut, Michael. Rhythm, Music and the Brain: Scientific Foundations and Clinical Applications, Routledge: N.Y., 2005, pg. 59.

[206] Thaut, Michael. Rhythm, Music and the Brain: Scientific Foundations and Clinical Applications, Routledge: N.Y., 2005, pg. 16.

[207] Thaut, Michael. Rhythm, Music and the Brain: Scientific Foundations and Clinical Applications, Routledge: N.Y., 2005, pg. 15.

[208] Thaut, Michael. Rhythm, Music and the Brain: Scientific Foundations and Clinical Applications, Routledge: N.Y., 2005, pg. 16.

executive system."[209] Clearly rhythm is an important component of the music within our bodies.

Rhythm provides patterns or pulses that are irregular or periodic. Our motor and nervous systems are sensitive to and quickly aroused by rhythm. Rhythm can make us dance in a frenzy or slow our hearts down. Rhythm sets the mood of a song, as well as animating a sometimes-lackluster melody. Rap music is the ultimate example of this. The rap melody repeats the same note over and over, while people groove on the rhythm!

Rhythm is influenced by the musical tempo. The "tempo" *(Italian for time and movement)* dictates the speed of periodic beats. This affects the mood of a piece and our energy levels as well. Fast tempos create energy, while depression or a peaceful meditation can be facilitated from slow tempos. In the body, the heart controls the tempo. Our heart races when we are frightened and slows down in a peaceful meditation.

Our own rhythms can be a more complete expression of who we are than we realize. Watch people's varied way of walking on a busy street. Some people bounce, others shuffle and a few march. Some are rigid, others flexible. Other variations include: jerkiness versus regularity of rhythm, or a calm rhythm versus a rushed one. Our personality and emotions can be reflected in the rhythm of our walk.

Words have rhythm. Languages have rhythm and tempos. The rate of speaking and associated movements often depicts the underlining meaning of our words. Our words may say

---

[209] Thaut, Michael. <u>Rhythm, Music and the Brain: Scientific Foundations and Clinical Applications</u>, Routledge: N.Y., 2005, pg. 16.

one thing, while our rhythm of words and body language can say another, revealing a deeper truth.

Rhythm patterns create characteristic feelings. Patterns of two beats mimic walking or marching, creating a feeling of a straight line. A pattern of three beats feels softer and directs energy inward. The 3-beat pattern is used for waltzes in which the dancers spiral around on the dance floor.

Rhythm expresses our own energy. Reinhard Flatischler, who developed a revolutionary approach to rhythm that combined pulse, breath, voice and rhythm,[210]reflects on the power of rhythm. "The drum returns my energy by translating it into audible rhythm and thus completes a circuit of energy that allows me to connect with my own power."

African and American Indian traditions use drumming to induce Shamanic journeys to cure physical, mental and emotional problems. I have a CD of African witchcraft music. On the inside cover, the Africans expressed sympathy for all Westerners who do not have access to their profound, healing rhythmic modalities. These Africans pitied Westerners who used hospitals and medical systems instead of their rhythmic music!

The Africans value drumming as a greater force, more than mere entertainment. Richard Bartlet, who authored <u>Matrix Energetics</u>, describes how rhythms induce a shamanic journey, "Repetitive drumming distracts the conscious mind, lulling the left brain into relinquishing its stranglehold over the prevailing view of reality. After much practice, temporary

---

[210]Flatischler, Reinhard. <u>The Forgotten Power of Rhythm, Taketina</u>: Mendocino, CA., 1992.

right-brain dominance occurs and the process Carl Jung calls 'active imagination' is allowed free reign. In Shamanic lore this is called a journey. In these journeys you may encounter mindscapes of a virtual territory of specifically identified terrain, which have been mapped out by conscious explorers for many cultures for thousands of years."[211]

Daniel Levitin gives another explanation for changes in consciousness induced by rhythm, "Music with rhythmic elements – played on drums, rain sticks, shakers, shells, stones, sticks, and hand claps –typically takes on a more regular, hypnotic quality that can induce trance states. Just how music induces trance states is not known, but it seems to be related to the relentless rhythmic momentum, coupled with a solid, predictable beat. When the beat is predictable neural circuits in the basal ganglia *(the habit and motor ritual circuits,* as well as regions of the cerebellum that connect to it, become entrained by the music. Neurons fire synchronously with the beat. This in turn shifts brain wave patterns, easing us into an altered state of consciousness that may resemble the onset of sleep, or the netherworld between sleep and wakefulness, or even a drug like state of heightened concentration coupled with increased relaxation of the muscle and a loss of awareness of time and place."[212] Repetition numbs our bondage to reality, opening us up to higher levels of consciousness.

Hazrat Inyat Khan was a teacher from India who started a Sufi Order in the West. He said, "When the rhythm in the

---

[211] Bartlett, Richard. Matrix Energetics: The Science and Art of Tranformation, Atria books: N.Y., 2007. pg. 70.
[212] Levitin, Daniel, J. The World in Six Songs: How the Musical Brain Created Human Nature, Penguin Group: N.Y., 2009. pgs. 213-214.

body is disturbed it can lead to illness, because it disturbs the whole mechanism that is going on, the order of which depends of the regularity of the rhythm. If a person suddenly hears something that causes fear, the rhythm is broken and the pulsation changes. Every shock a person receives breaks his rhythm. Once the rhythm is broken, it is most difficult to get it right again… The rhythm should be regained in a gradual process."[213]

Thaut suggests four applications of music and rhythm;

- Rhythmic stimulations have profound effects on motor control, speech, physiological and behavior functions.
- Rhythm can enhance learning, perception and language.
- Music can be used as an alternate transmission route for information in the brain.
- Music is a powerful emotional stimulus, which affects behavior, learning, perception and memory.[214]

**Rhythms in our Body**

Rhythm in the body is primarily created from the heart and brain, and these pulses animate the body's frequencies. Each heartbeat carries a frequency, just as each drumbeat creates a pitch. Sharry found that the brain and the heartbeat animate the energy of the body. She also discovered a pitch that keeps the heart beating in rhythm.

---

[213]Hazrat was born into a family of musicians in 1882. Khan, Inayat, Hazrat. The Music of Life, Omega Publishing: New Lebanon, N.Y., 1983. pg. 264.
[214] Thaut, Michael. Rhythm, Music and the Brain: Scientific Foundations and Clinical Applications, Routledge: N.Y., 2005, pg. 84.

Blood is pumped through the body according the rhythm of the heartbeat. Heart rates vary per individual, depending on age and size and other factors, but the average resting human heart rate is about 70 beats per minute. Heart rate varies significantly between individuals based on fitness, age and genetics.

Other body processes also create body percussion, such as breathing. Dr. Tomatis penned, "The vital act of breathing *(inhaling and exhaling)* follows a rhythm that varies with age, activity, thoracic development, stress and so on."[215]

Davis examines body pulses from another source. "Our brain waves also have their own rhythms and can average a pulse approximately every one tenth of a second."[216]

The heart creates the strongest body rhythm and can often entrain other pulses. Other rhythms in the body are cycles of replacement. Atoms, molecules, tissues, bones, skin, enzymes and cells are constantly being replaced and refurbished over time. The movement and activities of our organs and body systems, such as circulation, create characteristic sounds and pulses their own musical songs.

All body rhythm patterns interact, affecting each other. Waves generated from all body processes affect the rhythm, pitch and volume of each other.[217]

---

[215] Dr. Tomatis. The Ear and the Voice, The Scarecrow Press: Maryland, Toronto, Oxford, 1987. Translated into English in 2005. pg. 97.
[216] Davis, Dorinne. Sound Bodies through Sound Therapy, Kalco Publishing: Landing, New Jersey, 2004. pg. 228.
[217] Davis, Dorinne. Sound Bodies through Sound Therapy, Kalco Publishing: Landing, New Jersey, 2004. pg. 227.

Rhythmic patterns within larger patterns of sound are found in our body, just as the geometry of the solar system is reflected in the geometric alignment of our molecular structures. For example, the Fibonacci ratios mirror the ratios found in star systems, our bodies and in small conch shells!

> **"The Music of the Spheres**
> A harmonious universe is like a harp.
> Its rhythms are the equal repeated seasons,
> The beating of a heart,
> The going and returning of migratory birds,
> The cycles of stars and corn,
> The mimosa that unfolds by day and folds up by night,
> The rhythms of moon and tide,
> And apples that ripen and fall.
> Melody, accord, arpeggios are the harp of the universe.
> Unity behind apparent multiplicity.
> That is the music."
> *Ernesto Cardenal*

Cycles, which are rhythmic patterns, are found throughout the cosmos and in the human body. For example, a plant unfolds according to a rhythmical process of expansion and contraction.[218] Many healthy cyclical patterns or rhythms in the body reflect nature's cycles.

McTaggart discusses frequencies that emanate from our bodies that can interact with our environment, "Experiments in the 1940s by neuroanatomist Harold Burr from Yale University measured electrical fields around living things. Burr discovered electrical fields around all sorts of organisms - from molds, salamanders and frogs to humans. Changes in

---

[218] Goethe, quote from Francke, Sylvia. <u>The Tree of Life and the Holy Grail.</u> Temple Lodge: The Square Forest Row, England: 2007. pg. 24.

the electrical charges appeared to correlate with growth, sleep, regeneration, light, water, storms, the development of cancer and even with the waxing and waning of the moon."[219] Author David Burrows, in Time and the Warm Body, reflects, "Like music, daily life is made up of continuities, such as the circulation of blood, formed of discontinuities such as the heart beat: or continuities interrupted...like a conversation interrupted by a fire alarm."[220]

Scientist Fritz Alan Popp measured bio-photon emissions from a healthy student for nine months on the same place in her body. "The light emissions followed biological rhythms... Emissions seemed to follow other natural biological rhythms; similarities were noted by day or night, by week, by month as though the body were following the world's biorhythms, as well as its own."[221]

Cosmic cycles have been compared to a human's breathing rhythms.[222] The earth's breathing may be described as the alternating barometric pressure of day and night, or the sunset likened to exhaling and the sunrise to inhaling. The average person inhales 18 times a minute or 1080 times an hour. In a 24-hour period a person inhales and exhales approximately 25,920 times. This corresponds to the number of years it takes the sun to pass through each of our twelve constellations, a platonic year. Biological cycles also parallel tidal changes in the earth's magnetic field and the 28-day

---

[219] McTaggart, Lynne. The Field, The Quest for the Secret Force of the Universe, Harper Collins Publisher: N. Y., 2002, pg. 48.
[220] Burrows, David. Time and the Warm Body: A Musical Perspective on the Construction of Time, Brill: Boston, 2007, pg. 66.
[221] McTaggart, Lynne. The Field, The Quest for the Secret Force of the Universe, Harper Collins Publisher: N.Y., 2002, pg. 50.
[222] Theroux, Michael. From the Borderland Research Foundation. *"Microcosm and Macrocosm, in Rhythmic Formative Forces of Music."*

lunar cycle is similar to a 28-day menstrual cycle.[223] The circulatory system of a human being parallels the earth's alternating temperature differences of day and night, or in winter and summer.

Cosmic cycles and rhythms subtly affect us. Michael Therroux from the Borderland Research Foundation concluded, "The human organism is immersed in rhythmic formative force originating in the surrounding cosmos."[224]

---

"Humanity is a beautiful breathing instrument of music."
*Clement of Alexandria*

---

## Healing Rhythms

Hazrat Inayat Khan[225] reflects on rhythmic influences: "Life is rhythm. Rhythms may be divided into three stages and at every stage this rhythm changes the nature and character of life. One rhythm is mobile, the other is active and the third is chaotic. The mobile rhythm is creative, productive, and constructive and through this rhythm all power and inspiration are gained and peace is experienced. The advanced stage of this rhythm, the active rhythm, is the source of success, accomplishment of progress and maturation, the source of joy and fulfillment. And the third

---

[223] Becker, Robert, Dr. Cross Currents, The Perils of Electropollution, The Promise of Electromedicine, Penguin Group: New York, 1990. pg. 71.
[224] Theroux, Michael from the Borderland Research Foundation. "Microcosm and Macrocosm, in Rhythmic Formative Forces of Music."
[225] Khan, Inayat, Hazrat *(1882 –1927)* was the founder of Universal Sufism and the Sufi Order International. He initially came to the West as a representative of several traditions of classical Indian music. However, Khan's life mission was soon revealed to be the introduction and transmission of Sufi thought and practice to the West.

stage of this rhythm, the chaotic rhythm, is the source of failure and death, disease and destruction, the source of all pain and sorrow."[226]

Hazrat Inayat Khan continued to describe the relationship between the body and rhythm. "When the body is excited and the breath has lost its rhythm, and becomes irregular and uneven, a chaotic condition is created. When the body has regular circulation, proper rhythm and breath, then a person is capable of doing and accomplishing things. When a body is restful, comfortable and relaxed we are able to think; inspirations and revelations come; we feel quiet; we have enthusiasm and power."[227]

Rhythm within our body is also a communication system that can be likened to Morse code, a system of long and short beeps to communicate. The cycles in our bodies create a pulsation that contains more information than just a pulse, just as Morse code communicates more than just pulses.

Sharry notes that some of our body communication systems parallel Tesla's[228] idea of alternating current *(AC)*. Tesla pointed out the inefficiency of Edison's direct current, *(DC)*. The secret, he felt, lay in the use of alternating current, because to him all energies were cyclic. Why not build generators that would send electrical energy along

---

[226] Khan, Inayat, Hazrat. The Music of Life, Omega Publishing: New Lebanon, N.Y., 1983. pg. 100.

[227] Khan, Inayat, Hazrat. The Music of Life. Omega Publishing: New Lebanon, N.Y., 1983. pg. 100.

[228] Nikola Tesla (1856 - 1943) Tesla invented the alternating-current generator that provides light and electricity, the transformer through which it is sent, and even the high voltage coil of a picture tube. The Tesla Coil, in fact, is used in radios, television sets, and a wide range of other electronic equipment - invented in 1891, no-one's ever come up with anything better.

distribution lines first one way, than another? Direct current flows continuously in one direction; alternating current changes direction 50 or 60 times per second and can be stepped up to vary high voltage levels, minimizing power loss across great distances.

Dr. Becker reports that the "more primitive, analog data transmission and control system still exists in the body, located in the perineural cells and transmit information by means of the flow of semiconducting DC electrical current."[229] He reiterates, "A DC analog system of data transmission and control is, in fact, hidden within the central nervous system."[230]

Not only does our body employ DC current, but AC current as well. Sharry noted that Schwann cells have current running in both directions simultaneously, somewhat resembling AC current.

Frequencies create rhythm by periodically changing the volume of a note. Imagine a steady tone that gets louder three times a second. This pattern produces a rhythm. A repeated pattern in the volume of sound creates rhythm. Even harmonics, created from every frequency in our body, create a characteristic rhythm that our body is accustomed to. The volume of each successive harmonic note decreases proportionately, creating a rhythmic pattern.

The usual waveform of an AC power circuit is a sine wave. Audio and radio signals carried on electrical wires are also

[229] Dr. Becker, Robert O. Cross Currents, The Perils of Electropollution, The Promise of Electromedicine, Penguin Group, N.Y., 1990. pg 65.
[230] Dr. Becker, Robert O. Cross Currents, The Perils of Electropollution, The Promise of Electromedicine, Penguin Group, N.Y., 1990. pg. 62.

examples of alternating current. In these applications, an important goal is often the recovery of information encoded onto the AC signal. Nerve cells communicate to each other by acting as "transducers" creating electrical signals *(very small voltages and currents)* in response to certain chemical compounds called *neurotransmitters*, and releasing neurotransmitters when stimulated by electrical signals.

## BioAcoustic Rhythms

Frequencies create rhythm by periodically changing the volume of a note. Imagine a steady tone that gets louder three times a second. This pattern produces a rhythm. A repeated pattern in the volume of sound creates rhythm. Even harmonics, created from every frequency in our body, create a characteristic rhythm that our body is accustomed to. The volume of each successive harmonic note decreases proportionately, creating a rhythmic pattern.

The sounds that Sharry hears from people reflect rhythmic patterns as well as pitches. When the frequency dips or rises in a periodic fashion or the volume of pulse changes, a rhythmic pattern is created. Rhythm is created by repeated patterns of loudness and softness among frequencies.

BioAcoustic patterns reveal our personal biological rhythms. The architect of the frequencies in a voiceprint displays rhythmic patterns. The voiceprint's overall waveform reflects a portion of a cycle.

Sharry has observed a mathematical relationship between frequency and rhythm, which she is retaining as a proprietary secret. She hinted that changing the timing of the frequency formulation allows specific organs to be targeted for intervention.

Sharry studied rhythmic patterns of biochemical processes in the body such as the Krebs Digestion cycle by watching biochemical frequencies and rhythms change as they interacted. Proper rhythmic patterns of frequencies are essential in order for health to be maintained in the body.

If the rhythm of the sound was incorrect then the body will not incorporate the sounds properly. Sharry chooses not to disclose how these rhythmic periods are calculated, but her software utilizes the effective rhythm patterns.

Sharry's sonic formulas, called "sound presentations," need to be heard for certain duration to affect positive change. Many healing frequency formulas are presented in 30 to 60 second bursts, but this varies. When working with muscles, the FEs are effective in two-minute cycles. If the sounds are applied too long or too short of duration, then the effect will be incomplete.

Rhythm and music have far greater impact than we have previously understood. Research is changing our understanding of music. Thaut summarizes, "Based on new directions in brain research, a historical paradigm has occurred, moving music therapy from an interpretive social-science paradigm to a neuroscience paradigm based on music perception."[231] Thaut continues, "Many clinical studies have shown striking evidence that auditory rhythm and music can

---

[231] Thaut, Michael. Rhythm, Music and the Brain: Scientific Foundations and Clinical Applications, Routledge: N.Y., 2005, pg. 135.

213

be effectively harnessed for specific therapeutic purposes in the rehabilitation of patients with different neuropathologies. Such findings further underscore the complex ways in which music engages and communicates to the brain and in which the brain that engages in music can be – even in states of brain injury – changed by engaging in music."[232]

# Chapter Nine

# Frequency Interactions

## Heart and Brain Interactions

The frequencies of brain waves can be likened to melodies, while the heartbeat provides rhythm to animate its song. Melody and rhythm are in sync in pleasing music, and we feel healthy when they are in sync in our body too.

The heart provides a rhythmic beat and produces electromagnetic energy. The HeartMath Institute talks about the energy created by the heart. "The heart is the most powerful generator of electromagnetic energy in the human body, producing the largest rhythmic electromagnetic field of any of the body's organs. The heart's electrical field is about

---

[232] Thaut, Michael. Rhythm, Music and the Brain: Scientific Foundations and Clinical Applications, Routledge: N.Y., 2005, pg. 58.

60 times greater in amplitude than the electrical activity generated by the brain."[233] This field can be measured with an electrocardiogram. "The magnetic field produced by the heart is more than 5,000 times greater in strength than The Field, The Quest for the Secret Force of the Universe generated by the brain, and can be detected a number of feet away from the body, in all directions."[234] *(Waves travel spherically, not as a two-dimensional line representing a sound wave. Sound travels in all directions, creating a sphere that gets continually larger.)*

The HeartMath Institute gathers scientific information regarding the heart. They report, "Traditionally, the study of communication pathways between the head and heart has been approached from a rather one-sided perspective, with scientists primarily focusing on the heart's responses to the brain's commands. However, we have now learned that communication between the heart and brain is actually a dynamic, ongoing, two-way dialogue, with each organ continuously influencing the other's function. Research has shown that the heart communicates to the brain in four major ways: neurologically, bio-chemically, biophysically and energetically. Communication along all these conduits significantly affects the brain's activity. Moreover, our research shows that messages that the heart sends to the brain can also affect the brain's performance."[235] The energy from the heart and brain interact through the sonic wave pool of the body.

---

[233] www.HeartMath.org/ heart brain connections
[234] www.HeartMath.org/ heart brain connections
[235] www.HeartMath.org/ heart brain connections

When people experience positive emotions their heart rhythms become more coherent. Steady rhythms that are at the correct tempo also improve heart-brain synchronization. When our brainwaves and heartbeats are in sync, the Heart Math Institute[236] indicates that we receive physical and emotional benefits. These signals from the heart "may also modify cortical function and influence performance…shifting perception, mental clarity and heightened intuitive awareness."[237] When the heart and brain are aligned, we perceive greater wholeness - while solutions to problems come to us easier.

The heart-brain link makes sense when one considers that stresses, anxiety, uncertainty and fear cause our heart to race. These emotions trigger irregular, chaotic and incoherent rhythmic signals from the heart to the brain. When receiving these signals our brain stops maintenance functions and transfers energy to deal with a dangerous or stressful situation. Conversely, when we feel genuine hope, care and compassion, our heart sends harmonious and coherent signals to the brain, and then our bodies are nourished and repaired.[238]

Sharry has developed a frequency pattern that syncs both the heartbeat and brain waves! This frequency that the heart emits keeps it beating in rhythm and entrains brain waves. Although she will not reveal this healing rhythmic pattern or the mathematical association between these two organs, her software creates frequencies and rhythm that produce brain-heart synchronization.

---

[236] www.Heartmath.com
[237] www.Heartmath.com
[238] www.Heartmath.com

Nicole LaVoie, who authored <u>Return to Harmony</u> which describes her sound healing library, reported that each person has a fundamental frequency or, an average of all the frequencies within his mental, emotional and physical realms. She writes that the fundamental frequency, or the "soul note," is primarily produced when we speak from the heart. When we hum our soul note we "connect to source," creating a good time to make decisions. Humming this note brings joy and is empowering. Nicole reports that singing or hearing this note, one octave lower, releases "old energy blockages of core issues that we carry from lifetime to lifetime."[239]

Listening to a higher octave above this note helps one connect to higher energies and "the higher part of Self."[240] In order to facilitate cooperation in groups, Nicole averages every one's soul notes, and allows the group to entrain to this frequency, producing greater coherence in the group.

Our fundamental frequency is an average of all of our mental, emotional and physical frequencies. What we do when no one is looking creates FEs - mentally and emotionally. These frequencies become part of our overall signature tone or blueprint that we create throughout our lives. Over time consistent emotional and mental frequencies entrain and become incorporated within our physical bodies. Our signature tone is the accumulation of FEs that we thought, felt and experienced in the physical body.

---

[239] LaVoie, Nicole. <u>Return to Harmony: Creating Harmony and Balance through the Frequencies of Sound</u>, Sound Wave Energy Press: Pagosa Springs, CO., 1996. pg. 76.
[240] LaVoie, Nicole. <u>Return to Harmony: Creating Harmony and Balance through the Frequencies of Sound</u>, Sound Wave Energy Press: Pagosa Springs, CO. ,1996. pg. 77.

What we do in private is recorded in our internal frequency universe and we live with the ramifications. "We so what we reap" literally in a frequency sense. Behaving for the highest good in our secretive and dark experiences serves to bless ourselves. When our FE universe improves we uplift those we love. Perhaps, being the best person at all times is our greatest gift to others.

## Energy Connections

Dr. Becker's research indicates that, "Magnetic and electromagnetic fields have energy, carry energy and are produced by electrical currents. When we talk about electrical currents flowing in living organisms, we also imply that they are producing magnetic fields that extend outside the body as well and can be influenced by external magnetic fields."[241] In the all-pervasive world of frequencies we are not isolated or separate from our environment.

The heart's electromagnetic field envelops every cell of our bodies and extends out in all directions around us. The cardiac field can be measured several feet away from the body by sensitive devices. "Research shows our heart's field changes distinctly as we experience different emotions. It is registered in people's brains around us and apparently is capable of affecting cells and DNA studied in vitro."[242]

Interactions can take place between the energy of the hearts and brains of two people touching or in close proximity.

---

[241] Becker, Robert, Dr. Cross Currents, The Perils of Electropollution, The Promise of Electromedicine, Penguin Group: New York, 1990, pg. 69.
[242] www.Heartmath.com

Intriguing research from the HeartMath Institute shows that electromagnetic signals generated by the heart have the capacity to affect others around us. In specific, one person's heartbeat can be registered in another person's brain waves.[243] This communication is stronger when one's heart is generating a coherent rhythm.[244] With this method we can intuitively perceive what other people are feeling.

Douglas Dean conducted research study suggesting that communication at higher energetic frequencies take place constantly at an unconscious level.[245] "The conscious personality fails to perceive the interconnectedness of all life at subtle energy levels. His finding suggests that humans may be in continuous psychic communication with other individuals at higher levels of consciousness, in addition to their everyday verbal exchanges."[246] On the subconscious level we may have built-in cell phones!

Fritz Alan Popp, a biophysicist from Germany, created a machine to measure photon emissions from living organisms. We are told by Mc Taggert that, "It began to dawn on Popp that these emissions had a purpose outside of the body. Wave resonance wasn't simply being used to communicate within the body, but between living things."[247]

---

[243] HeartMath Institute, *"The Electricity of Touch: Detection and Measurement of Cardiac Energy Exchange Between People"* by Rollin McCraty, PhD, Mike Atkinson, Dana Tomasino, BA, and William Tiller, PhD.

[244] HeatMath Institute, *"The Electricity of Touch: Detection and Measurement of Cardiac Energy Exchange Between People"* by Rollin McCraty, PhD, Mike Atkinson, Dana Tomasino, BA, and William Tiller, PhD.

[245] D. Dean. *"Plethysmograph Recording as ESP Response,"* International Journal of Neuropsychiatry, September/October, 1966.

[246] Dr. Gerber, Richard. Vibrational Medicine, The Number One Handbook of Subtle-Energy Therapies, third edition, Bear & Co: Vermont, 2001. pg. 255.

[247] McTaggart, Lynne. The Field, The Quest for the Secret Force of the Universe, Harper Collins Publisher: New York, 2002. pg. 53.

Author Ted Levintin discusses the role of music in interpersonal communication. "In Africa, music is not an art form as much as it is communication. Singing together releases oxytocin, a neurochemical now known to be involved in establishing bonds of trust between people."[248]

Levintin probes into studies contrasting music and subconscious interpersonal communication and says, "Two individuals who are asked to synchronize their finger tapping on a desk, synchronize more closely than when asked to synchronize with a metronome. This may seem counter intuitive, because the metronome is far steadier in its beat and therefore more predictable. But the studies show that humans accommodate one another's performance, a situation of co-adaption. They interact with one another, but not with the metronome, leading to a greater drive to coordinating."[249]

Dr. Bittman published a study on the effects of group drumming. He scientifically demonstrated that participation in group drumming increased the activity of specialized white blood cells that destroy cancer cells and virally-infected cells.[250] Think about that, the rhythm and connectivity people shared in group drumming sessions improved people's immune system.

---

[248] Vernon Reid of the rock group Living Colour said the sentence about Africa. Levitin, Daniel, J. The World in Six Songs: How the Musical Brain Created Human Nature. Penguin: N.Y., 2008. pgs. 50-51.
[249] Levitin, Daniel,J. The World in Six Songs: How the Musical Brain Created Human Nature, Penguin: N.Y., 2008. pgs. 50-51.
[250] http://www.mind-body.org/bittman.html , Alternative Therapies, Jan. 2001.

People broadcast a rich spectrum of vibrations that attract a corresponding spectrum of experiences through resonance.[251] This introduces the study of how experiences affect vibration. Clearly vibrations on a subconscious level affect our environment and vice versa.

Negative emotions from people collectively create electromagnetic fields, generating global stress. Incoherent waves of energy emanate from an individual to those nearby and ultimately can join with negative energies of many people. The feeling or energy can journey around the globe. Global stress and incoherence are intensified by instant mass media reports of natural disasters, social upheaval and economic turmoil. During a time of crisis, one can feel the atmosphere of concern, worry and fear. For instance, many have recorded that before war erupts in a country, music stops and the silence is brimming with feelings of dread.

Collectively, positive emotions such as hope, care, compassion and appreciation generate a coherent wave producing a global electromagnetic field. The Global Coherence Initiative engages people to project heart-felt compassion, care and love to the world. Many believe this spawns energy that results in new solutions for world problems. It "builds a reservoir of positive energy that benefits the planet."[252] They suggest that each time a person raises his positive emotional energy - the entire world benefits. "By living from your heart and expressing higher emotions you lift the heaviness of the local and global

[251] www. Montalk.net
[252] Global Coherence Initiative with the Heart-Math Institute

collective frequency realm. Nothing lifts gravity like levity and love."[253]

The Global Coherence Initiative continues, "The scientific community is just beginning to appreciate how The Field, The Quest for the Secret Force of the Universes generated by living systems and the ionosphere interact with one another. For instance, the earth and the ionosphere generate a symphony of frequencies ranging from 0.01 to 300 hertz. Some of the large resonances occurring in the earth's fields are the same as those of the human heart and brain."[254]

Scientists have discovered that changes in the earth's magnetic field are associated with: changes in the brain and nervous system, athletic performances, memory, synthesis of nutrients in plants, number of traffic violations and accidents, heart attack/stroke mortalities and incidences of depression/suicide. The "geomagnetic conditions affect the rhythms of the heart stronger than all the physiological functions studied so far."[255]

Not only does the Global Coherence Initiative suggest that life is affected by the earth's geomagnetic fields, but that the earth's fields can be affected by human emotions.

Roger Nelson from Princeton University used random number generators to show that human emotions interact with a global energy field. The largest change in random generators occurred during the Sept. 11, 2001 attacks on the World Trade Centers. Two National Oceanic and

---

[253] The Nexus Seven. The 33 Arks of Soul Resonance. Montalk website.
[254] Global Coherence Initiative with the Heart-Math Institute
[255] Global Coherence Initiative with the Heart-Math Institute

Atmospheric Administration space weather satellites that monitor the earth's geomagnetic field also displayed a spike at the time and for several days thereafter, "indicating stress waves possibly caused by mass human emotions."[256]

## Regional Energies

There are multitudes of frequencies in our environments that collect and influence the sounds that Sharry hears, our health and even global trends.

People respond differently to sounds in different geographical locations. A location has its own overall frequency that is composed of energy from people, language, industry, pollution, geology, weather and other influences. These frequencies combine with and affect the local people and their taste in music.

Sharry believes that this energy creates the sounds emanating from the ground that she hears in different locations. For example, she hears a G# coming from the vicinity of Ohio and an A in London. She noted that the A frequency improved her vision, so much so that she didn't need glasses while in England.

Sharry observed that the pitch coming from the ground in the United States, when converted to a color, is the same color as blue jeans, which people in the United States love. She suggests that subtle pitches of a location can influence people's color preferences.

---

[256] Global Coherence Initiative with the Heart-Math Institute

It seems far-fetched that tones radiate from the ground, but many people can relate to experiencing the absence of such sounds. When a fresh snow has fallen the silence is deeper. Snow muffles subtle noises coming from the earth. In the winter there are also fewer animals and plants contributing to these subtle frequencies that we are not conscious of. Hence, it feels silent and still after the snow falls. We have a famous Christmas carol associated with snowy winter called, "Silent Night."

The average pitch and tempo of a language vary, as well. For example, the average pitch in the French language is about 436 cycles per second and in American English it is 440 cycles per second. The French speak at a lower averaged pitch than Americans and utilize unique rhythm patterns, tempos and musical inflections. Each language possesses intricate and unique patterns of melody, harmony and rhythm. These vibrations subtly influence the population.

An article by Fosar and Blundorf reports that our DNA can be influenced and reprogrammed by words and frequencies.[257] According to Russian research, DNA that is not used for building proteins serves as data storage and for communication. The Russian linguists found that genetic code follows the same rules as our human languages. More specifically, alkalines of our DNA follow grammar and rules similar to those found in languages. They concluded that

---

[257] Fosar, Grazyna and Bludorf, Franz. Vernetzte Intelligenz. (book) (Article) DNA Can be Influenced by Words and Frequencies – Russian DNA Discoveries. http://www.souldofdistortion.nl/dna1.html

human languages did not appear coincidentally but are a reflection of our DNA.[258]

Russian biophysicist and molecular biologist Pjotr Garjajev reports that living DNA substances *(in living tissue, not in vitro)* will always react to language-modulated laser rays and even radio waves if the frequencies are correct. It is normal for our DNA to react to language. This would explain why hypnosis and affirmations can have a strong effect on people. Esoteric teachers have known for ages that our body is programmable by words, thoughts and language. Of course the frequency has to be correct, which explains why not everyone experiences the same degree of success with affirmations and hypnosis.[259]

Author Mary Desaulniers writes, "Russian researcher Peter Gariaev has uncovered the linguistic and psychic capabilities of "junk" DNA... According to the findings of Russian scientists, the genetic code follows the same rules found in human languages. By modulating certain frequency sound patterns onto a laser ray, they were able to influence DNA frequency and genetic information...Perhaps the most interesting corollary of their discovery is that simple words and phrases may work just as well as laser beams."[260]

Energy from local soil and rocks contributes to local electromagnetic fields. The energy emanating from a granite

[258] Fosar, Grazyna and Bludorf, Franz. Vernetzte Intelligenz. (book) (Article) DNA Can be Influenced by Words and Frequencies – Russian DNA Discoveries. http://www.souldofdistortion.nl/dna1.html
[259] Fosar, Grazyna and Bludorf, Franz. Vernetzte Intelligenz. (book) (Article) DNA Can be Influenced by Words and Frequencies – Russian DNA Discoveries. http://www.souldofdistortion.nl/dna1.html
[260] Mary Desaulniers. Article found at: www.suite101.com/writer_articles.cfm/mdesaulniers, 2010.

rock is different than from quartz, shale or sand. Minerals found in rocks have unique universal frequency-equivalents. Further, the earth's molten iron core generates the magnetic field around the planet. In summary, geological factors create energy in a location, which subtly affects us. Being at the beach feels different than spending time in New York City or Siberia.

Another contributing factor to regional energy fields is the frequency of electrical currents utilized in a country *(electrical/magnetic frequencies from cell phones, TVs, microwaves...)*. These currents are different in various countries. For example, in the United States electricity is delivered at 60 hertz and in the United Kingdom it is delivered at 50 hertz.

Color influences individuals. Energies from color contribute to a "feeling" of a specific location. For example, a desert "feels" different than a seaport. The desert-scape includes yellows and browns, while the seascape boasts of blues and greens. The color of the landscape is one of many factors contributing to a local atmosphere, which subtly affects the people there.

A friend of mine conducted an experiment with Kirlian photography,[261] which records a visual representation of

---

[261] "Aura Cameras are used to give individuals a visual representation of their bioenergetic state. Based on such biofeedback technologies and galvanic skin response and skin temperature, aura cameras measure these physiological inputs and then convert this information into digital displays through a computer interface. The resulting display is typically a depiction of what is traditionally known as the human aura and chakra." "Kirlian photography refers to a form of photogram made with a high voltage. It is named after Semyon Kirlian, who in 1939 accidentally discovered that if an object on a photographic plate is connected to a source of high voltage, small corona discharges *(created by the strong electric field at the edges of the*

energy. He took repeated Kirlian photographs of the same person at almost the same time with the only difference being the color of clothes that she was wearing. This single difference produced a change in the colors of the person's bioenergies in the resulting Kirlian photograph.

The jungle feels different than a desert, reflecting various levels of moisture in the air. I can smell and "feel" a large body of water, such as a river, lake or ocean before I see it. Different weather patterns, including amount of sunshine, precipitation, wind, temperature and barometric pressure also contribute to local energy fields.

Another example of environmental energy is created by the earth's rotation, which continuously creates electromagnetic impulses called spherics that have a determining effect on our weather.[262] Spherics can also modify the structure of protein molecules.[263] Sunlight and sunspots also influence the earth's electromagnetic energies.

Electromagnetic waves from our air interact with sound and other factors. "Sound propagates in the air at the rate of approximately 700 miles per hour, depending on air pressure and temperature. This process involves countless collisions between the atoms and the molecules that form the earth's atmosphere. Each collision creates friction between the air components, resulting in heat, more accurately described as electromagnetism. The amplitude of the electromagnetism is

---

*bject)* create an image on the photographic plate."
*ttp://en.wikipedia.org/wiki/Kirlian_photography*
[262] Cousto, Hans. The Cosmic Octave, the Origin of Harmony, LifeRhythm: Mendocino, CA., 2000. pg. 33.
[263] Cousto, Hans. The Cosmic Octave: The Origin of Harmony, LifeRhythm: Mendocino, CA., 2000. pg. 33.

a function of the sound pressure level, the local temperature and air pressure, the latter dictating the number of collisions that occur."[264] There are two variables of sound-generated electromagnetism: frequency and what the frequency travels through and interacts with, such as weather conditions. Analog signals, being identical *(analogous)* to electrical signals generated in nature, are highly susceptible to interference from natural phenomenon *(such as weather and sunspots)*.

Environmental electromagnetic waves interact with humans. Davis underscores this point, "The Schumann Resonance theory suggests that the entire *(human)* body vibrates at the fundamental frequency of approximately eight cycles per second in a relaxed state *(same as an alpha brain wave)*... The earth also vibrates at this frequency. As a result, a synergistic relationship develops between the charged layers of the earth's atmosphere and the human body."[265]

Davis continues, "Similarly, the energy fields around a tree change in advance of weather patterns and other atmospheric conditions. If weather disturbances affect the earth's atmosphere, perhaps it also accounts for the behavioral changes seen in some learning disabled children prior to certain types of storms."[266]

Pollution, noise levels and types of industry activity impact the local energy fields. Further, the characteristic attitudes of

---

[264] Reid, John Stuart. "*The Special Relationship between Sound and Light.*" Journal of Subtle Energies and Energy Medicine, Vol. 17, number three.
[265] Davis, Dorinne. <u>Sound Bodies through Sound Therapy.</u> Kalco Publishing: Landing, New Jersey, 2004. pg. 228.
[266] Davis, Dorinne. <u>Sound Bodies through Sound Therapy.</u> Kalco Publishing: Landing, New Jersey, 2004. pg. 228.

people contribute energy to these large wave pools. The people of Japan, New York City and rural Appalachia all create different local energy fields. Also, one can feel or sense the difference between a friendly place and one in which one is not welcomed.

History can contribute to the local energy-pool. Sites of historical atrocities *(such as Auschwitz, Germany and Gettysburg, USA)* emanate a chilling and somber feeling, which correlate to horrible energies that people felt there at an earlier time. Likewise, people travel to sacred sites, churches and mosques as they crave the holy and uplifting feelings associated with these places.

Motorola Corporation published a listing of recorded sounds coming from space. For over ten years they recorded these daily subtle sounds. These frequencies change throughout the day. Different frequencies recorded from space interact with frequencies in our bodies.

Different organs, body parts and body processes have varying densities *(such as brain waves versus bones)* and different frequencies. The incoming sounds affect them differently. External wave interactions can support or stress individual body processes and organs.

Ancient music systems varied as the time of day and season changed to provide balance to listeners as local energy varied. It feels different in the morning than it does in the heat of an afternoon. It feels different in summer with the contributing sounds and the energy of plants, than it does in the winter. Ancient music was written to balance the human energetic system with incoming energies from space and nature.

In contrast, frequencies of cell phones, microwaves, electricity, electromagnetic waves, polluted foods, polluted water, polluted air and unhealthy habits create stress in our personal frequency systems. Dr. Becker cautions, "All abnormal, manmade electromagnetic fields, regardless of their frequencies, produce the same biological effects. These effects, which deviate from normal functions and are actually or potentially harmful, are the following:

- *Increases in the rate of cancer-cell division*
- *Increase in incidence of certain cancers*
- *Developmental abnormalities in embryos*
- *Alterations in neurochemicals, resulting in behavior abnormalities such as suicide*
- *Alternation in biological cycles*
- *Stress in responses in exposed animals that, if prolonged, leads to declines in immune-system efficiency*
- *Alterations in learning abilities*"[267]

In summary, there are many variables in our environments that influence our internal frequencies. Some of these are:

- Sunlight
- Electromagnetic energy from the sunspots
- Molten iron in the earth's core
- Weather
- Star light
- Level of vegetation
- Amounts of moisture in the air

---

[267] Becker, Robert, Dr. Cross Currents, The Perils of Electropollution, The Promise of Electromedicine, Penguin Group: New York, 1990, pgs. 214-215.

- Characteristic thoughts, feelings and attitudes of a population
- Intensity of electrical current, other energy sources and local industry
- Rhythm and pitch of the local language or dialect
- Pollution and environmental toxins
- Proximity of power plants, airports and places with excess energy, noise and manmade, abnormal electromagnetic energies
- Type of ground rock and soil composition
- History
- Local environmental color

On a subtle level we interact with our environment to a greater degree than we ever imagined.

## Healing Frequency Patterns

In India's ancient spiritual practice, a guru assigned a mantra to a devotee and asked him to repeat it thousands of times. The mantra incorporated the energy that a devotee needed for harmony and balance. A mantra *(that Sharry suggests were mostly based on age categories)* represented a devotee's ideal signature sound. The mantra repetitions created a great deal of this needed energy for the devotee, becoming part of who he or she was.

Today, we travel all over and are affected by energy in different locations, which have different resonating tones. This interaction alters our own frequencies. In addition, we meet a great variety of people who influence our signature frequency. The environment, traveling, mass media, people we meet and other factors influence our frequency needs. A complex web of internal and external acoustic signals interacts with our own unique frequencies. The ideal mantra in the twentieth century may change more often than it did in ancient times.

The body craves pitches and rhythms that facilitate internal harmony. Since the environment affects our internal body frequencies, our frequency needs vary in different locations. This is why different music is appealing in contrasting locations. People are instinctively attracted to music that on some level provides a form of healing. Listening to music that you love improves your well-being. Sometimes I buy a new musical CD and enjoy it over and over again. If I listen to it too much, I become "saturated" with its sound and then I am ready to listen to new music. My body absorbed what it needed and it is no longer drawn to the music. On a subtle level, the music has changed me and I now desire something else.

We assume we like a song because it is a personal preference. On a subconscious level music is a set of numbers. BioAcoustics suggests that these numbers enable the body to complete needed internal mathematical equations. Our body creates a sense of pleasure that correlates to the FEs that we need.

Many agree that numerical patterns found in nature when converted to frequencies are beneficial to us. Leonardo De Pisa, better known as Fibonacci, observed principles found in musical harmony were organized according to that of branching, flowering and spiraling patterns in nature. He observed the Fibonacci series, in which adding two adjacent numbers gives the next number in the series: 1, 1, 2, 3, 5, 8, 13, 21, 34, 55 and all the way to infinity.

The ratio of neighboring Fibonacci numbers approaches phi *(1.618).*[268] These ratios are found in our bodies, the spiral of a seashell and in billions of stars in distant galaxies.

---

[268] Phi is the symbol for the golden ratio. "The golden ratio has fascinated intellectuals for at least 2,400 years. Some of the greatest mathematical minds of all ages, from Pythagoras and Euclid in ancient Greece, through the medieval Italian mathematician Leonardo of Pisa and the Renaissance astronomer Johannes Kepler, to present-day scientific figures such as Oxford physicist Roger Penrose, have spent endless hours over this simple ratio and its properties. The fascination with the Golden Ratio is not confined just to mathematicians. Biologists, artists, musicians, historians, architects, psychologists and mystics have pondered and debated the basis of its ubiquity and appeal. The Golden Ratio has inspired thinkers of all disciplines like no other number in the history of mathematics." *Mario Livio,*
*The Golden Ratio: The Story of Phi, The World's Most Astonishing Number*

- Luca Pacioli *(1445–1517)* defines the golden ratio as the "divine proportion" in his *Divina Proportione.*
- Johannes Kepler *(1571–1630)* describes the golden ratio as a "precious jewel:" "Geometry has two great treasures: one is the Theorem of Pythagoras, and the other the division of a line into extreme and mean ratio; the first we may compare to a measure of gold, the second we may name a precious jewel."
- Charles Bonnet *(1720–1793)* points out that in the spiral phyllotaxis of plants going clockwise and counter-clockwise were frequently two successive Fibonacci series.
- Martin Ohm *(1792–1872)* is believed to be the first to use the term golden section to describe this ratio, in 1835.  E
- Edouard Lucas *(1842–1891)* gives the numerical sequence now known as the Fibonacci sequence its present name.
- Mark Barr *(20th century)* suggests the Greek letter phi (φ), the initial letter of Greek sculptor Phidias's name, as a symbol for the golden ratio.
- Roger Penrose *(b.1931)* discovered a symmetrical pattern that uses the golden ratio in The Field, The Quest for the Secret Force of the Universe, the Quest for the Secret Force of the Universe of periodic tilings, which led to new discoveries about quasicrystals."
  http://en.wikipedia.org/wiki/Golden_ratio

Major chords approximate the Fibonacci numbers 1, 3, 5 and 8 in a modified form. The next number in the Fibonacci series is 13. When the 8th and 13th tones are played together, they create the 8/13th interval. The 8/13th interval is believed by some to harmonize and thereby raise our consciousness[269] and precipitate mankind's next evolutionary step.

The Fibonacci ratios, if drawn, reveal a spiral, similar to the one found in a nautilus shell. In contrast, Western music creates a circle when drawn due to equal-temperament adjustments. Many ancient traditions believed that listening to the "spiral" pattern in sound enabled one to "quicken" his soul and rise closer to God. In contrast, the Western scale creates spiritual progress that can be likened to a dog chasing its tail.

The Fibonacci numbers found in nature can be converted into tones. My CD, "Paint Your Soul," with my original musical compositions, uses the Fibonacci frequencies, including the 8/13 interval.[270]

One does not hear the exact Fibonacci frequencies in our music today, because the frequencies are in between our smallest intervals in the musical scale that we use. People do not receive the benefits of these precise tones.

---

[269] Consciousness defies simple definition. It has been defined loosely as a constellation of mental attributes such as subjectivity, self-awareness, sentience, and the ability to perceive a relationship between oneself and one's environment. Consciousness may involve thoughts, sensations, perceptions, moods, emotions, dreams, and an awareness of self. http://en.wikipedia.org/wiki/Consciousness

[270] Sample this music at www.jillswingsoflight.com. Receive complementary mp3's and sound healing newsletter at www.jillshealingmusic.com.

The "Paint Your Soul" CD creates the pure tones of this spiral pattern by using tuning forks designed to create the exact Fibonacci frequencies. The tones twinkle continuously in the background of this soothing and fluid music.

## Geometric Shapes

Like most people, I believed that inanimate objects do not make sounds. Chairs, 2-D shapes and other objects appear silent to me. Only living things make sounds. Yet, water, fire and air can create sounds and they are not alive. I later heard sounds coming from things that I had previously believed to be silent, like deep space; but now I marvel at NASA's recordings of space sounds. Sharry hears otoacoustic emissions streaming out of people's ears and these sounds can be recorded with sensitive devises. I never would have dreamed that tiny sounds streamed forth from our ears! Sharry hears different sounds emanating out of the ground in various locations. Sharry also hears sounds emanating from shapes, even 2-D shapes. She also hears sounds from photographs and handwriting.

Sharry is not the only one insisting that sounds and shapes are related. Masuro Emoto froze water while exposing it to music. He then photographed the water as it froze and published pictures of the resulting crystalline structures. His images documented beautiful crystal shapes that formed when water was exposed to classical music, and distorted images that were created from heavy metal sounds. This showed that different sound vibrations, in close proximity to the freezing water, affected the tiny crystalline shapes within the frozen water. In this way, he correlated shapes with sounds.[271]

As was mentioned earlier, Hans Jenny, a Swiss physicist, put sand on a metal plate and attached a sound generator to the bottom of the plate. Certain sounds created recognizable 2-D shapes in the sand. He filmed many shapes being formed by sound vibrations, such as:

- Intricate geometric patterns
- Mandalas
- Flower patterns
- Biological forms
- Powerful archetypes
- Pictures that look like stained glass
- Patterns found in crop circles[272]

Jenny also associated sounds and specific shapes.

Sharry is able to voice a sound similar to the whistle made from a crystal bowl. She gradually increases a frequency, until she hits one note that creates an echo. When this special pitch is sung the room appears to sing. This frequency is amplified by the shape of the room. Sound reverberates off the walls and reflects back so as to increase its volume.

---

[271] Emoto also theorized that the resulting shapes in the water might have reacted to underlying feelings that the water may have been exposed to. Books by Masuro Emoto; The Hidden Messages in Water *(by Masaru Emoto and David A. Thayne),* Love Thyself: Message from Water III, Restore Your Well Being, Water Crystal Healing: Music and Images to Restore your Well-Being.

[272] Mattson, Jill. Ancient Sounds Modern Healing, Wings of Light: Oil City, Pa, 2006. pg. 46.

Sharry told me that a square room produces a frequency of a C. When singing in a square room a C will increase in volume so much that it appears to sing back to you. Other notes in a square room will not. In a parallel manner, the pitch of a D is emitted from a room that is nine by eight feet.

The pattern given to me by Sharry is below:

| Shapes and Sounds | | |
|---|---|---|
| Pitch | Natural Harmonic Scale Ratios | Dimensions of the Room |
| C | 1 | Square (1) |
| D | 9/8 | 18 x 16 |
| E | 5/4 | 10 x 8 |
| F | 4/3 | 8 x 6 |
| G | 3/2 | 6 x 4 |
| A | 5/3 | 10 x 6 |
| B | 15/8 | 30 x 16 |
| In between B-C | | circle |

The ratios used to create these exact notes are the same as pitches in the harmonic scale *(a just intonation scale)*. This scale is based on the natural division of a vibrating string into seven harmonic parts.

In ancient Egypt, healers wrote special symbols, letters and shapes on materials and submersed them in water. The Egyptian stories tell tales of healing that occurred when the water was swallowed. The ancient Egyptians energized the water by exposure to shapes, glyphs and later, words - reportedly, affecting the wellness of the person.

The ancient South Americans put flowers in water to imprint the vibration of the flower upon the water that they then drank. Water has been used to imprint information which can be incorporated into a person when he or she drinks it.

Sharry noticed that the sounds coming from the geometric shape of the Maltese or Knights' Templar cross[273] were familiar to her. The familiarity of the sounds attracted her to this design. She commonly uses these very tones in BioAcoustics! The Maltese cross replicated a common healing frequency combination.

Sharry's healing frequencies often utilize complementary tones or colors, which equate to the musical interval of a minor sixth. Sounds Sharry heard coming from the Templar cross were similar to musical intervals of three, six and nine notes apart.

The 1-3-5 triad, which is used in our current musical system, was not always the basic pattern for a chord. A 1-3-6 triad was branded "The Devil's Triad" in the Middle Ages. This chord included the interval of a minor sixth. Sharry frequently uses this interval to balance troublesome voice spikes. The Catholic Church prohibited the healing interval of a minor sixth to be played, according to a book written by

---

[273] The Maltese cross has four V-shaped arms joined together at their tips, so that each arm has two points.

Penelope Gouk,[274] preserving the healing secrets for themselves. *(See Appendix B)*

Sharry had the unique childhood experience of finding an object with three interlocking triangles, all sharing one side. She discovered that this shape produced a shadow of a Templar cross, as seen below.

**Sharry's Rendition of the Templar Cross**

The Templar Cross design was found on ancient pottery dating from 6,000 BC in ancient Turkey.[275] Throughout history this symbol was thought to represent many things, such as the four directions *(north, south, east, west),* the four elements *(fire, air, water, earth),* the symbolism of the

---

[274] Books by Penelope Gouk:  Musical Healing in Cultural Contexts, Enlightenment, and  Representing Emotions:  New Connections in the Histories of Art, Music and Medicine.
[275] http://www.angelfire.com/falcon/codex_morpheu/cross.html

immortality of the serpent *(representing wisdom),*[276] and it has been associated with the goddess Venus *(the feminine energy).*[277]

Sharry had this geometric shape constructed in metal. From one angle the sculpture looks like a design of interwoven triangles, from another it appears to be a series of X's making a square pattern. At a specific angle it gives off the shadow of the Maltese cross.

Since Sharry hears sounds coming from shapes, she developed an appreciation of sacred geometry. Sacred geometry, an ancient belief system, teaches that certain geometrical and mathematical proportions are likewise found in music, light and cosmology. Sacred geometry professes that unique healing and spiritual properties radiate from special designs.

Today, definitions of sacred geometry are broad, ranging from mathematical to esoteric in nature. Here is an esoteric definition of sacred geometry: "Sacred geometry is a variety of grid systems organizing aspects of consciousness and the energy relationships that support the consciousness field."[278] This definition relates the energy of certain shapes to levels of consciousness.

Throughout antiquity, certain shapes were believed to create powerful energy that could be used for targeted purposes. For example, the swastika symbol was used in antiquity to denote good luck. Archaeological evidence of swastika-shaped

---

[276] The Geometry Behind the Maltese Cross   http://sacredcirclecosmos.com

[277] http://www.magdalenemysteries.com/venus_templars.html

[278] http://sinclair.quarterman.org/sacredarchitecture.html

ornaments dates from the Neolithic period. It occurs mainly in the modern day culture of India, sometimes as a geometrical motif and sometimes as a religious symbol. It remains widely used in Eastern religions such as Hinduism and Buddhism.

Though once commonly used, because of its iconic usage in Nazi Germany the symbol has become stigmatized in the Western world, even outlawed in Germany.[279] Hitler was aware of the energy associated with this symbol.

"Sacred architecture" refers to any building system that enhances spiritual awareness, effects and processes by incorporating select shapes in the building design. Sacred geometrical shapes, such as the Templar cross, are used in:

- Sacred architecture - temples, mosques, megaliths, monuments, sacred structures and churches
- Sacred spaces such as altars and tabernacles
- Meeting places such as sacred groves, village greens and holy wells
- The creation of religious art, iconography, using "divine" proportions[280]

**Colored Time**

Donna Eden developed "energy medicine" techniques and has taught over 50,000 people worldwide to understand the body as an energy system. Donna Eden, like Sharry Edwards, teaches that people have signature colors *(a signature color is*

---

[279] http://en.wikipedia.org/wiki/Swastika
[280] Using the golden ratio, Fibonacci numbers or other numerical patterns found in nature.

*a higher octave of our signature sound).* Donna, a clairvoyant, sees auras with her naked eye, which she differentiates from signature colors. Signature colors stay with us for our lifetime, but aura colors change with our current emotions, physical and mental conditions. She witnesses that aura colors change around people as they go through their life, but their signature color remains consistent.

Donna describes the personalities and typical strengths and challenges associated with each signature color. Her descriptions of challenges and attributes associated with colors are similar to Sharry's descriptions on the "Color, Tones and Signs" chart on page 260 and also to typical astrological characterizations of people. Each color reflects one's life lessons.

In addition to echoing many concepts that Sharry embraces, Eden declares that the predominant color energy around people changes throughout time. Donna noticed that people born from about 1890 to the early 1930s predominantly radiated the signature color of green, which enabled people to take risks and show their brilliance. They march to their own drummer. Their life experiences challenged them to be their own person. People with a green signature color had to struggle to overcome impatience and the desire to be right. Donna says the energy of green creates learning opportunities about prosperity. Within this time frame, the United States grew rapidly in prosperity and also experienced the opposite side of the prosperity coin, the Great Depression.

Donna saw most people's signature colors change to blue in the era of 1927 to 1960, particularly the women. Blue energy is nurturing. This was the age of welfare, Medicare and

Social Security. Mothers who radiated the color blue often had many children. Many parents provided opportunities for their children that they never had. "Spare the rod and spoil the child" ceased to be good advice for parenting. For example, when a child came home with a bad report card, he was no longer whipped, but he received a tutor instead.

There are lessons associated with blue energy. People who radiate blue energy let other people off the hook, as they are enablers. The Holocaust was made possible during this time period by the Germans' enabling of Hitler's rise to power. People with blue signature colors are born optimists. They do not set structures and boundaries, but their life is enhanced if they learn to. They have difficulty letting go of people and things they are attached to. People with this energy need to stick to their guns and not do what other people want them to.

Around 1960 the new generation primarily radiated the signature color of violet. This color correlates to the emotions of empowerment and spirituality. During this time policies of tyranny and oppression fell, the Berlin Wall was torn down and Eastern European countries gained their freedom. The hippies and flower children promoted peace, and the war in Vietnam came to an end. On the other hand, searching for an ideal such as peace became disillusioning if one couldn't maintain internal peace. Many turned to altered states and drugs for this euphoric feeling. The difficult learning experiences of the violet energy are reflected in dealing with terrorism, which undermines empowerment and reflects world conflicts. People radiating this color are learning about power, within the world and within themselves. They have healthy egos; yet, they are searching for spiritual values.

As time passes, the frequency of the new generation's signature color changes allowing civilizations to learn new lessons. Ancient and esoteric mystery schools also profess that the energy of a color is predominantly active during designated time periods. This energy produces the emphasis reflected in the dominant activities of the civilization. The people who live during this time have opportunities to grow when they learned the lessons of the predominant color energy.

Ancient mystery schools[281] describe thoughts, emotions, challenges, blessings and lessons associated with colors. They describe lessons that people can experience and attributes that they can develop by focusing on a specific color vibration:

| Color | Lessons and Attributes |
|-------|------------------------|
| Violet | Freedom, Ceremony, Mercy, Purity and Transmutation |
| Green | Truth, Healing, Abundance and Science |
| White | Purity, Discipline and Harmony |
| Pink | Love, Adoration, Creativity and Compassion |

---

[281] "A mystery school is a university for the soul, a school for the study of the mysteries of the inner nature of man and of surrounding nature. By understanding these mysteries, the student perceives his intimate relationship with divinity, and strives through self-discipline and devotion to become at one with his inner god." Theosociety.org.

| Yellow | Wisdom and Understanding |
|--------|--------------------------|
| Blue | Power, Will, Protection and Faith |

The mystery schools also taught that great avatars demonstrated the lessons associated with the vibration of a color. Buddha taught the lessons of the green "ray," while Jesus provided his life as an example of mastering the golden "ray."

Let's review what we have explored about colors! Colored lights have been effective in changing the chemistry within people's bodies. For example, blue light is applied to the skin to cause a chemical reaction in blood circulating under the skin, effectively lessening bilirubin levels[282] in some types of neonatal jaundice. Donna Eden professes that people radiate colors that influence civilizations during certain time periods. Colors impact minute energies in our bodies, subtle interactions with others, and even global trends.

Waves affect us on tiny molecular and huge cosmic levels. Yet, the patterns of influence are similar. The wise philosopher of antiquity, Hermes Trismegistus, is quoted as saying, "As below so above, as above so below." His meaning is that from the whole universe to tiny atoms, from a star in the sky to a firefly, from the sun to the heat within a

---

[282] Bilirubin *(formerly referred to as hematoidin)* is the yellow breakdown product of normal heme catabolism. Heme is found in hemoglobin, a principal component of red blood cells. Bilirubin is excreted in bile and urine, and elevated levels may indicate certain diseases. It is responsible for the yellow color of bruises, urine, and the yellow discoloration in jaundice. http://en.wikipedia.org/wiki/Bilirubin

cell, there is an immense chain. The language of frequencies, expressed as colors, sounds and other types of energy, connects us all.

If one records a voice and raises it up three octaves, the sound is reminiscent of crickets. If the recording is raised up five octaves, it mimics bird chirps. Taken up two octaves further, it resembles whale sounds. Taken up even farther, these sounds become similar to the tones that are recorded from the stars. In some way, we speak the same language, but on different octaves. We are truly in one "uni-verse," meaning one verse or one voice.

# Chapter Ten

# Musical Astrology

The German scientist, Fritz Albert Popp, uncovered mechanisms of cell communication. "Popp showed in his experiments that weak light emissions were sufficient to orchestrate the body. The emissions had to be of low intensity, because these communications were occurring on a quantum level, and higher intensities would be felt only in the world at large."[283] Weak light emissions from a portion of the electromagnetic spectrum are used in the body to facilitate internal communication.

---

[283] McTaggart, Lynne. The Field, The Quest for the Secret Force of the Universe, Harper Collins Publisher: N.Y., 2002. pg. 47.

Dr. Becker[284] describes an analog current system found within the central nervous system.[285] This system, the perineural cell system, is activated prior to nerve impulses, appears to make actual decisions and regulates one's level of consciousness.[286] This analog system of body communication is powerful, indeed, if it controls consciousness.

Both Becker and Popp agree that low-intensity energy has a significant effect on the human organism. The body picks up analog, low-intensity energy from the stars and sunspots. NASA releases recorded star sounds. John and Christian Byrd from the Motorola Corporation published cycles of frequencies from space.[287]

Many writings from antiquity describe the use of music to balance changing subtle energies from space. When we do not harmonize with the orchestra of planet-sounds, our bodies can become inefficient, or perhaps fall into a state of disease or "dis-ease."

Pythagoras believed that musical scales should be based on astrological energy, such as the vibrations created by planetary movements. He hypothesized that the mathematical proportions of musical intervals should predict the movement

---

[284] Dr. Robert Becker is a pioneering researcher in electricity and regeneration. He is an orthopedic surgeon and a professor at N.Y. State University, Upstate Medical Center and at the Louisiana Sate University Medical Center. He has authored The Body Electric and Cross Currents, The Perils of Electropollution, The Promise of Electromedicine.

[285] Becker, Robert, Dr. Cross Currents, The Perils of Electropollution, The Promise of Electromedicine, Penguin Group: N.Y., 1990, pg. 62.

[286] Becker, Robert, Dr. Cross Currents, The Perils of Electropollution, The Promise of Electromedicine, Penguin Group: N.Y., 1990, pg. 65.

[287] BioAcoustics has incorporated these frequencies into its data banks.

of the planets in our solar system. Kepler confirmed that the ratios of the farthest and closest point of the elliptical orbits of the planets created whole number ratios, used in just intonation scales.

Pythagoreans studied music to gain insights into the mathematical underpinnings of the physical world.[288] Kitty Ferguson, who wrote, <u>The Music of Pythagoras</u>, tells us, "The Pythagoreans used music to heal the body and to elevate the soul, yet they believed that earthly music was no more than a faint echo of the universal 'harmony of the spheres.' In ancient cosmology, the planetary spheres ascended from Earth to Heaven like the rungs of a ladder. Each sphere was said to correspond to a different note of a grand musical scale. The particular tones emitted by the planets depended upon the ratios of their respective orbits, just as the tone of a lyre-string depended upon its length. The music of the spheres was never a fixed system. Many variant schemes existed because each philosopher approached it …from a different perspective."[289]

The low levels of electromagnetic energy changes continually. In Chinese acupuncture theory, energy concentrates on a section of the body and then this intensity moves around the organs following a clock-like pattern, responding to environmental energies that change throughout the day. For example, from 11:00 a.m. to 1:00 p.m., the heart's energy is at its peak. At 5:00 p.m. to 7:00 p.m., the kidneys' energy flow is at its greatest. The best time to treat an organ is when the energy flow is the greatest. It has also

---

[288] Ferguson, Kitty. <u>The Music of Pythagoras</u>, Walker: N.Y. 2008. Pg. 130.
[289] http://www.skyscript.co.uk/kepler.html#ch

been postulated that jet lag is caused by the interruption of this natural body clock.

Dr. Gerber relates this cycle of biological energy to the cosmos. "It is possible that some of our innate biological rhythms are reflections of higher subtle energetic rhythms. The subtle energy rhythms are, in turn, in resonant synchrony with the cosmic cycles of the universe."[290]

Western medicine is exploring the timing of various treatments. "The idea of optimal treatment relating to time of day is only recently explored in Western medicine. There is now significant evidence to support the concept of an internal clock. This internal timepiece, which governs many bodily functions including cyclic enzymatic activity within the brain, also seems to have an effect on drug toxicity… Cancer researchers have discovered that drug therapy administered during early morning hours had the least toxic effects on experimental animals."[291]

Sharry points out that the energy recorded from space changes every couple of hours during the day, creating changes within our own subtle energy as the day progresses. This may explain the conclusive research findings regarding the timing of cancer treatments.

Astronomy anticipates energy from the moving planets, the sun and the moon. The movement of planets can be likened to a water boat that makes waves in its path. Astrology claims

---

[290] Dr. Gerber, Richard. Vibrational Medicine, The Number One Handbook of Subtle-Energy Therapies, third edition, Bear & Co.: Vermont, 2001. pg. 184.
[291] Dr. Gerber, Richard. Vibrational Medicine, The Number One Handbook of Subtle-Energy Therapies, third edition, Bear & Co.: Vermont, 2001. pgs. 183 -184.

to predict future influences based on the electromagnetic energy created by waves resulting from the ongoing movements of the planets and these energy interactions as they transit through space. Astrology describes the influence of energy created from these movements as their energies arrive on earth and interact with our subtle energy, influencing us emotionally, mentally and physically.

Numerous traditions have understood astrological energy since the 3rd millennium BC. Astrology has played a role in the shaping of cultures, early astronomy, the <u>Vedas</u>, the <u>Bible</u> and various disciplines throughout history. Although today many people do not take astrology seriously, this was not the case in ancient history.

In ancient times people practiced a form of "musical astrology." In this healing art of the ancient Chinese and Hindu cultures, the leaders regulated the instruments and music heard during the year to balance people's finer energies. The music and the harmonics were altered to balance people's energy with the subtle energies coming from planetary movements. *(Harmonics vary in volume from different instruments. By changing the instruments that you listen to, you change the intensity of harmonics that you hear. At certain times of the year, wood instruments, metal instruments, reed instruments, or drums were exclusively played to keep people in balance with seasonal energy.)* This was believed to have a harmonizing influence on the civilization.

Ancient documents refer to the early Chinese systems of "musically playing the stars." Historical documents describe restricting music that people heard to influence their emotional and mental responses to a ruler, and in essence this provided a controlling factor over the people. This information was safeguarded to preserve these powerful secrets that could influence entire civilizations.

Documents reveal that astrological signs were assigned specific frequencies. "The tone system of ancient China, the 'Lu' scale, consisted of twelve notes obtained by successive fifths[292] *(each note was about five of our notes apart).* Each of the twelve Lu were assigned a month or constellation of the zodiac… During a given month, it was only permitted to play music based on …a scale stemming from the corresponding Lu."[293] In the ancient cultures both the musical system and the calendar were intimately connected.

In the 1600s scientist Johannes Kepler sought evidence for harmony in the universe, as described by Pythagoras and others. Kepler found that the movement of planets creates a scale that was linked to simple, whole numeric ratios.[294] In his book, Hermonices Mundi, the Five Books on Musical Harmony, Kepler calculated the angles of the planets *(as measured from the sun)* from their extreme positions in elliptical orbits during a twenty-four-hour period. A system of simple intervals emerged, sixteen in all, which are musical consonances or intervals with whole number ratios *(two of the*

---

[292] "Naturally for the sake of practical music making they are transposed into a narrower compass." *(into our hearing range)* Godwin, Joscelyn edits Hans Lauer. Cosmic Music: Musical Keys to the Interpretation of the Universe, Inner Traditions: Vermont, 1989. pg. 185.

[293] Godwin, Joscelyn edits Hans Lauer. Cosmic Music: Musical Keys to the Interpretation of the Universe, Inner Traditions: Vermont, 1989. pg. 185

[294] Godwin, Joscelyn. Cosmic Music: Musical Keys to the Interpretation of the Universe, Inner Traditions: Rochester, Vermont, 1989. pgs. 111-112.

*intervals were not whole number ratios).*[295] He offers this as proof of harmonic laws in the cosmos.

If we take Kepler's diatonic musical scale[296] and reduce it mathematically through octaves, these waves correspond to the brain wave patterns of alpha, beta, theta and delta. Think about that. The movements of the planets create frequencies and our brain waves emulate that wave pattern.[297] Isn't that astounding? [298]

Four hundred years later, a pair of Americans detected a form of music from the heavens. "In 1993 Hulse and Taylor landed the Nobel Prize for discovering binary pulses – stars which send out electromagnetic waves in pulses. The most sensitive equipment located in one of the world's highest places, high on a mountain top in Arecibo, Puerto Rico, picks up evidence of their existence through radio waves."[299]

[295] Godwin, Joscelyn. Cosmic Music: Musical Keys to the Interpretation of the Universe, Inner Traditions: Rochester, Vermont, 1989. pg. 117.

[296] A diatonic scale is a seven note musical scale comprising five whole steps and two half steps. Between each of the two half steps are either two or three whole steps, with the pattern repeating at the octave. The modern major and minor scales are diatonic. http://en.wikipedia.org/wiki/Diatonic_scale

[297] Sylvia Francke said, "The harmonics of the diatonic tempered musical scale, in frequencies below normal hearing range, correspond to brainwave, cluster patterns." Francke, Sylvia. The Tree of Life and the Holy Grail, Temple Lodge: England, 2007. pg. 200.

[298] Brain waves are measured as frequency and magnetic potential. When magnets are attracting, coming close together and increasing in kinetic energy, the magnets are decreasing in magnetic potential energy. The kinetic energy increases, because of "The Law of Conversation of Energy," which states that energy can't be created or destroyed, only change forms. It's like ladling soup into a bowl. All the soup is still there, it just came out of the pot, and into the bowl. The pot is symbolic of one form of energy and the bowl of another. *answers.yahoo.com electromagnetic energy*

[299] McTaggart, Lynne. The Field, The Quest for the Secret Force of the Universe, Harper Collins Publishers: N.Y., 2002. pg. 88.

Author David Tame reports, "The sun itself has been described as a 'great musical instrument' by Dr. Martin Pomerantz of the Bartol Research Foundation...They have detected oscillations on the sun's surface which they believe originate from acoustic of vibratory waves inside the fiery sphere. Eighty tones or different kinds of vibrations have been observed, with periods of two to eight minutes.

Tame continues, "These oscillations, as well as radio waves of space have been transposed into audible sound. The results, though interesting, cannot really be said to correspond to music as we know it. However, Saturn's magnetosphere produces waves which when transposed into sound, have been described as a slow dreamy melody. When Voyager 2 drew close to the ringed world it picked up the whines and hisses of the magnetosphere and beamed them back to earth."[300] When speed up they consisted of a melody.

The movement of planets creates low vibrations that affect our subtle energy. The earth also emits low levels of electromagnetic energy from the spinning core of molten iron way below the surface. Energies from the sun distort the earth's field with high-energy solar winds. The interaction of the earth's magnetic field *(from the molten iron)* and the solar winds *(from the sun)* combines into electromagnetic energy, which is comprised of low frequencies.[301]

Dr. Becker describes cosmic magnetic influences on life. "The strength of the Earth's magnetic field averages about

---

[300] Tame, David. The Secret Power of Music: The Transformation of Self and Society Through Musical Energy, Destiny Books: Vermont, 1984. pg. 236.
[301] Becker, Robert. Dr. Cross Currents, The Perils of Electropollution, The Promise of Electromedicine, Penguin Group: New York, 1990. pg. 174.

half a gauss, and worse yet, its daily charge is less than 0.1 gauss. Compared to a magnet that holds a refrigerator door closed, this is peanuts, indeed. There is simply no way that such a small charge in The Field, The Quest for the Secret Force of the Universe could influence even a compass needle. However, Professor Brown's[302] experiments in the Woods Hole Marine Biological Laboratory indicate clearly that living organisms have the ability to somehow sense these minute daily cycles in the earth's magnetic field and to use them to time their biological cycles."[303]

Dr. Becker continues, "Twenty years later we know that living things have the capacity of detecting and obtaining information from such low-strength fields as the steady geomagnetic field and its cyclic fluctuations."[304] Dr. Becker believes that this is how animals differentiate between north and south for migrations and other purposes.

It has been proved that the subtle energy systems in our body detect and obtain information from geomagnetic fields. Similarly, astrologers profess that our subtle energy systems are influenced by electromagnetic energy that originates in space.

## Sounds of Planets, Sun and Galaxy

German physicist, Hans Cousto's life's work has been to apply his scientific training to unlock deeper links between the stars and frequencies. He believes there is a deep spiritual

---

[302] Professor Frank Brown of the Woods Hole Marine Biological Laboratory in Woods Hale, Ma.

[303] Becker, Robert. Dr. Cross Currents, The Perils of Electropollution, The Promise of Electromedicine, Penguin Group: New York, 1990. pg. 71.

[304] Becker, Robert. Dr. Cross Currents, The Perils of Electropollution, The Promise of Electromedicine, Penguin Group: New York, 1990. pg. 72.

harmony in the design and flow of the universe. Music is an expression of this harmony.

In his book <u>The Cosmic Octave, The Origen of Harmony</u>, Cousto shares his revelations: "It was the result of a way of seeing things which moved me to combine the old teachings of harmonics with new findings in physics and other sciences. The result is an all-encompassing system of measurement with which it is possible to transpose the movements of the planets into audible rhythms, sounds and color. This basic system of measurement clearly demonstrates the harmonic relationship that exists between different kinds of natural phenomena in The Field, The Quest for the Secret Force of the Universes of astronomy, meteorology and microbiology."[305]

Cousto explains his system of measurement, which, "like the harmony of music, is inherent in the general structure of all beings."[306] Cousto links the orbital and rotational motions of the stars and planets to specific frequencies for each celestial body. He then translates these celestial frequencies into audible pitches through the principal of octaves.

Hans Cousto reveals that the time period of planet rotation is equal to the inverse of the frequency of the planet.[307] With this formula, he calculated the frequencies of our moon, sun, earth and the other planets in our solar system.

---

[305] , Hans. <u>The Cosmic Octave: The, Origin of Harmony,</u> LifeRhythm: Mendocino CA., 2000. pg. 10.
[306]Cousto Hans. <u>The Cosmic Octave: The Origin of Harmony,</u> LifeRhythm: Mendocino CA., 2000. pg. 10.
[307] Cousto, Hans. <u>The Cosmic Octave: The, Origin of Harmony,</u> LifeRhythm: Mendocino, CA.,. 2000. pg. 18.

The Biosonic website,[308] developed by John Beaulieu, N.D., Ph.D., lists benefits of Cousto's planetary tones:

**Sun-tone**: Enhances a sense of strength, motivation, self-identity, vitality and radiance. It promotes enthusiasm, assertiveness and determination. *(light green...126.22 Hz)*

**Moon-tone**: Promotes emotional tranquility, softness and intuition. It enhances feelings, the feminine energy and a flowing flexibility with life. *(orange...210.42 Hz)*

**Earth-tone**: Enhances the deep security and safety of Mother Earth. It is the cosmic sound of "om." It grounds and centers us. *(orange red...194.18 Hz)*

**Mercury-tone**: Strengthens cooperation and understanding. It sharpens communication skills through reason, writing and speaking with confidence. *(blue green...141.270 Hz)*

**Venus-tone**: Enhances an ability to feel, love, receive and share, and have close relationships. It enhances creativity. It also increases our love of pleasure, harmony and self-appreciation. *(yellow orange...221.23 Hz)*

**Mars-tone**: Builds strength, desire, motivation and action. It brings out decision-making abilities and assertiveness, while strengthening our courage and sexual nature. *(blue...144.72 Hz)*

**Jupiter-tone**: Promotes openness, trust, optimism, good fortune and brings a jovial sense of laughter. It helps one to be receptive to grace and adventure in life. *(red...183.58 Hz)*

---

[308] www.biosonics.com. John Beaulieu, N.D., Ph.D., founded a "Sound School" in 1985 to promote artistic, healing, and scientific dialogue on sound as well as develop the relationship of sound to energy medicine and consciousness.

**Saturn-tone**: Develops discipline and setting limits with others and ourselves. It helps us to be structured, organized and responsible. *(blue...147.85 Hz)*

**Uranus-tone**: Enhances ability to make life changes through inspiration, insight and freedom of expression and without self-imposed limitations. *(orange...207.36 Hz)*

**Neptune-tone**: Creates spiritual experiences and emphasizes compassion. It supports our dream life, artistic nature, music, art, dance and creativity. *(orange...211.44 Hz)*

**Pluto-tone**: Helps us face our deepest secrets and brings light to the darkness. The energetic forces of Pluto help us let go of old patterns, bringing a rebirth in consciousness.[309] *(blue green...140.25 Hz)*

The tones that Cousto calculated for the planets and the sun are singing on tuning forks that twinkle in the background of my deeply moving, musical and fluid "StarDust" CD,[310] which may be sampled at www.jillswingsoflight.com and www.jillshealingmusic.com. Cousto's and Sharry's frequencies for these colors are reciprocals implying frequency differences perhaps resulting from different brain hemisphere usage. I have embedded both left and right brain formula of these star tones in StarDust CD.

A strong vibration, in close proximity, causes a lesser vibration to match itself. When we hear the sounds of the stars *(raised up octaves into our hearing range)*, we entrain the star tones. Just as we see the gorgeous "starscape" at night, the songs of the stars can twinkle inside of us.

---

[309] BioSonics.com Planetary Tuners
[310] Listen the music at www.jillswingsoflight.com. Free samples and complementary sound healing newsletter at www.jillshealingmusic.com

In addition to these planetary tones, I created tuning forks of the frequencies representing hydrogen, oxygen, nitrogen and carbon...elements that make up our bodies and the same elements that are found in the stars. These tones also float in and out of the heavenly StarDust music.

Here are a few reactions from these musical compositions and tones:

- "Your music is as close to the sounds I experienced in my near death experience than anything I've ever heard. Hope my story makes you feel like a little angel." *Judy F*
- "When I listen to the 'Star Dust' CD, my air purifier turns off as the air is pure, and the air smells really wonderful." *Scott K.*
- "I was taken by the haunting beauty of the vocals and by the cascading effect of the music. It seemed to create rhythmic surges of consciousness - as if my attention was being swept in and out like the waves on the ocean that were also a part of the music." *Jeff C*
- Your music represents one of my most intriguing encounters with music: It brought tears to my eyes at first, and weeks later, still leaves me in a state of contemplative quietude after listening." *Judy S*
- "I find your music so hard to describe - so beautiful, just not of this world - too special to be earthly." *Tillie S*

I am a channel, much like the late Edgar Casey, whose channeled information has been credited with establishing the use of many herbal remedies. Through channeling experience, [311] I learned to identify great beings before they

---

[311] When one channels he alters his consciousness and allows a spirit to speak through him.

spoke, because I recognized their distinctive energy. In a similar example, if you close your eyes and pretend that your mother is sitting next to you, you can recall what she "feels" like. Her "feeling" is always characteristically the same. I discovered that these distinctive "feelings" of specific beings could be captured during recording sessions. In silence I taped the presence of these divine beings during channeling and I could later "feel" their presence in the recording. My music contains such channeled energies. Inside the cover of the Star Dust CD you find the names of the channeled beings for each song.

## Astrological Signs, Colors and Musical Notes

Sharry has developed fascinating uses of low level energies from space. Our bodies are hardwired to create a sense of pleasure when it sees or hears whole number ratios. Some just intonation scales use these ratios that follow the elliptical orbits of planets. Are these the seeming secret patterns of music that affect our consciousness?

Sharry developed the following chart that shows relationships between colors, musical notes and astrological signs. There are twelve astrological signs that correspond to the twelve half-notes in our musical scale. Sharry also compares the energy of astrology to a color palette.

## Color, Tones and Signs

| Signature Color | Signature Tone | Astrological Sign |
|---|---|---|
| Orange | D | Gemini |
| Orange yellow | D# *(or Eb)* | Cancer |
| Yellow | E | Leo |
| Yellow green | F | Virgo |
| Green | F# *(or Gb)* | Libra |
| Green blue | G | Scorpion |
| Blue | G# *(or Ab)* | Sagittarius |
| Blue violet | A | Capricorn |
| Violet | A# *(or Bb)* | Aquarius |
| Violet red | B | Pieces |
| Red | C | Aries |
| Orange red | C# | Taurus |

Sharry correlates astrological energies and low level frequencies with the vibrations inside our bodies. The vibrations from the planets interact with and strike resonance with the frequencies within us. This interaction influences our personality traits and health attributes. Any predominance of a frequency creates characteristic health strengths and challenges, along with dominant personality traits.

Our signature tone, color, astrological sign and dominant emotional characteristics are harmonically and mathematically related. Sharry's principals of brain dominance, colors and frequencies apply to astrological energies as well. Sharry reflects that about 40 percent of the time a person's signature note matches his astrological sign. An additional 40 percent of the time this same person's voice reflects a missing note that is six notes away from the note of his astrological sign *(or the complementary color)*. The remaining 20 percent of the time the pronounced and missing tones will vary with brain dominance. Sharry correlates these percentages to brain dominance. As we noted earlier, 40 percent of the general population is right brained. Forty percent is left brained. Twenty percent is whole brained.

My astrological sign is Capricorn with a correlating signature tone of A. Yet, when Sharry tested me with her freeware program nanoVoice, my signature tone had moved to a G# *(the light reciprocal of A).*

A signature tone produces energy, which describes one's passions and influences. When a portion of one's mission in life is accomplished, Sharry observed that the signature tone is harmonized or balanced. Another tone may then become dominant as we embark on an additional life mission. Sharry hinted that if all of a person's tones are harmonized that it maybe time for him to pass on or link to a group that supports one's higher mission.

An altered signature tone changes an individual's characteristic health and emotional patterns. For example, the note associated with an A, enabled me to be highly intuitive, read between the lines and put myself aside for others. I was no longer radiating an A. Sharry described the personality traits associated with G #: "wants to make a difference, likes to help and satisfy others, hands on, and time-conscious." *(The color chart on page 147 has a brief personality description associated with each musical note.)* Sharry informed me that the predominance of G# within my energy drives me to create useful physical products using words. Meanwhile, I was interviewing Sharry to write this book! Sharry suggested that the steps involved in the writing of books would eventually balance the high volume of G# in my voice.

Sharry also pointed out that I am attracted to people with a predominance of D in their voice, as this tone is an interval of a minor sixth away from my predominate G#. The G# provides me with harmonizing balance.

A signature tone of G# attracts different people than an A. The G# will also create different coincidences than the signature tone of A. As our signature tone varies, so does our life path. These imbalances attract the lessons and adventures of our lives.

Subtle frequencies recorded from space correspond to elements. Sharry suggests that when the Frequency-Equivalent of zinc is received from space, people with colds get better quicker, as if they have taken zinc supplements. Sharry provides information to counter the negative energy on www.nutrasounds.com in her weekly "Keynotes" column. A sample of this is on the page 264.

Astrology gets minimal respect today, but for thousands of years many highly evolved people, including the wise men from the <u>Bible</u>, used information about influences from the stars to make personal struggles triggered by subtle energy easier to navigate. Sharry's sound healing system creates tones to counter difficult geomagnetic, environmental, planetary and cosmic energies… which is not too dissimilar than the ancient Chinese's musical feng shui.

Different frequencies coming from space interact with our physical bodies and emotions. At times these frequencies help us and at times they make our life more difficult. Let's say we already had too much G# in our voice and we receive even more of the frequency of G# from space. These waves combine and our imbalance is aggravated. When some people have failing health they usually report "good days and bad days." These changing subtle energies from space can explain these experiences.

Ancient wisdom acknowledges benefits from overcoming personal challenges. Likewise, a body builder exercises his muscles against resistance, such as weights. When we overcome negative emotional energy, we increase our emotional strength. As we overcome our negativity and obstacles our subtle energy becomes stronger.

Insights about the impact of astrological energies altered my perception of free will. Energies from the cosmos influence my emotions - without my conscious knowledge. What I am attracted to is established - without my conscious awareness. We have free will over our reactions to feelings, personality traits and coincidences. Yes, I have free will, but many of my feelings, personality traits, attractions, coincidences and opportunities are influenced by energies outside of my consciousness.

### Sharry's Key Note Frequency Report for March 17-18-19

Time to pay attention to circulation issues – oxygen, blood viscosity, vein and capillary health... especially for those with cholesterol rooted issues. More discomfort associated with lower leg circulation may be noticed until the 20th. Supplementation with niacin, folic acid, choline, inositol and a decrease in fatty foods may be helpful. Bil, an enzyme/herb combination by Theryzyme has been known to assist when the unfriendly fats in the body become troublesome. Because of the slowdown of circulation, people prone to gout may be more easily sent into an episode...especially when changes in the weather take them into dramatic temperature changes. This is often a thyroid issue.

Conversion of chemical energy to muscle energy is stressed during these few days, but will open up into a surge of physical energy by the 21st when more mineral frequencies become available. You may feel a bit guilty because of your lazy "spell" but it is just Mother Earth expressing waves of energy flux. You will move along quite nicely beginning to build momentum around the 23rd. Magnesium may speed this interaction. Food containing magnesium includes chocolate, brown rice and soybeans. Vulnerable muscles for this time are the wrist and psoas muscles. There is a vulnerability to Influenza on the 18th but may be offset by bioflavonoids.

This is a time to get things on the table about expectation as you move forward into the fruition stage of what you have planned. It is much more important NOW that you lay the foundation of what is to be done in terms of who will be responsible for what factions of completion.

Guilt will lie with what you said. Worry with what you have not done. We are within a few days of balance toward a new beginning. Take advantage of the next few days to complete the old so that you can start anew. You have until late on the 21st to finish-up any old business.

This line of thinking gave me insights into "sacred contracts." Carolyn Myss coined this term, which became popular from several of her books.[312] "In short, a sacred contract is an agreement your soul makes before you are born," Myss explains. "You promise to do certain things for yourself, for others, and for divine purposes. Part of the contract requires that you discover what you are meant to do."[313] The energy from the stars holds clues as to how we are directed to our life's work and sacred contracts.

At the time of our conception, astrological energies could be a deciding influence on the selection of our individual DNA, which produces our inherited personality. Theoretically, a spirit could choose the time of his conception, so that cosmic energies would impact DNA *(life blueprint)* to create a specific personality trait. Theoretically, a spirit could orchestrate important life relationships by coordinating conception times with planned partners, which would trigger attraction to designated people. I have read accounts in antiquity in which marriage partners were determined by astrological compatibility, which is harmonious with such an idea.

Subtle energy from the stars influences our health, emotions and interactions with other people. People in ancient times understood this and interpreted the significance of astrological influences. Some scientists are now discovering the ways stellar energy influences our lives. Sharry and others

---

[312] Myss, Carolyn. Sacred Contracts, Awakening your Divine Potential and Finding Your Sacred Contract.

[313] "Decoding our Sacred Contract requires us to become fluent in the language of symbols and archetypes so that we can interpret dreams, understand the meaning behind 'coincidences,' and learn to follow our intuition. There are other authors who write about pre birth planning, such as Robert Schwartz in Your Soul's Plan: Discovering the Real Meaning of the Life You Planned Before You Were Born.

also interpret this influence and create tools to manage and understand this energy.

## Conclusion

In Part II we unveiled foundational premises of BioAcoustic biology and related them to music, color, math, brain dominance, the environment and astrological energies. In Part III we will explore a myriad of ways to personally use this information for an enhanced life.

# PART THREE
# APPLICATIONS

# Introduction to Applications

Part Three describes options to harness benefits from sound, as an intrinsic healing modality. Although this section is not a complete survey of sound healing applications, included are techniques that can be mastered with a reasonable level of commitment. Applications presented here include Sharry's services and free personal applications – many originating in antiquity.

Sharry's incredible applications and her discoveries, birth hope for physical maladies and gives us tools to manage our emotions. A significant portion of Sharry's energy is spent to train people to use her system, to release people from imbalances that define and diminish their lives. Chapter 2 reviews Sharry's services and educational opportunities.

I view Sharry's nanoVoice as her most powerful free gift to people to date, so there is a dedicated chapter *(Chapter 3)* on this alone. This freeware program gives us a better understanding of ourselves from the inside out. The nanoVoice can also be used to obtain deeper psychological and emotional underpinnings of the people that influence and interact with us.

We listen to music a good portion of our lives, without any thought to its specific impact on our health and emotional well-being. As we are exposed to music regularly it behooves us to give careful consideration to selecting beneficial music. Chapter 4 explores information to help you select your listening choices.

I included free techniques of using your voice to make powerful life changes. I selected ones that mimic and expand on the sound healing techniques pioneered by Sharry. We can easily assume that due to her special hearing, we cannot use sound as she does; however, we can do much along the lines of what Sharry does.

People in ancient civilizations understood the benefits of special sounds. In Chapter 5 we will discover toning, an ancient art to daily tune-up and loosen stuck energy.

A revered practice in many ancient societies was listening to tiny sounds heard during silent repose. A meditative exercise described in Chapter 6 includes methods to hear subtle sounds - for significant personal benefit.

Since keys to our health, intellect and emotional well-being can be found within the pitches of our voice, why not develop our speaking voice? The final sound healing applications described in Chapter 7 teaches how to change our speaking voice for lasting and significant personal benefits.

I had written a book sampling a variety of sound healing techniques before I met Sharry at a conference where we both were speakers. The depth of her discoveries attracted me like a magnet ...I wanted to learn more. Shortly after our encounter I began writing this book; however, my quest for learning about the potency of sound and music, started many years earlier.

Over an eighteen-year period I have pursued my love of studying secrets hidden in hundreds of volumes of antiquity. Most were about secret societies, like the Tibetan monks, Christian monks, Druids, ancient Egyptian mystics, ancient Chinese, and more... Not only did I uncover ideas from many cultures and ages, but it vastly opened up my thoughts and heart. Occasionally, these secret societies wrote about using sound as a profound tool to transform people's consciousness and to improve their minds, bodies and spirits.

In ancient mystery schools much sound information was restricted to verbal communication and selectively given to the upper hierarchies of students. Since people could use sound to control and harm others, its powers were only trusted to a few proven people. Each mystery school allowed bits of this information to be disclosed in writing. I read so many secret societies' doctrines that I cumulatively gathered sound healing techniques, amassing voluminous secrets to transform your world with sound.

I used these ancient techniques in my own musical compositions to rebirth these benefits and the wonderful art that flourished eons ago. With the aid of clairaudient hearing I employed a form of cosmic plagiarism, copying the music I seemed to magically hear in my head.

I also found myself interviewing scientists and sound healers, confirming the effectiveness of many of life-changing techniques. My book, <u>Ancient Sounds - Modern Healing,</u> is a result of that research.[314] This unique volume takes the reader on an extraordinary journey filled with secrets from age-old cultures, along with the latest findings from today's scientific community. Together, they reveal that sound can alter a person's brain waves, increase relaxation, eliminate stress, aid the healing process and help us to become happier, healthier and more productive.

With this background, it is easy to see how exciting Sharry's depth of observations, replicable results, and methods of using sound to empower our lives was tantalizing to me!

In Part Three, Applications, we will focus on the magic within sounds to enhance our personal power. With patient attention we can sense subtleties and nuances in sound, revealing people's intent, emotions and health. By listening to our own sounds we hear our body's symphony leading us to greater depth of understanding and peace within. More than ever before, we can understand sonic influences and use them constructively.

This science of sound is just beginning to unfold, and in time it will be universally accepted. Right now, it is as if sound can be used like a magic wand to bestow blessings. May the magic of sound always uplift you!

---

[314] Available at www.jillswingsoflight.com

# Chapter One

# Sound Health Services

Sharry has numerous websites that provide education and sound healing products. She offers her frequency gifts in a variety of forms.

On her website you can learn how to create a voiceprint. After sending this to Sound Health you can acquire a report of pertinent information contained in your voice. For example, you may want a report on the nutrition that your body needs right now, or perhaps which of your muscles are in danger of being hurt versus which ones would be improved by strength training. Perhaps you want to know if you are at risk for a vaccination's side effects. A review of the various software packages listed in Part One of this book defines areas in which you can receive information. The cost varies with the depth of services needed. The hourly rate varies between $40 and $125 at the time of this writing.

Many people take the next step and get a sound presentation *(a sonic formula that is programmed into a tone box for you to listen to).* Sharry has trained many qualified practitioners throughout the world that can analyze your voice and create a sound regiment for you. Their locations and contact information is available on her website.

The software available from Sound Health contains a comprehensive set of sonic formulas collected from 30 years of experiences. Some people have taken pieces of Sharry's methods and data to create other sound healing services. Some have developed helpful products, while other's services are shoddy and potentially harmful. Using a trained BioAcoustic practitioner that uses Sound Health's latest software and databases helps avoid these pitfalls!

If you want Sharry's expertise, you can schedule a session to sonically address your issues. Her fee is $125 per hour at the time of this writing. Many sound presentations can be completed in about four hours over two days, depending on the circumstances. A follow up visit is essential!

When a session is scheduled with Sharry, plan to spend two days in Athens, Ohio, or nearby. Your "sound diet" is tested in person: you must be present for this portion of service. On the first day, several voiceprints are taken, while you discuss a variety of topics. The voiceprints are analyzed and researched while you wait.

Shortly after, you listen to test tones in the sound lab. The low frequencies pulse in rhythmic beats, as if someone is tapping a finger on a drum.

You listen to tone trials in a separate room than the administrator, just as the x-ray technician leaves the room when you get an x-ray. One person's tones may not be beneficial to the next.

While you listen to the tones, staff observes and measures your reactions with biofeedback equipment, such as a pulse oximeter or a temperature gauge. Different types of information are used to determine the length of time needed for listening: your heart rate, blood pressure, pulse, oxygen saturation levels, body temperature and muscle testing. Personal reactions are also analyzed, including whether or not you like the tones, body language, relaxation, symptom changes, expression of emotions, tingling or tightening of muscles, fidgeting, dizziness, clenching teeth and comparisons of how you feel when the tones are turned off. A good rule of thumb is that if you like the sounds, they are beneficial. This information helps determine the length of listening time and selection of tones.

More sound is not always better. Over listening corrects the problem and then continues to produce a new imbalance.

Based on the results of tone test trials, sonic formulations are programmed into a sound box referred to as, a sound presentation. You can purchase the portable, reusable sound box *(currently $450),* or you may borrow one for a limited time under certain conditions. Listening times will be prescribed. Perhaps you can get started that day or night if you sleep alone. Listening duration is reduced over time as the body incorporates the FEs into its own sound matrix. Sound treatment can be required for several days to many months, depending upon the severity, layers of the problem and chronic nature of the problem.

Your brain assimilates these sonic remedies into its maintenance regime. When the body no longer needs the tones for support, you will begin to dislike the tones - that is the ultimate goal for the sound presentation.

Periodic assessment is a critical aspect of sound healing. Sharry requires that you return to Sound Health to complete a second set of voice samples. Sharry observes the impact of your listening and reexamines a new voiceprint. Your tones and listening times will be refined, based on the results.

The voiceprint delineates your chronic, current and predictive health issues. Most people schedule a session to target a specific health concern. However, important predictive information may be revealed. For example, Sharry described a woman who came in for chronic pain, which Sharry helped reduce during that session. Sharry had observed that the woman was developing a far more serious disease. Shortly thereafter, the woman's regular physician diagnosed this condition for which she then scheduled an additional visit.

Each person's matrix of sounds is unique. A BioAcoustic frequency formula that helps one person is not transferable to another. Sharry cited a case in which a girl used her twin's frequencies for a similar ailment, but her sister's frequencies made her sicker instead. One would think that the frequency formula would be transferable, but our bodies are extremely complex. There are too many variables for one person's sound protocols to work on another.

Improperly using BioAcoustics can create problems. Some frequencies can take your heart into rhythm and others take it out of rhythm. Sounds not properly combined with the right rhythms may prove ineffective. Sounds not accounting for brain dominance may also be problematic.

BioAcoustics should not be used for many health issues, especially emergencies such as, but not limited to poisoning, traumatic bleeding, appendicitis and heart attack.

Sharry has the following disclaimer on her website: "Human BioAcoustics, as originated by Sharry Edwards, M.Ed., does not diagnose or prescribe for medical or psychological conditions nor does it claim to prevent, treat, mitigate or cure such conditions. Human BioAcoustic researchers do not provide diagnosis, care, treatment or rehabilitation of individuals, nor apply medical, mental health or human development principles."

Neither the FDA nor the AMA considers BioAcoustics a medical technique. The primary emphasis is research.

## BioAcoustic Courses

BioAcoustics courses[315] teach how to analyze a voice and create a sonic presentation. This enables you to become a practitioner, researcher, and instructor to help your family, friends and yourself. The courses are available on line or on site, usually in Albany, Ohio.

Learning how to regularly balance your inharmonious tones is an excellent way to remain healthy during this time of soaring health costs. Sharry wants people to understand how their bodies work *(acoustically speaking)*. She presents us with this training opportunity so we can take a strong role in maintaining our health and harmony.

There are numerous BioAcoustic courses, internships, continuing education classes, forums and an annual conference to further develop professional level skills. Many become BioAcoustic practitioners after taking the five day Level Two course. Some people work in clinics or

---

[315] More information is available at www.nutrasounds.com.

complementing medical or alternative health service, while others develop their own practice or business. BioAcoustic clinicians charge between $40 per hour and $400 per hour for sound sessions. Physicians usually charge the higher rates. There are no standardized fee schedules for practitioners.

At NutraSounds.com you can view contact information for practitioners with a good reputation. Practitioners in this network are required to submit case studies to Sound Health, enabling them to gauge the reliability of their work and to contribute to research efforts.

Collective information is analyzed and additional databases are created from hundreds and hundreds of studies. Sharry is the hub of the BioAcoustic Internet. The research, ideas and discoveries of what works from all of the practitioners and researchers come into Sound Health. The staff and Sharry review the data.

Being a BioAcoustic practitioner is not for everyone. It is a science in the making. Your observation, interpretation and good judgment are required to apply the principals. Voluminous amount of materials must be learned. The processes are not easy to understand at first, requiring patience and commitment.

### The Annual Conference

An annual training session - where practitioners review research, new techniques, marketing strategies, new product and databases - is held once a year in Albany, Ohio. Some topics presented during the 2009 three-day event will give you a flavor for this annual training event: classes on cancer, hair regrowth, eye health, migraines, epilepsy, diabetes, the spine, iodine, frequencies for the new epidemic the swine flu, human chorionic gonadotropin hormone *(HcG)* diet, golf and sports nutrition, correcting chemical processes in the body, presentations on time-saving techniques, new products, teaching and marketing ideas, new employment opportunities and legal updates. Practitioners share their findings and contributions to the science of BioAcoustics.

## The Guardians of the People Network

Sharry has established a network called "Guardians of the People; Health for the People, by the People" to support a grass roots effort to spread alternative wellness opportunities to your family, friends and clientele.

Membership in this group provides on line training and up to 12 computer programs to help you co-create a community network for health and wellness. Trained members can educate others regarding nutrition, weight management, muscle trauma and on other health issues.

Another agenda proposes the use of sound health techniques to identify at risk people for vaccinations. Sharry's program, PreVac, can help evaluate the readiness of the body to appropriately process a vaccine. This grass roots effort aims to spread the usage of this program so people can make informed decisions regarding vaccinations.

Write SharryOnAir@gmail.com to receive more information and investigate GuardiansofthePeople.com. At the time of this writing, yearly membership is $55 with a monthly membership of $40 that includes at least one software program, one class each month and newsletters.

## Other Information

Information on BioAcoustics can be found at:

- Nutrasounds.com *(profiling and class information)*
- SharryEdwards.com
- Soundhealthoptions.com
- NanoVoice.org *(nanovoice software)*
- Soundhealthinc.com
- Vocalprofiling.com
- JBAB.org, *(the Journal of BioAcoustic Biology, which posts articles on this developing science)*
- Many videos on YouTube.
- Dozens of authors have written about Sharry in their books and information appears on many journals and sites.

# Chapter Two

# The nanoVoice

Sharry gifts the world with her personality profiler software - the nanoVoice. It provides powerful information about our emotions that can make a critical difference in our lives. This information holds crucial keys for personal growth with the cumulative effect of positively impacting our society.

The effect of emotions influences us more than we acknowledge. For example, the soaring cost of health care is a top priority in the world. The root cause of many diseases lies in stressed emotions. In another example, war and famine have worldwide, devastating effects. If people maintained inner peace and harmony, would fewer people allow war? If most people displayed compassion, could we reduce world famine? If people mastered their emotions to a greater extent, think of the incredible progress we could see in eradicating the problems listed above.

The lack of emotional control is linked to crime, delinquency, domestic violence, sexual/physiological abuse, substance abuse and many other insidious problems. How many businesses falter from people whose egos are out of control? What is the cost of ignoring the healthy maturation of our emotions? The development of positive emotions is crucial not only for the individual's development, but also for the well-being of our civilizations.

One of life's biggest challenges is to discover our unique contributions in life and to pursue this path. To collectively face the unrivaled challenges of the twenty-first century, more people must achieve this potential. Only in this way can the optimum future of humanity be realized.

Our gifts are as unique as our fingerprints, but are not easily recognized nor developed. The secret to uncovering our life purpose lies within our feelings. It feels good to develop our natural talents. Following feelings provides an intuitive journey that can reveal our highest destiny.

All people have experienced pain. In response many dull their feelings. When we harden ourselves to diminish pain we also disconnect with feelings that make us happy. The shell we construct to protect us also isolates us from joy. Numbing one emotion diminishes our overall ability to feel, to be aware of what makes us happy.

Fulfilling a personal calling is ultimately satisfying, provides unrivaled energy and cultivates joy. Yet, it gets even better. Experiencing positive emotions on a regular basis enhance optimum health.

Emotions drive our actions. Consider that determination, will, consistency, courage and fortitude fuel our successes, giving us power. In contrast, negative emotions of depression and hopelessness rob us of life energy.

The cliché that strong people do not show emotions is the root cause that renders them powerless. Yet, we subconsciously block emotions out of our conscious mind. It's extraordinarily difficult to manage feelings that we are unaware of.

I discovered first-hand the operating patterns of our subconscious mind by teaching people to play the violin. Initially, learning to play violin demands more commitment than is required for other instruments such as guitar or piano. To play a single note a student must simultaneously control at least six skills. Violin students perform all skill areas simultaneously, but they consciously concentrate on only one.

The skills that the students are not paying attention to go "underground" in their subconscious minds. For example, while a student concentrates on bowing, he plays out of tune.

There are default settings for motor coordination that occur without our conscious awareness. Without our awareness, the brain averages the requirements for all motor actions. Beginning violinists play slow notes faster and fast notes slower. They average the length of time for both. The same is true for dynamics: beginners play all notes at the same volume, with no variation between loud and soft. Instinctively students place their fingers equidistant apart on the strings, as they play out of tune. This occurs without conscious thought or awareness.

Beginners stop bowing while they think about what finger to place down. They are not aware of the silence they create, altering the music's rhythm. The brain deems note recognition more important than timing. It stops one activity so the person can concentrate on what it deems most important. I have never met a student who is aware of these default processes. They just conclude that playing the violin is hard.

Our mind, like a computer, operates programs in the background while we focus on one thing. Likewise, many subconscious emotions run in the background, affecting our health and behavior. When we get a virus on our computer, it insidiously and quietly works in the background, while we carry on…unaware. So it is in our lives, as the impact of negative emotions can quietly cause us to crash, physically, emotionally and behaviorally. In order to master these hidden emotions, we need to be aware of them.

We experience complex thoughts, feelings and behaviors, but we are only fully conscious of one of these activities at a time. We subjugate feelings while we are preoccupied with other things. Our society minimizes emotions and encourages us to ignore them and act as if we are too strong for them to bother us. Paradoxically, pushing emotions into our subconscious mind makes it easier for us to be controlled, while strength quietly slips away.

Underground emotional energy influences our health and creates emotional habits. It is not only unpleasant feelings that we wish to deny that find their way into our subconscious minds, but also routine thoughts and feelings that we experience all day long.

We spend our formative years in school, developing our rational minds, but our emotional development receives little formal attention. High divorce rates, job loss, employment stress, accidents, deaths, personal struggles, changing hormones, financial problems and health issues challenge everyone's emotional health. Yet, as a society we stubbornly treat the development of our emotions as a low priority. Perhaps since emotions are invisible, we falsely believe they don't exist. Meanwhile, emotions continually affect the bottom line of our health, happiness and well-being.

The nanoVoice is a valuable tool to help us see what is going on in the "underground playground" of our subconscious feelings and thoughts. The ability to master emotions is contingent on our awareness of them. We do not eliminate negative feelings by ignoring them. Only after we identify and address them, are we able to release them.

The nanoVoice paints our conscious and unconscious feelings in concrete numeric form. Below are examples in which knowledge of our subconscious feelings can spur our growth.

- People unknowingly project their subliminal feelings onto others. For example, a habitual liar is quick to perceive that another is lying, and an angry man easily finds another who picks a fight. A person withdraws, not allowing anyone to get close, while he perceives that others have abandoned him. We miss the connection when our own feelings *(our own frequencies)* wind up in our perceptions of others.

- We clothe dark feelings in an acceptable light. For example, anger is often disguised as a righteous reaction.

- Subconscious expectations set up interpersonal booby traps. We do not voice our expectations, yet are disappointed when they are not met. It's easier to avoid misunderstandings and disappointments when we acknowledge our expectations.

- Our unconscious feelings can trigger other people's behavior. For example, Bob believes that he is "no good" and radiates this feeling. Those nearby feel this energy, subconsciously pick up on it and act accordingly. Subtly, Bob conditioned others to treat him with low regard.

- A person is rarely aware that his ego directs a situation, although this happens often. When we are not conscious of it, our ego is extraordinarily hard to manage.

It is difficult to know ourselves from the inside out.

Just like second-hand smoke inflicts damage on those nearby, so do our toxic emotions. Yet we steadfastly believe that we can hide our feelings without any impact on others.

Sharry's nanoVoice illuminates subtle emotions so we can better navigate emotional challenges.

## How to Use the nanoVoice

The nanoVoice is a scaled-down version of software called nVoice. nanoVoice is a free download available at www.nanoVoice.org. Instructions and free nanoVoice classes are also offered online.

The nanoVoice creates a graphic document when you speak into a microphone connected to your computer. The resulting time domain voiceprint shows component pitches found in our musical scale that are counted and included in bar graphs.

A specific emotion, such as love or anger, always feels the same because it carries a unique, invariant universal energy or frequency. When a person experiences a specific emotion, it registers as the same frequency on a voiceprint.

In the nanoVoice print each musical note in a scale is associated with specific emotions. For example, a tall bar graph representing the pitch of C indicates excess power, independence, ego, self-direction, excitement and physical motivation. Even though these feelings may be subconscious, they are revealed in the resulting voiceprint. There is more in your voice than you realize. The chart on page 147 shows which emotions are linked to each pitch in your voice.

Emotions are linked to various organs and systems in the body by octave resonance. The nanoVoice also displays which body organs and processes are stressed.

The nanoVoice program provides four to five paragraphs assessing your personality data. The full version of the software, the nVoice, creates a four to five page assessment. Both explain the pitches and colors that were created by your voice sample and how they relate to your emotions and health.

## Purposes of the nanoVoice

Personality programs such as the nanoVoice have a multitude of applications. They identify our natural talents, strengths and capabilities, encouraging us to better utilize them. Simultaneously personality profilers identify our weaknesses, enabling us to convert them into strengths.

Psychologist Carol Ritberger comments on our subconscious emotions: "We are to the world a physical and a personality presence. We learn to deal with our physical presence from the day we are born, but our personality presence impacts us to a greater extent, and frequently we are oblivious to that impact."[316]

Sages throughout history report how difficult it is to "know thyself," but these wise sages did not have access to the nanoVoice. Special pitches reveal subconscious expectations,

---

[316] Ritberger, Carol, PHD. <u>What Color is your Personality?</u> Hay House: Carlsbad, CA., 2000 . pg. 37.

difficulty with openness, or desires to make a difference. The recording reveals areas in which we are emotionally stuck. Viewing our underlying fear depicts our confusion, sheds light on indecision and depicts ego issues. Accessing buried feelings gives us profound insights to acknowledge, resolve and release negative emotional habits.

Voiceprints taken throughout the day vary, reflecting our natural changing emotional states. Different information emerges when we discuss various topics. Cumulative data from many discussions depicts overall emotional patterns. We can observe how often an emotional problem is present on a variety of issues. For example, anger may show up in ten of ten voiceprints or only one of ten voiceprints. The FEs of repeated negative feelings accumulates, creating physical as well as emotional problems.

When conflicting information surfaces in a voiceprint, the same conflict exists in our emotions. When we weigh the pros and cons of a decision, each emotion associated with the options registers in the voiceprint. The predominant strength of each emotion is reflected in the number of hits of each pitch *(height of the associated bar on the bar graph)*, showing the intensity of that emotion.

Sharry records speeches of political candidates, world leaders and celebrities, giving us illuminating information about them. For example, a voiceprint report from Princess Dianna is included in the nanoVoice download packet. Sharry occasionally reviews voiceprints of political candidates and people in the news on her weekly radio show.

The nanoVoice is useful for group dynamics, work disputes and family/marriage/relationship counseling. It provides foundational information to plan strategies in negotiations and to anticipate people's actions and reactions. The nanoVoice creates an objective review of people. Understanding how people are hard-wired makes it easier to accept that differences are just that - differences - nothing more.

The nanoVoice can explain our attractions and aversions to people. We will be drawn to a person who radiates the missing frequencies in our voice. If we have too much of a frequency and we meet another person with an abundance of this same frequency, we will be repelled. Ever wonder why opposites attract? It's well worth the time to use voiceprints to understand our subconscious sonic interplay.

Our brain hemisphere usage affects our attraction and repulsion of other people. In Part Two we discussed that the right and left hemispheres of our brain process frequencies in an inverse manner. For example, we can be attracted to someone when we are using our right brain hemisphere and repulsed when we are utilizing our left brain hemisphere, even if it is the same person.

The nanoVoice voiceprint reflects which brain hemisphere a person is using. Red and yellow bar graphs reflect left brain usage, while green and blue colored bar graphs mirror right brain usage. Another way to note brain dominance is that people using their right brain hemisphere create tones on the right half of a nanoVoice graph. Conversely, frequencies on the left half of the graph reflect the usage of the left brain hemisphere.

Here is an interesting application of using frequencies to manage our attractions. To get over the death of a loved one or the loss of a lover, listen to the signature tone of the missing person, which eases the heartache. If you do not know the lost person's signature tone, listen to the tone associated with this person's astrological sign. If you enjoy the sound of the tone, listening would help you to let go. If the astrological sign doesn't work, try using the reciprocal or light reciprocal frequency *(see Part Two)*.

Valerie Hunt, Ph.D., measures electromagnetic energy in people's energy fields. She reports that some people can overpower others and sap their energy. In some relationships two people's energy fields blend, each becoming stronger.[317] The Nanovoice is a handy tool to predict results of energy interactions. For example, a person with a predominance of C energy is learning to control his ego. Another individual, who radiates G# energy, tends to see himself as not physically important. When in a relationship, the C personality needs to learn not to overpower the G# personality which must develop boundaries and self-esteem.

Leaders in The Field, The Quest for the Secret Force of the Universe of psychology attest that our personalities affect more than just relationships, they affect our health as well.[318] Carol Ritberger, PhD, reports, "Current research in the areas of behavioral medicine and psycho-neuro-immunology *(the study of how emotions affect the immune system)* reveals a

---

[317] Trivieri, Larry, Jr. Health on the Edge, Penguin Books: New York, 2003. pg. 196.
[318] Ritberger, Carol, PHD. What Color is your Personality? Hay House: Carlsbad, CA., 2000. pg. 9.

direct correlation between personality and illness."[319] Ritberger continues, "As a matter of fact there are very predictable personality characteristics that can predispose a person to hypertension, heart disease, asthma, cancer, allergies, auto-immune disorders and many other related illnesses."[320] Science confirms what we know from our personal experiences: improving emotional problems enhances our health.

The nanoVoice can be used to support your health. Taking a voiceprint before and after consuming a medication will show its immediate impact. Does the medicine balance and harmonize tones? We can also note the impact of certain foods through voiceprints. If our body needs the food, our voice coherence should improve. *(Increased voice coherence is shown when each bar graph is similar in size.)* Imbalance in our voice reveals that our body does not want or cannot use the nourishment offered. After we discuss or touch a food that we may have an allergy to the resulting voiceprint may reflect a significant decrease in balance. If our voiceprint is missing a frequency, we can sing or listen to the absent or weak tone. We can harmonize ourselves on many levels by simply singing our weak or missing notes. A follow up voiceprint will display the impact of our sonic remedy.

Sharry relayed a story about discovering predictive behavior within the voiceprint. While conducting a role-playing exercise in a class on perceptions, she divided students into two groups. One group told the truth and the other team

---

[319] Ritberger, Carol, PHD. <u>What Color is your Personality?</u> Hay House: Carlsbad, CA., 2000. pg. 9.
[320] Ritberger, Carol, PHD. <u>What Color is your Personality?</u> Hay House: Carlsbad, CA., 2000. pg. 10.

intentionally lied. Without knowing who was in each group, Sharry could readily "hear" the truth-tellers. This piqued her curiosity. She reviewed everyone's voiceprints, noting the balanced presence of A# and E pitches when the student spoke truthfully and the absence or an imbalance of these pitches when one lied. For example, in a 45-second voice recording a person hits each note an average of 42 times. If A# recorded 80 times and E showed up 20 times, they would not be in balance. This person was not telling the truth.

After further experimentation, Sharry realized that the A# and E pitches are absent in situations other than lying, such as avoiding uncomfortable feelings or discussing a fearful or uncertain topic. The absence or imbalance of A and E are linked to a state of denial – and we may not be aware of this.

Here is an example of how we can use this information. Nicki was considering an important life change – returning to college. After discussing this, her voiceprint showed no E and A# pitches, reflecting her indecision. Without understanding why, she may have procrastinated and never pursued this goal. Nicki realized that if she was serious about returning to college, she needed to delve deeper into her feelings. This reflection brought to the surface her worry about driving her kids to school and getting to her classes on time, because of the distances involved. To resolve the conflict Nicki moved to be closer to both schools. After she moved the balanced A# and E pitches appeared in Nicki's voiceprint.

## The Personality Colors

Our personality is like our automatic pilot, habitually processing information, making consistent decisions and creating our emotional climate. Our personality is made up of both traits and characteristics. Our traits are our hard-wired, emotional responses. Ritberger details, "Traits are genetic coding that determines the way our brain develops and functions around mental processes, which is how we gather and process information and make decisions."[21] Traits develop our strengths and weaknesses, dictate how we perceive things and predispose us to certain attitudes, values, beliefs and motivations. Traits also shape what irritates us, direct how stress affects us, influence our self-esteem and shape our coping mechanisms. Characteristics, in contrast, are behaviors that we have learned from life experiences.

Each colored bar on the nanoVoice print relates to specific personality traits and weaknesses. As we saw earlier, doubling a given frequency creates octaves. This multiplying effect can be repeated many times to form octaves of much higher frequencies. FEs of emotions can be doubled by octaves until they are in the range of wavelengths of color. In this way Sharry correlated colors with personality traits. She also drew upon her research and experiences in college matching colors with personalities.

The classification of personality trait by color is a non-threatening, reflective means to analyze people. The hues within a given color represent a personality trait or type *(for example, blue, blue-green and blue-yellow are all hues of blue)*. Sharry points out that our language verifies links between colors and emotions. For example, "He was green with envy." "She was so angry she saw red." "Her sadness made her blue." At the time of this publication, even the

---

[21] Ritberger, Carol, PHD. <u>What Color is your Personality?</u> Hay House: Carlsbad, CA., 2000. pg. 7.

Internet's *Wikipedia* reports that the color of money is equivalent to the pitch of an F or F#, which correlates to the color of green.

Effects of color are very real. Dr. Max Luscher[322] believed that colors have an emotional value and that a person's reaction to color reveals his basic personality traits. His research provided conclusive evidence that colors create the same psychological, emotional and physiological reaction in people.[323]

The nanoVoice program depicts frequency bar graphs in one of four colors. Each color reflects our habitual method of responding to the world around us…our core personality traits.

- **Red** - A person with red personality traits engages in reactive behavior, gut-level reactions and rapid-fire thinking and actions. A person with red traits has a desire to act - before extensive planning and examination of his words and actions. People who see most of their pitches graphed in red are flexible when happy and immutable when "wronged" or hurt. These people like to be in relationships that they are in control of and know everything that is going on. They don't want to be told

---

[322] Dr. Max Lûscher developed a famous color test during the early 1900s. He has devoted his life to the study of how color affects behavior. The test is based upon fundamentals in color psychology. With years of research by color psychologists the characteristics of certain colors has been identified to cause an emotional response in people. He studied the response from hundreds of thousands of test subjects around the world in order to isolate how certain colors make us feel. By doing the reverse, using the colors people prefer to determine how people feel, we can get some interesting indicators about a person's current emotional state.

[323] Ritberger, Carol, PHD. <u>What Color is your Personality?</u> Hay House: Carlsbad, CA., 2000. pg. 44.

what to do or think. They perceive their desire to control is their way of helping others. These people are physical and assertive, especially if pushed. Their mental processing is sequential. People with red traits tend to think of what is wrong and not what is right. They are hard workers, detail oriented and structured.[324] These people like to see and do things before the rest of the crowd. They like to do things for the community. Sharry classifies the red personality as a *fireman's mentality.*

- **Green** - People with green personality traits live in a world of hopes and dreams for the future. They believe that intangible things are vital in life. With rich imaginations, they are creative and their minds work quickly. People with these traits, see a bird's-eye view of situations. They primarily think with the left hemisphere of their brains. They also get caught up in their visions and intuitions, and can distort their perceptions to fit their dreams. With their highly developed intuition they read between the lines of what others say. People with green traits stand back while carefully selecting and planning their words and actions. They are slow to react without good reason. These people are driven by a need to be liked, often attracting co-dependent or abusive relationships. They avoid conflict and use their intuition to steer clear of it. Green personality types are champions of the downtrodden, the environment and human rights. A green personality type pushes himself physically. People with green traits have an intense desire to make

---

[324] Ritberger, Carol, PHD. <u>What Color is your Personality?</u> Hay House: Carlsbad, CA., 2000. pgs. 71 - 85.

their lives count.[325] Sharry summarizes these people as representing a *farmer's mentality*.

- **Yellow** - Yellow personalities are self-reliant, self-made, self-respected, self-motivated, self-starting, and self-fulfilled. They like things their way and their lives center on their goals. Yellow personality types believe that they can do anything if they put their mind to it. They are challengers and natural leaders. They are original thinkers who dare to do things differently. People with yellow traits use their intelligence and develop many competencies. They think, plan and organize their words and actions in a logical fashion. Their drive for perfection creates a critical and authoritarian streak, while they can be impractical, condescending and overly conceptual. They do not need critics, because they already judge themselves and rarely see a need for improvement. They can always "spin" an explanation to justify their actions. People with yellow traits have sharp mental processing, an intellectual outlook and a logical and cautious approach to life.[326] These people can be sensitive if comfortable with their own lives, but demanding and whining if they are not secure. Sharry feels that these people have a *lawyer's or planner's mentality*.

- **Blue** - These people are caretakers and put others' needs before their own. These people are loving, sensitive and concerned about other's needs. They do not have to be in charge, but are often put in charge because of their high

[325] Ritberger, Carol, PHD. <u>What Color is your Personality?</u> Hay House: Carlsbad, CA., 2000. pgs. 119 - 133.
[326] Ritberger, Carol, PHD. <u>What Color is your Personality?</u> Hay House: Carlsbad, CA., 2000. pgs. 103 - 117.

level of empathy. When their emotions are not under control, questioned or abused, they can experience addictive disorders. The negative side of blue is being temperamental and flying off the handle at little things. They need to know they are appreciated. They manage spiritual resources well, but they tend to give things away. They are skilled at communicating and have an overall love for humanity. They have an ability to put others first with a spiritual or emotional outlook *(possibly a naive perspective)*. Sharry sums this category of people as **spiritual leaders**.

The bars representing frequencies in our nanoVoice print are colored. The colors change with the content of our discussions, because we apply different emotions and mental processes in various situations. The colors indicate which method of processing information we are using and how we will react to situations regarding that topic.

We can apply interpretations of the characteristics of colors to various topics. For example, if we talk about sex, yellow bars in the graph reveal a person whose physical sex includes heavy mental overtones. In contrast, the person's whose nanoVoice print depicts red bars displays spontaneous sexual activity and responses. The color blue appears when a person adds emotions to their physical expressions, while the color green reflects a person who is interested in long-term commitment and planning for the relationship.

Each bar graph also represents a musical note. The chart on page 147 describes the personality traits associated with each note. We can match the characteristics of a musical pitch and color. For example, a voiceprint shows a high, red bar graph of the note C. The musical note C indicates self-power, ego, self-direction, leadership, excitement and physical motivation. The color red reflects a reactive personality. When we combine the influence of the color red and the note of C, we can predict that this person will use their ego or strength to get their way without much thought to the outcome. They will act immediately on establishing what they think is right.

If the same high C is green, we can combine the characteristics of the musical note and the qualities associated with green. This person sees the big picture and uses experience and intuition to manage and accomplish things. They have the necessary qualifications, but avoid management conflicts. With their intense desire to make a difference they can be workaholics, perhaps with little regard for the time commitments of others.

If the extremely high C is yellow, the person may believe they should get their way, as they are most qualified to know what is best. They are initiators and organizers, but tend to believe that they know what is best for everyone, disregarding others' opinions.

If the very high C is blue, this person is likely to be an emotional leader who champions a cause to benefit others. Their approach will be more charismatic than rational.

Multiple colors can be revealed on the voiceprint, revealing a person's multifaceted outlook and approach to that topic.

Although we all experience the entire gamut of emotions, when we have feelings outside of our core personality for an extended time we feel stressed. Emotions push us into doing what is beyond our normal motivation. These challenging times force us to be flexible, which can improve our personality characteristics, or cause emotional and psychological problems.

When our vibratory spectrum lacks certain frequencies there is nothing within our vibratory spectrum to repel challenges. We essentially manifest that which we most need to experience. Every learning experience offers choices in how to proceed; there are always opportunities to climb the frequency scale. Once a lesson is learned, the new equilibrium state no longer invites those types of experiences/lessons.

Spiritual growth is the never-ending expansion of one's energy to encompass deeper and wider aspects of all energetic mastery, to increase the vibrancy and strength of one's being. This involves enriching and expanding one's vibratory spectrum. The richer the spectrum, the closer it moves toward white light, containing all colors, encompassing greater consciousness.

In summary, the voiceprint can be used as a reflective tool to understand ourselves; it can reveal how we process information and emotions in a variety of situations as well as reveal this information about others' behavior.

The nanoVoice makes us more aware of:
- Subconscious feelings - relating to specific topics
- Our methods of processing information *(such as the way a "blue" person would respond to a situation versus a "red" person)*

- Our habitual reactions to people and events
- Understanding other people on a deeper level
- Areas of uncertainty *(the absence of the notes A# and E in our voiceprint give us clues about underlying reservations and fears.)*
- Hemisphere of the brain we are utilizing most

# Chapter Three

# Emotionally Healing Music

Categorizing music as entertainment or a mood setter is a recent development, since the Renaissance period. This is a significant aspect of music. Music subtly massages emotions, or motivates us to dance, march or relax. An effective movie soundtrack enhances the drama and draws in the viewer. A movie would be greatly diminished without it. Music amplifies the actors' and observers' emotions.

Conventional music contains FEs, as does BioAcoustic software. Beyond the widely accepted notion that music affects our emotions is the unacknowledged power of frequencies to shape our health and thinking. Scientists have mathematical models of how rhythm can result in improved motor function.[327] Rhythm "excites, moves and gives order

---

[327] Thaut, Michael. <u>Rhythm, Music and the Brain: Scientific Foundations and Clinical Applications</u>, Routledge: N.Y., 2005, pg. 112.

to our feelings, thoughts and sense of movement."[328] Music improves speech, language and cognitive rehabilitation.[329] The work of G. E. Mueller and Schuman *(1894, but confirmed by recent scientists)* says that, "The metrical organization *(of music)* makes it easier to remember verbal material."[330] Thaut discusses even more benefits."Rhythm may also be one of the central processors to optimize our gestalt formulation in the basic process of learning and perception."[331]

Just as we ingest medicine and supplements for specific physiological benefits, music can be tailored for specific benefits. Music already does this, we are just not conscious of its impact. Emotions, musical notes and physical matter are energies that influence each other through resonance.

We blindly expose ourselves to FEs that impact our healthy thoughts and emotions. Levitin details many physical benefits from simply listening to good music. "Immunoglobulin A (IgA) is an important antibody that is needed for fighting colds, flus, and other infections of the mucous system. Several recent studies show that IgA levels increased following music therapy. In another study, levels of melatonin, norepinephrine, and epinephrine increased during a four-week course of music therapy, and then returned to pretherapy levels after the music therapy ended. Serotonin *(a naturally occurring hormone in the brain)* helps to regulate

---

[328] Thaut, Michael. <u>Rhythm, Music and the Brain: Scientific Foundations and Clinical Applications</u>, Routledge: N.Y., 2005, pg. 59.
[329] Thaut, Michael. <u>Rhythm, Music and the Brain: Scientific Foundations and Clinical Applications</u>, Routledge: N.Y., 2005, pgs. 165 – 202.
[330] Thaut, Michael. <u>Rhythm, Music and the Brain: Scientific Foundations and Clinical Applications</u>, Routledge: N.Y. 2005, pg. 7.
[331] Thaut, Michael. <u>Rhythm, Music and the Brain: Scientific Foundations and Clinical Applications</u>, Routledge: N.Y. 2005, pg. 16.

the body's natural sleep/waking cycle and is effective in treating seasonal affective disorder. It is also putatively linked to the body's immune system because some researchers believe that it increases cytokine production which in turn signals T-cells to travel to the sites of the infection. Both norepinephrine and epinephrine affect alertness and arousal and activate reward centers in the brain. All this from a song."[332]

Many ancient civilizations, such as the ancient Chinese, believed that those who controlled the music controlled the population. They guarded their musical concoctions as a security measure and policed their provinces. Even as late as the Middle Ages the Catholic Church proclaimed musical "do's and don'ts" and restricted chords and scales. Also in this time period kings hired musicians, prescribing music to satisfy their personal tastes.

In recorded history individuals first dictated musical selections during the Renaissance. Musicians could make a living from public performances.

Classical composers created eloquent, emotional and artistic pieces of music. The power of their compositions is evident by their enduring popularity. Research has shown that classical music produces a wide array of benefits. Here are a few examples:

- Listening to Mozart helped patients perform better in sight tests.[333]

---

[332] Levitin, Daniel. The World in Six Songs: How the Musical Brain created Human Nature, Penguin Group: N.Y., 2009. pgs. 98-99.
[333] http://news.bbc.co.uk/2/hi/health/4920658.stm

- Reports document a winemaker exposed his grape plants to classical music, resulting in better wines.[334]
- Music, particularly Mozart, showed a therapeutic effect on epilepsy[335]
- A popular study showed that students, who listened to Mozart prior to tests, scored higher marks in intelligence, as published in *Nature Magazine* in 1993.[336]

Research is accumulating evidence, documenting a multitude of benefits produced by music. Certain music raises attentiveness, focus and concentration. You can feel in charge with confident sounding music and transfer this feeling, temporarily at least, to life. Playing music early in life facilitates the development of neural pathways associated with language, memory and spatial development. Stimulating linguistic rhymes, dances, intricate movements and play in the early years are essential to developing and uniting the emotions, mind and body.

Sound affects us with a myriad of powerful influences. Music holds a bountiful array of FEs with potentially broad effects on our physical, biochemical and emotional selves. We unknowingly immerse ourselves in this energy-altering wave stream without any thought to its impact. Wise people will consider what kind of music they listen to.

Music can aid us in targeted areas. Perhaps music of the future will be consciously composed to:

---

[334] http://www.upi.com/ConsumerHealthDaily/view.php?StoryID=20051013-06014.
[335] http://news.bbc.co.uk/hi/english/health/newsid_1251000/1251839.stm
[336] The study by Rauscher, Shaw and Ky, entitled *"Music and Spatial Task Performance."* (See Campbell, _The Mozart Effect_®, pages 28, 303, 305-306.)

- Transform negative emotions into positive ones
- Stimulate emotional sensitivity
- Enable people to feel emotions that benefit mankind, such as forgiveness, gratitude or compassion
- Encourage heroic acts
- Open our hearts
- Enhance and integrate health
- Vibrate and invigorate our cells
- Create healthy subtle energies
- Develop targeted concrete and subtle energies
- Clarify and sharpen our minds
- Increase awareness

In our modern day, Sharry worked with James Marshall, who wrote a song,[337] named, "Le Ciel," with the frequencies that would kill the swine flu.

I share Sharry's deep desire to diminish negative emotions, while reinforcing positive ones. I do this with music. A girlfriend introduced me to the "flower essences." I was thrilled when the flower essences provided inspiration for emotionally healing music.

Some indigenous tribes of South America used flower essences to enhance their health and emotional states. They believe that the energy of a flower is a gift to mankind through which a person can receive a specific emotional healing energy. One can feel the cheerfulness of a daisy or the beauty of a rose; each flower possesses unique energy.

---

[337] http://shop.babynaynay.com/product.sc?productId=3

Applied properly, the essence of a flower can be transferred to an individual. Indigenous tribes devised an ancient process to capture the essence or energy of a flower. They soaked the flower in purified water during early morning sunlight. The water imprinted the flower's essence.[338] People drink the captured water, taking in the flower's signature energy.

A person ingests the flower essence to receive a desirable emotion that the flower emulates. For example a fearful person drinks rockrose flower water to uplift his fearful energy and to transform it into trust.

A man named Gurdudas describes the flower as the highest concentration of life force in the plant, representing the crowning energy of the plant. The actual flower essence is an electromagnetic pattern, an etheric imprint, or as he said, "the intelligence of the flower."

Dr. Richard Gerber reflects on the flower essences in his book, Vibrational Medicine. The flower essences "utilize the energetic storage properties of water to transfer a frequency-specific, information bearing quantum of subtle energy to the patient in order to effect healing at various levels of human

---

[338] Dr. Jacques Benveniste is a medical doctor who discovered scientific properties of water, which defy explanation by the tenets of mainstream physics. His science, Digital Biology, is based upon two breakthrough observations that he can prove in experiments that have been duplicated by other scientists:

1. If a substance is diluted in water, the water can carry the memory of that substance even after it has been so diluted that none of the molecules of the original substance remain.

2. The molecules of any given substance have a spectrum of frequencies that can be digitally recorded with a computer, then played back into untreated water and the new water acts as if the actual substance were physically present.

http://www.spiritof maat.com/ archive/dec3/ bveniste. htm

functioning."[339] He continued, "Flower remedies are used primarily to balance the mental and emotional energies of the individual which, if unbalanced, will predispose to, as well as exacerbate, the various physical manifestations of illness."[340]

Unlike conventional drugs, which work on the physical level, the frequencies of the flowers rehabilitate emotional, mental and spiritual energies. Improvements in these areas filter down to upgrade one's physical health. With improved emotions a person's resilience to disease is strengthened and internal harmony is increased.[341]

Dr. Edward Bach, a pioneer in flower essence remedies, noted important personality patterns resulting in 12 lifelong paths that people experience. He believed that people could find their essential nature in one of these personality descriptions. Then he identified flowers with the vibratory energy to upgrade these emotions. He called this collection of flowers, "Soul Flowers."

Each personality path is characterized by a challenging emotion. The soul flowers can help people overcome these challenges by raising the energy of a difficult emotion and transforming it into a virtue.[342] Each flower helps a person master a problematic emotion to obtain the corresponding

---

[339] Gerber, Richard, Dr. Vibrational Medicine, The Number One Handbook of Subtle-Energy Therapies, third edition, Bear & Co: Vermont, 2001. pg. 282.
[340] Gerber, Richard, Dr. Vibrational Medicine, The Number One Handbook of Subtle-Energy Therapies, third edition, Bear & Co: Vermont, 2001. pg. 282.
[341] Gurudas. Flower essence and Vibrational Healing, channeled by Kevin Ryerson, Brotherhood of Life: Albuquerque, New Mexico, 1983.
[342] Adapted from: Barnard, Julian. Bach Flower Remedies: Form and Function, Lindisfarne Books: Great Barrington, MA., 2004. pg. 139.

virtue. Bach claimed that our soul advances by perfecting the flower's associated virtue.[343]

Dr. Bach was an extreme sensitive who intuited his selection of healing flowers. Today there is quite a process to match a flower with a specific emotion. Specialists observe flower essence properties including the plant's structure and form, growth pattern, color, chemical properties, herbal uses, as well as energetic properties. These qualities are then correlated with specific human emotions. They test the preliminary indications in clinical settings. This clinical study of the use of essences is called empirical research, or research based on experience. Homeopathic remedies have been successfully verified during the last two centuries.

The soul flowers help overcome these emotional difficulties:

### The Gentian Flower
*Turns doubt into trust*

### The Cerato Flower
*Turns self-doubt into inner-certainty*

### The Clematis Flower
*Avoiding reality to living in the moment*

### The Mimulus Flower
*Turns fear-of-the-world into trust-of-the-world*

### The Impatience Flower
*Turns impatience into patience*

---

[343] Adapted from: Barnard, Julian. <u>Bach Flower Remedies: Form and Function,</u> Lindisfarne Books: Great Barrington, MA., 2004. pg. 139.

**The Vervian Flower**
*Turns inflexibility into broad mindedness*

**The Water Violet Flower**
*Turns isolation into togetherness*

**The Scleranthus flower**
*Turns inner conflict into inner peace*

**The Rock rose flower**
*Turns panic into heroic courage*

**The Centuary flower**
*Turns passive service into active service*

**The Agrimony flower**
*Turns pretend harmony to inner peace*

**The Chicory flower**"[344]
*Turns demanding love to giving love freely*

Bach claimed that people incarnate on earth in "soul groups." People dedicated to the mastery of an essential virtue for humanity comprise one soul group. An individual can contribute to the evolution of our communities, but the soul group can potentially achieve success across the planet. As we transform our individual emotional challenges into virtues, we strengthen these divine essences on earth.[345]

---

[344] Mechthild and Scheffer. Encyclopedia of Bach Flower Remedies, Healing Arts Press: Rochester, Vermont, 2001. Pgs. 44, 58, 62, 76, 81, 95, 120, 128, 152, 172, and 185.

[345] Adapted from: Barnard, Julian. Bach Flower Remedies: Form and Function, Lindsisfarne Books: Great Barrington, MA., 2004. pg. 139.

## Musical Vibrations of Flowers

I composed 12 Healing Flower Symphonies using the frequencies and inspiration of the soul flowers. Each symphony creates energy for the emotional transformation as if the listener just ingested the physical flower essences.

I obtained the FEs of the soul flowers with the help of an advanced practitioner of vibratory medicine. The process included the use of a sound oscilloscope and a special microphone that made a recording. When a flower petal was near the microphone, a graph of a pitch was created on the computer screen. I duplicated this sound and embedded the appropriate flower frequency into each Healing Flower Symphony. In this manner I incorporated the FE for each flower into the Healing Flower Symphonies.[346]

Sharry gives us an illustration of giving a person the vitamin niacin. A skin flushing occurs with the use of niacin supplements. She can provide the FE of niacin to a person and the same nutritional benefit is achieved and the skin flushing will also occur. Likewise, the emotional benefits of the flower remedies can be passed through the FE of the associated flower.

In addition, I utilized my intuition and opened myself to the feelings emitted by each soul flower. When composing music

---

[346] Another method to accomplish this has been used by Dr. Jacques Benveniste. He records a signal from a substance by using a microphone without a membrane, just an electromagnetic coil. He plugs the electronic coil into the female receptacle of the sound card of a computer. Then he puts the molecules in water in a test tube next to the coil. When those millions of molecules vibrate, it's enough for the coil to pick them up. http://www.spiritof maat.com/ archive/dec3/ bveniste. htm

that replicated the feeling of trust, I considered that trust is deeper than a feeling; it is a "knowing," an absolute assurance. Then I envisioned our heartbeat - something that we have heard subtly, but steadily throughout our lives - something that we took comfort from our mother's heartbeat in the womb. This sound is reminiscent of the feeling of trust. After taping the sounds of a heartbeat, I composed a symphony around this reassuring beat. Then I immersed myself in the feeling of trust and let the musical composition flow from me. The final symphony contains the FE recorded from the particular flower being captured, together with the original composition expressing the emotions of the flower.

Each flower essence supports the transformation of a negative emotion into the mastery of it. Initially it seemed counterintuitive to musically create the negative emotion that each soul flower was to remedy. Later, I observed people who repeatedly listened to melancholy and sad music, and then watched them discard negative emotional baggage which then opened them up to positive feelings. This idea was anything but flawed.

I gained this important insight about emotional transformations as I played violin for elderly people in a supported living home over the course of a year. When they listened to the music, it received their full attention as nothing else competed for their focus. Their complete attention made the music more potent.

I watched patients who appeared frozen sit in cradled positions with never a glance or word to anyone else. Two months into my visits a gentleman fell flat on his face on the floor. Anxiously I ran to help him and noticed that no one else even glanced his way. After playing violin for three months the residents had not spoken a word to me. No one so much as glanced at me or anyone else.

This group was able to speak, but chose not to. I wondered why all the people had retreated so deeply. I reflected that after years of pain people are hesitant to be vulnerable and ope, lest they get hurt again. Invisible yet insidious pain, gathered after years of life's trials, weighed them down and eventually creating stagnation in their emotional bodies. They were spending their final years in a nursing home, where their isolation grew.

After about four months of performing a small change began to occur – a few talked to me. At first, I attributed this to them warming up to me. Interestingly, several months later they started talking to one another. Soon they regularly engaged in social chatting. Now I was certain; the music played a vital role in their healthy emotional improvement. The music stirred old pain, bringing it to the surface. It enabled them to reconnect with feelings that they had long ignored, leading to an emotional catharsis. They loosened the grip of the pain and let it go. Releasing this storehouse of dark energy allowed them to reach out and include others in their lives. It was amazing that when they were exposed regularly to emotional, live music that it had such a significant impact on their behavior.

The right brain hemisphere processes music without words. The right hemisphere also processes patterns, context, creativity, spatial awareness, and recognizes faces, places and objects. The left brain hemisphere handles speech, analysis, time and things in sequence. It recognizes letters, numbers and words.

Listening to violin music triggers right brain hemisphere usage. This gives people access to their emotions, while bypassing painful memories as it does not process identifying information. The residents experienced sad emotions expressed through a violin solo, without remembering who hurt them. Just feeling the sorrowful emotion over and over again was enough to gradually release it.

I questioned if music could increase the intensity of a difficult emotion. I concluded that the answer depends upon one's intentions. To illustrate how our feelings follow our direction, imagine walking into a room in which someone is:

• Furious with you
• Angry with a stranger
• Angry at himself

In all cases you can feel anger, but you can also feel where it is directed. One can target an emotion to a certain person and this carries on sound. Can you not tell the difference between a "hello" when a person is angry or happy with you?

People report incredible healings, especially regarding releases of negative emotions after listening to the Healing Flower Symphonies. Here are two examples:

• I had an extraordinary healing episode as a result of listening to *The Healing Flowers Symphony* CD. The music touched an annoying fear that I have held for many years. As a highly analytical person I have been very consciously aware of this fear, yet I had also been keenly aware that it had no logical basis. But I have never attempted to deal with it. I have treated it like a thorn in my side, which I was destined to carry. After listening, this perennial fear simply dissipated as if it had been dissolved by the music. I know it was the music that was responsible *(the "self-healing" aspect notwithstanding)* because of the extreme resonance that occurred between that fear sensation and specific sections of the song. I was left with a sensation of extreme well being that manifested emotionally as a quiet effortless peace that had displaced the fear and seemed to seep into my whole being, and mentally as a picture of Mother Earth coddling me in her arms as if I were a small child being rocked to sleep. It was an extraordinary experience." *Keith David Henry Theoretical Metaphisicist*

- "I was afflicted with a bad cold. That evening I could not sleep and no medicine was working. I played the Healing Flower Symphonies and shortly everything that was blocking my respiratory system, throat and digestive system removed itself from my body. I had an immediate full recovery. The next day I talked on my radio show with a regular voice and energy. Jill's music is truly powerful, and is on the cutting edge of a rediscovery of ancient remedies that heal the body, mind and spirit." *Gary Purifory, Co-Owner of CLN Radio*

In my experience at the nursing home, I intended for people to release painful emotions when I played violin. I doubt they considered anything other than fleeting feelings and thoughts generated by the music. In a year's time everyone appeared to socially improve. My intention to enable them to shed emotional baggage is clearly effective. I noticed that people who were not ready to acknowledge their own negative emotional habits, let alone release them, found the releasing portions of this music disturbing. Those who did not have a the associated negative emotion experienced no difficulties listening. For example, a patient person easily listened to the impatient music, while an impatient person did not.

Negative feelings do not disappear by pretending that we do not have them, just like we do not get rid of a bad habit by ignoring it. To eliminate a bad habit, we acknowledge it and choose a better behavior. Likewise, after we feel and let go of negative emotions, then we can practice and strengthen healthier feelings.

With this experience in mind, I feel it is just as important to release negative emotions as it is to build positive ones. Some people are so full of pain, there is little room or desire to incorporate positive feelings.

Daniel Levitin describes a positive biological response to sad music, "When we are sad, many of us turn to sad music. Why would that be? On the surface of things, you might expect that sad people would be uplifted by happy music. But that is not what research shows. Prolactin, a tranquilizing hormone, is released when we're sad. Sorrow does have a physiological purpose and it may be an adaptive response, which is to help us conserve energy and reorient our priorities for the future after a traumatic event. Prolactin is also released after orgasm, after birth, and during lactation in females. A chemical analysis of tears reveals that Prolactin is not always present in tears – it is not released in tears of lubrication of the eye, or when the eye is irritated, or in tears of joy: it is only released in tears of sorrow. David Huron suggests that sad music 'tricks' our brain into releasing Prolactin into the safe or imaginary sorrow induced by music and the Prolactin then turns around our mood."[347]

Each flower's essence deals with the yin and yang of life's conflicts. I start each symphony immersed in the negative emotional qualities of the corresponding flower. The Healing Flower Symphonies musically weave in and out of painful emotions such as fear, distrust and insecurity. The music transports the listener to an emotional space that corresponds to negative feelings they have stored subconsciously. To receive the benefits, the listener must not ignore feelings, but relive them and then let them go. As the emotion leaves the listener, he will feel it as it passes out of his body. There are no short cuts to releasing pain. These flower symphonies are not intended for "pansies!"

After the emotional catharsis the flower symphony evolves into triumph, giving the listener a transforming experience of the flower's corresponding positive virtue.

For example, one flower's energy addresses the "pleaser" personality, one who is always nice, but not sincere. This person readily approves of others to appear pleasant or to avoid conflict. Their true feelings are hidden and an unhealthy emotional pattern persists.

---

[347] Levitin, Daniel. The World in Six Songs: How the Musical Brain Created Human Nature, Penguin Group: N.Y., 2009, pgs. 132 -133.

Each note of this flower symphony begins in tune, but in a fraction of a second it bends out of tune. This happens so quickly that the listener is not aware of the intonation problem, but the sour after-vibration leaves an unsettling feeling. The music creates a pretending to be nice feeling, just like the person with a pleaser personality.

The intonation problem is only noticeable when this section of the music is contrasted with the remainder of the symphony that is pure and in-tune for the entire length of the notes. The melody transitions into deep, calm and pure harmony *(sounds like harmony but isn't)*. The contrast between pretentious harmony and the real thing is obvious. In this way, listeners can:

- Be conscious of their feeling of wanting to please
- Realize how much better it feels to be sincere than agree with everyone and everything
- Honor their own beliefs

The music of the flowers enables us to practice good attributes, such as peace or patience. Repeatedly feeling the emotions associated with a desirable attribute makes this pattern permanent. When we feel a certain emotion, people near us feel it too and associate that emotion with us. For example, a person who is often in a peaceful state is described as peaceful. The mastery of a difficult emotion creates a virtue!

Plato *(428-347 BC)* noted that music evoked admirable emotions of virtue, courage and restraint.[348]

---

[348] Ferguson, Kitty. The Music of Pythagoras, Walker and Co: N.Y., 2008.

To sum up, we can harness energy created by music to help us in many ways. The Healing Flower Symphonies are an example of music crafted to achieve a specific benefit.

Appendix A describes the Healing Flower Symphonies in more detail.

Listen to the Healing Flower Symphonies at www.jillswingsoflight.com. A free mp-3 sample of these symphonies is also available at www.jillshealingmusic.com.

# Chapter Four

# Toning

*Toning* is the use of the natural voice of the human body. We use it every day. We also tone when we groan, sigh, cry, moan, laugh, say "ahhh" or "ouch."

The karate master cries out as he strikes. The weight lifter grunts as he lifts. Why? Because the spontaneous release of natural tones multiples and focuses his energy and power. Self created tones affect us from the inside out!

"Ouch!" Why do we do scream in pain? Sound instinctually releases pain from our bodies, but we forget to credit sound.

Natural tones, such as grunts, groans, moans, screams, laughs, yawns and sighs balance our voice and internal sonic wave pool. Sounds such as "mmm" and "ahhh" harmonize and balance harmful, stressed frequencies. Without our conscious direction we produce spontaneous sounds and effectively improve internal harmony. Sharry recommends toning these sounds to decrease headaches, sinus pain and ear/nose/throat infections.

Ancient mystic groups chanted the names of god, carefully crafted with rich vowel sounds. Each vowel sound creates emphasis and abundance of various harmonics. Health issues occur when certain harmonic patterns within our bodies are distorted and diminished. People believed the names of gods connected them to divine energies, but these sounds also restored harmonic structures within their minds, bodies and emotions.

Valerie Hunt, Ph.D., [349] who has degrees in biology, physiological psychology, science education and physical therapy, reflects, "At a young age we begin the process of repressing natural sounds and thus begins our journey of learning to be vehicles of storage, rather than what we are naturally meant to be, which are vehicles of expression. Toning helps us to express again - by using these natural sounds to release pent-up or blocked energy and re-establish a

---

[349] Valerie Hunt established in the 1950s neuromuscular patterns of anxiety and anger at a time when the only physiological research of emotions was chemical and behavioral. In the 1960s she added to The Field, The Quest for the Secret Force of the Universe, the Quest for the Secret Force of the Universe of behavior psychology with her discovery of neuromuscular nerve stimulation patterns related to nonverbal communication, In the 1970's she developed a high frequency device, AuraMeter, to record electrical energy from the human's body surface. Trivieri, Larry, Jr. Health on the Edge, Penguin Group: N.Y., 2003. pg. 185.

natural flow of energy. This leaves the physical body feeling peaceful and cleansed."[350]

In Part Two Technical Details, we discussed how the voice frequencies in the electromagnetic wave range are distributed in the predictive and in the warning stages. Slower vibratory cycles of sound have not solidified into a physical problem in our body, yet. They are still pliable, easily molded and harmonized. Toning enables us to balance these tones before they become problematic.

Hunt observed that when the body's electromagnetic pattern is disturbed, disease and malfunction develop.[351] A flexible range of electromagnetic energy creates health. She reports that people need a large quantity of energy in the various electromagnetic energy bands. She refers to this quantity of energy as "power." People with "power" in the lower ranges will be physically active and have a dynamic life. Lower frequencies keep the cells and organs working together. Power in the middle ranges of this spectrum enables people to handle intellectual issues and gives them problem-solving abilities. Power in the upper ranges enables people to go into higher ranges of consciousness and utilize wisdom and conceptual thinking. The ideal is to have the full range of electromagnetic frequencies.[352] Toning gives us power in all of these frequency ranges.

Hunt measures people's energy in the electromagnetic spectrum. People with cancer suppress their emotions, staying in what they perceive to be positive emotions. They do not

---

[350] http://www.toning.org/toning.html
[351] Trivieri, Larry, Jr. Health on the Edge, Penguin Group: N.Y., 2003. pg. 187.
[352] Trivieri, Larry, Jr. Health on the Edge, Penguin Group: N.Y., 2003. pg. 192.

have a full spectrum of electromagnetic energy, going from low to high frequencies. Hunt generally describes cancer patients, "They are sweet, lovable people. That is their emotional orientation. They aren't aggressive, and they don't have the lower frequencies that have to do with tissue vitality. Without tissue vitality, the cell becomes cancerous. But the difficulty is that some of these people would rather die than give into the very intense, angry, and hostile emotions that they have."[353] Toning enables us to reach all frequency levels, empowering ourselves on many levels: spiritual, physical, mental and emotional. Free flowing energy is essential to good health and positive well-being.

Toning is an ancient, sound healing practice. Sharry has long employed a form of this technique. We may not have her special abilities to voice sine waves, but toning creates sounds to heal and soothe others and ourselves. At the end of this section a brief description of how to tone is provided - so you can practice healing with your voice too!

The frequencies of feelings combine with sounds. Our subconscious feelings are part of our spoken words. The quality of our tone communicates our underlying intent and the feelings beneath our words. For example, the "hello" we say to someone we love is different than the "hello" we say to someone we do not like. Our emotional communication is clearly included in our tone of voice, speaking louder than our words.

When we consciously censor our spoken words, these censored ideas remain in our tone of voice. We may not even be aware of these subtle underlying feelings, but some sense

[353] Trivieri, Larry, Jr. Health on the Edge, Penguin Group: N.Y., 2003. pg. 186.

them. Animals can become adept at reading our tones and seem to understand the words we are speaking.

We often suppress voicing our deep feelings. Many times we do not speak our truth, as we are taught to be polite or kind instead. Sometimes the truth is painful or we do not want to acknowledge that we are angry. Those who suppress negative feelings are deemed polite and kind. Let's look at an example of the habitual white lie. How often do we tell people we feel fine, when we are not? Or "nothing is new," when we do not want to share something new? Or that we like something, when we do not?

Sometimes we forget what our truth is, because we have hidden it in our subconscious minds. Sound carries our hidden feelings back to us. Our tone of voice is a communication link to our subconscious mind.[354]

When our feelings and words are not in alignment, we create dissonance in our bodies. In contrast, speaking our truth sets us free.

## Toning for Health

Toning *(a glissando sound)* creates all FEs that our voice can produce. It bathes us in the full gamut of enriching sounds. This gives our brain a fertile frequency bank to select from and eventually duplicate needed frequencies.

When we cannot keep our thoughts and moods positive, sound can reestablish coherent frequencies in our bodies, refresh our energies and improve our health. Toning clears

---

[354] Dewhurst Madock, Olivea. The Book of Sound Therapy, Simon and Schuster: 1993.

stuck negative energies, repressed thoughts and buried feelings. Sound can restore the body's natural resonance. Toning gives us an entire body tune-up!

Laurel Keyes writes that, "The purpose of toning is to restore the vibratory pattern of the body to its perfect electromagnetic field, so that it will function in harmony with itself."[355]

Laurel Keyes writes about a small group of people who toned vowel sounds while imagining the tone going through another's body. Laurel reports tumors healed, cancers cured and other marvelous effects from this technique.[356]

When we tone, we sing vowel sounds while changing our pitch. Vowel sounds carry our feelings, especially the ones we hide from ourselves. Vowel sounds such as "ooooooh" and "aaaaaaaah" are emotionally expressive and good to use when toning. In contrast, consonants help us express thoughts.

### Toning for Others

1. Face another individual or imagine him across from you.
2. Close your eyes.
3. Relax, keep your teeth apart and muscles loose.
4. Tune into your own feelings and put your thoughts aside.
5. Set your intentions. Expect to clear energy blockages in the other person. *(Placebos are often effective because a positive belief is a powerful energy. It is important that you believe you can heal another - intention is critical.)*

---

[355] Keyes, Laurel Elizabeth. The Creative Power of the Voice. De Vorss Publishers: CA., 1973.
[356] Keyes, Laurel Elizabeth. The Creative Power of the Voice, .De Vorss Publishers: CA., 1973.

6. Pretend the tone starts below the other person's feet and passes up into his feet, legs and traveling through his body, moving towards his head.

7. Utter the lowest pitch of any vowel sound that you can. Utter a sound such as "ooooooooohhhh" and then VERY SLOWLY let the tone smoothly rise in pitch. Keep singing the vowel sound as long as you comfortably can. Take a breath whenever necessary and resume on the same pitch that you left off at. Only let the pitch rise when it easily and effortlessly rises up. If you push, even a little to raise your voice, then go down to a lower pitch and remain there until the pitch rises, as if it did so on its own.

8. Listen carefully to your sound as it slowly rises. There will be cracks in the sound and places where the sound is uneven, softer or weaker. When this occurs, stay on this pitch, and then repeat sliding just above and just below the pitch until your voice is smooth and strong.

9. A cracking pitch corresponds to a place in the other person's body where an energy blockage is occurring. If you are unsure of where this spot is, do not worry; just correct the cracking in the tone and the energy blockage will clear.

10. If you feel in your imagination that the tone goes right or left, as well as up or down, honor that feeling. If you cannot imagine this, have faith that the negative energy is clearing.

11. After you reach the top of the head, extend the toning up for about three feet and then allow your tone to slowly decrease in pitch. Imagine the tone coming down through the person's body.

12. Use your imagination and see your tone run through the person's body from top to bottom, bottom to top, and again as necessary until you get a smooth, strong siren tone without any cracking or soft spots. Go up and down until your voice smoothly and easily glides up and down.

13. Laurel Keyes reports that she tones on average for 15 minutes per person. If someone is seriously ill, Laurel tones with others and for longer time periods. She may continue toning every day for several weeks.

14. Toning increases in power when more people tone - to aid the same person at the same time.

15. Feel gratitude for being able to raise the energy in another person's body.

## Toning for Yourself

1. Close your eyes and imagine that your body is a black ink well. As you utter tones visualize clear water coming into the ink well with each breath, until you and the ink well are pristine clear.

2. Let out a vowel sound *(any one you feel comfortable with)* or even groan on the lowest pitch that you can. For example, you could utter the vowel sound, "aaaaaahhhh."

3. Let your body speak, not your mind. Do not worry about how you sound, but concentrate on how the sound makes your body feel. Be entirely absorbed in your sound and let it rise from within you, as if this sound is separate from you. You are just observing the sound.

4. Imagine the tone begins below your feet and works its way up the body until it reaches the top of your head, and then above your head three feet. This could take 15 minutes to 30 minutes or more. The first time that you tone, it may take longer to clear built-up energy blockages. Tone daily for increased improvements.[357]

5. As you imagine your tone going from your feet to your head, the pitch of your tone will also rise. Allow the tone to rise in pitch when the body wants it to. The pitch will glide

---

[357] Health is not a black and white issue. There are many degrees of sickness and health. Your health can get better and better!

up effortlessly when it is ready. Never push to raise your voice.

6. Any area in which the pitch takes a while to rise, or where your voice cracks or skips tones, is an area with an energy blockage. Do not get louder to break through the energy blockage: that only produces a quick fix. Gently continue toning and give your voice all the time it needs to raise in pitch. If you stay on a pitch for 5 to 10 minutes or more, then you are receiving a great healing!

7. If your voice doesn't rise right away, imagine seeing your tone going right or left in your body and finding a path eventually that leads upward. Honor the path the tone wants to take.

8. Direct feelings of harmony and well-being to the spot where you imagine the blockage to be. Imagine pure and beautiful light filling this area. Believe that you are healing. Love your body.

9. Once you tone above your head, then reverse directions and let your voice slide down while you are singing the vowel sound. Imagine the sound going down your body and up again until your voice is crystal clear and smooth.

10. If you do this regularly, you will feel energized, refreshed and healthier. Watch negative emotions melt from your thinking!

The first time I toned, I unknowably had an energy blockage at the bottom of my feet, as I was not grounded. I assumed that toning did not work, because I toned for ten minutes without my voice rising and easily sliding up on its own. After the tone worked through the blockage at my feet, my voice slowly climbed.

While you tone, notice which sounds you like best. Are there sounds that make you smile, relax, breathe easier and you simply enjoy? These frequencies will produce a vibrating sensation and perhaps reduce the pain of a headache, sinus, ear or throat pain. Continue to tone these sounds. This is your body's way of saying that it needs these frequencies. Ideally, hum them until they no longer appeal to you.

Which vowel sounds do you prefer? Remember that a tone carries with it a spectrum of more or less audible harmonics. The peculiar sounds a clarinet produces resonate only with only odd numbered harmonics. The flute's pure sound concentrates its energy in the root note. In contrast, the soft sounds of the French horn create a weak fundamental and a strong second harmonic. Likewise, each vowel creates different harmonics.

Joscelyn Godwin emphasizes just how much the energy of a pitch lies in a harmonic and relates that, "Dayton Miller found that the resonance of the vowels ma, maw, mow, and moo amplify a single harmonic as much as 90 percent of the total energy of the sound."[358]

Recall that Sharry has documented harmonic series within the body. Faults in the harmonic series are paralleled with health issues. The vowel sounds that you enjoy the most will be the ones that your body prefers to strengthen internal harmonic series.

I experimented with toning when I had a headache, following Sharry's method. I cannot make the special sounds that she

---

[358] Godwin, Joscelyn. The Mystery of the Seven Vowels: In Theory and Practice, Phanes Press: MI., 1991. pg. 13.

does, but I allowed my voice to slide up and down. Amazingly, I found one tone that accentuated the pain of my headache. It was a painful discovery, but it was a discovery nonetheless. After finding this tone I continued to allow my voice to slide around and I found another tone *(about six musical notes away)* that got rid of the headache. I also noted that humming seemed to send tones into the head region more so than singing a tone did.

I used the nanoVoice reports to strengthen my toning. I toned during my nanoVoice recording and my voice slid in and out of every pitch in my voice range. The notes that I got stuck on when I toned were the weak or overabundance tones *(or the reciprocals)* documented in my voiceprint. It was as if my voice needed more of the frequency that it stayed on or got "stuck" on for any length of time. I continued to sing the missing notes. I felt more energized and less tempted to slip in to a "down" feeling when I toned a missing frequency.

Toning also had an immediate effect on the predictive frequencies within my voice, providing improved coherence. Repeated toning corrected frequency patterns in the acute range of frequencies, but I have yet to budge the chronic voice coherence imbalances after many toning sessions.

I suspected that my weak tones were due to harmonic faults. I continued with experimentation. As a singer, I know several techniques to produce fuller harmonics in the voice, as this produces a warmer, thicker and richer sound. One way is to stand straight and concentrate on the sound reverberating within your spine. This makes your tones fuller and richer, as it strengthens the harmonics in your voice. The second method to enhance harmonics is not only breathing deeply, but to let your belly feel as if it was so relaxed that it was falling on the floor. The third technique is to pull back the skin on your forehead, as if you were raising your eyebrows. These singing techniques can be employed at the same time as toning and amplify the positive effects of toning. Employing these exercises improved the rate at which my voice gained coherence.

# Chapter Five

# **The Sounds of Silence**

Many people feel uncomfortable with silence. We live our lives surrounded by lawnmowers, traffic, TVs, sirens, mp3 players and horns. We hear little silence let alone subtleties of sound that are only apparent during silence.

Many find comfort with constant noise. The TV endlessly talks to them. Do we escape silence to avoid feeling alone or vulnerable? Do we not want to be alone with our feelings and innermost thoughts?

Spiritual leaders have long revered silence.

- "Silence is the altar of God."[359]
- "Be still and know that I am God."[360]

---

[359] Paramahansa Yogananda
[360] Old Testament, Bible.

- "When we go into the inner chamber and shut the door to every sound that comes from life without, then the voice of God will speak to our soul, and we will know the key note of our life." [361]
- " My Soul counseled me and charged me to listen for voices that rise neither from the tongue nor the throat,
  Before that day I heard but dully, and naught save clamor and loud cries came to my ears,
  But now I have learned to listen to silence,
  To hear its choirs singing the songs of ages,
  Chanting the hymns of space, and disclosing the secrets of eternity."[362]

We may not be able to hear otoacoustic emissions as Sharry does, but there are beneficial sounds that we can focus on.

Focused inner listening amplifies the sounds of our heart, circulatory and respiratory systems and our subtle chorus of inner sounds. The ability to perceive these subtle inner sounds and receive associated benefits can be developed.

Mystics profess that as one journeys towards enlightenment, a series of subtle, internal sounds may be heard in quiet meditation.

People have professed to hear the:
- Pounding of the surf of the sea
- Humming of bees
- Tinkling of soft bells
- Ringing of soft bells

---

[361] Hazrat Inayat Kan. <u>Music of Life</u>, Omega Publishing: New Lebanon, N.Y., 1983.
[362] Kahlil Gibran

- Chirping of crickets
- Babbling water of a brook
- Rumbling of thunder
- Roaring of a lion
- Blowing of a conch shell
- Gong of a big drum
- Strings of a harp
- Tone of a flute
- Sound of bag pipes
- Absence of all sound[363]

The Bible also refers to this inner hearing: "And I heard the voice from heaven. Like the sound of many waters, like the sound of loud thunder, the voice I heard was like the sounds of harpers playing on their harps."[364]

The Rosicrucians, a mystic group, believed the famed "music of the spheres" that Pythagoras and many other historical giants wrote about corresponded to the frequency-equivalents of the human spine. They measured and weighed each vertebra of the human spine, discovering that the ratio of weight between each vertebra was the same as the ratio between the notes of the chromatic scale. The weights of the vertebra corresponded to the harmonic series. They believed that when both hemispheres of the brain were synchronized or in harmony that a vibration was created in the spine and heard inside the head, creating the "Music of the Spheres."[365]

[363] Van Dyke, Deborah. Traveling the Sacred Sound Current, Sound Current Music: Bowan Island, B.C. Canada, 2001, pg. 147.
[364] Bible. Revelations 14:2.
[365] LaVoie, Nichole. Return to Harmony: Creating Harmony and Balance through the Frequencies of Sound, Sound Wave Energy Press: Pagosa Springs, Co., 1996. pgs. 87 - 88.

Many sages credit the proper use of sound with great wisdom. It offers profound spiritual growth and puts pilgrims on the spiritual fast-track. Below are quotes from a variety of spiritual disciplines, reflecting on the power of sound and our hearing abilities.

- Origen[366] described hearing as a "readiness of the soul towards God."
- "True inner hearing has not been perfected until one can hear the sounds in a seed, in a leaf... When one unites with the 'archetone,' giving life to all forms, he unites with the cosmic music of the universe. Finally, one unites with the tone of his own direct star from whence he came."[367]
- "Upon the wings of sound, the way of higher evolution is traveled."[368]
- "At first only the light works, but when one goes deeper into creation there is sound. When one is face to face with spirit, what is first expressed is the light or what one first responds to is light; and what one responds to next, and what touches one deeper, is sound."[369]
- "While information and knowledge, the fruits of pursuing the light, provide relative peace and spiritual progress, they pale in comparison to the higher God attributes of truth, love, wisdom and freedom and power which the

[366] According to some sources, Origen *(C185-351)* was a key figure in the First Council of Nicaea, disagreeing with the emperor, Constantine.
[367] Colton, Ann Ree. The Archetypal Kingdom quoted from Van Dyke, Deborah. Traveling the Sacred Sound Current, Sound Current Music: Bowan Island, B.C. Canada, 2001. pg. 144.
[368] Tibetan Master Djwhal Khul *(in works by Alice Bailey)*
[369] Khan, Inayat, Hazrat. The Music of Life, Omega Publishing: New Lebanon, N.Y.. 1983. pg.. 45.

awakened Sound Current imbued within the sincere seeker of truth… These attributes are enlivened by bathing in the audible Life Stream."[370]

- "Sound is a tremendous occult *(meaning hidden)* power. It is such a stupendous force that the electricity generated by a million Niagara Falls could never counteract even the smallest potentiality of sound when directed by proper knowledge."[371]

- "For there is nothing in this world that can help one spiritually more than music. Meditation prepares, but music is the highest for touching perfection."[372]

- "Since the difference between one dimension and another is its rate of vibration, the key to the transformation of the spirit lies within the music." [373]

- "It is not a fairy tale that the saints used to speak with the trees and plants. You can speak with them today if you are in communication. Man has the same privilege today, if he realizes that he is privileged."[374]

- "There is a time to rend and a time to sew, a time to keep silence and a time to speak."[375]

- Pythagoras and Plato said that the nature of the soul is sound.

- "The person who has found the keynote of his own voice has found the key of his own life."[376]

---

[370] Sikh Guru Nanak

[371] Blavatsky,Helena. The Secret Doctrine.

[372] Khan, Inayat, Hazrat. The Music of Life, Omega Publishing: New Lebanon, N.Y., 1983. pg. 140.

[373] Pritchard, Evan. The Temple Within, from Van Dyke, Deborah. Traveling the Sacred Sound Current, Sound Current Music: Bowan Island, B.C. Canada, 2001.

[374] Khan, Inayat, Hazrat. The Music of Life, Omega Publishing: New Lebanon, N.Y., 1983. pg. 44.

[375] Ecclesiastes 3:,. Bible.

[376] Khan, Inayat, Hazrat. The Music of Life, Omega Publishing: New Lebanon, N.Y., 1983. pg. 275.

The science pioneered by Sharry Edwards points to sound as the premiere vehicle to receive emotional and physical improvements. In parting Sharry describes a method for listening to inner subtle sounds, our signature sounds. Other words that mystics substitute for signature sounds could be aura, prana or chi. Some religions refer to this sound as the Holy Spirit, the Original Sound and a group called the Ecks associates this sound with God.

To hear our signature sounds, focus attention on a sound that is nearby. Next, adjust your hearing to listen to a sound that is far away. Continue changing your listening focus, going back and forth. This eventually creates a high pitched sound, similar to a ringing sound in our ears. This is our personal sound. This sound feeds our bodies and energies, improving the coherence of our voice.

Another way to access your signature sounds is to plug your ears and then listen carefully to subtle internal sounds. Find whatever means works best to block out extraneous sounds, such as using earplugs or placing a pillow over the ears. All that matters is that outside sound is effectively blocked out and that you are comfortable and able to concentrate.

Alternatively, you can imagine that each sound you hear can be locked away in an imaginary bag that completely muffles the sound. One by one put the sound of traffic, the refrigerator, the airplane flying overhead and so on into the sound tight bag. Let all these sounds go and then listen for the sound that comes from within.

When we screen out distractions we amplify our subtle inner sounds. In contrast, when we ignore these subtleties, they fade into the background and seem to disappear altogether. To benefit from this gift, we must give it our deepest attention. We are a part of the miracle!

Many sit quietly in meditation for quite some time before they perceive these subtle sounds. As they focus on slight sounds, they hear their nervous or circulatory systems, heartbeat or other internal sounds.

Tinnitus is not a common condition. Tinnitus usually results from inner ear damage. The little "sounds of silence" could be confused with tinnitus. With tinnitus someone hears the same pitch, volume and quality of sound all the time. You can amplify these subtle sounds at will simply by focusing on them. These sounds change depending on the time of day, how you feel and with your state of consciousness.

While in a meditative state, pretend to hear tiny sounds. Trust your imagination to amplify extremely soft, subtle and high-pitched sounds. Internal sounds may be mechanical sounding, like a ringing in your ears, the white noise on TV or it could sound like nature…such as the ocean, crickets or rain. As you focus on internal sounds they become louder. Close your eyes and move into the sounds with your feelings. Allow sound to come around you, like a cloak.

At first listen you may hear one sound, but with additional concentration you may hear that the tone is comprised of a multitude of softer and shorter frequencies. Just like a white light can be divided into a rainbow of frequencies, internal sounds can be divided into component pitches and patterns.

Can you separate the sounds coming from each ear? By focusing your attention on one ear the sound will increase in that ear. You can now pan the sounds back and forth between your ears. After I do this several times I focus the sounds in the center of my head. Internal sounds are now like surround sound. I imagine these sounds to be filled with light and expanding to encompass my entire head and the area around it. I imagine I have a halo of sweet sounds.

Over time these subtle sounds morph. What begins sounding like a cricket may end up ten minutes later resembling the sound of the ocean. I went through many months that I only heard crickets and then suddenly my internal sounds were similar to the howling of the wind.

It was fascinating to play with these sounds. If I heard a dominant sound, I chanted along with it, increasing the volume of my inner hearing. Singing an octave below the pitch grounded me, giving me a feeling of solidity and power. Humming the octave above appeared to increase my intuition and connection to spirit. Toning, while focusing on these inner sounds, seemed to bring me into balance.

I focus on my signature sounds in quiet moments, but I can also hear them while shopping or doing the dishes. When I focus on these sounds it is as if I twisted the volume button and pumped up the sounds.

Various traditions in antiquity, suggest that chanting the phrase, "I am that I am," prepares one to hear the sounds of silence. The actual sound of this phrase varied from language to language, but each included long vowel sounds that resonated subtle feelings within our being. The audible resonance and the internal feelings of being one with our creator combine to raise our overall vibrations so we can to better hear the sound of silence. According to experts on mantras, Brian and Ester Crowley, participating in sacred sound improves our intuition, consciousness and inner hearing.[377]

The actual sounds of many ancient languages were considered potent and are still used for spiritual purposes, from Sanskrit mantras to Latin masses. Correct pronunciation and our internal feelings of "tuning in" to God are said to free the mind, give the body vitalizing energy, release healing forces from within and improve our ability to hear the sounds of silence.

## Chanting I Am That I Am[378]

|  | *Egyptian* | *Sanskrit* | *Hebrew* |
|---|---|---|---|
| ***Phrase*** | *Nuk-Pu-Nuk* | *Tat- Twam Asi* | *Ehyeh Asher Ehyeh* |
| ***Interpretation*** | I Am He I Am | That and this are One | I Am that I Am |
| ***Pronunciation*** | N'uhk P'oo N'uhk | That Th-wam Ah-see | Ay-yeh Ah-shehr Ay-yeh |

---

[377] Crowley, Brian and Ester. Words of Power: Sacred Sounds of East and West, Llewellyn Publications, Minn.1991. Preface.

[378] Crowley, Brian and Esther. Words of Power: Sacred Sounds of East and West, Llewellyn Publications, Minn., 1991. pgs. 300 -301.

## Meditating to Hear the "Sounds of Silence"

People may have to increase their meditation skills to be able to listen to silence for a half-hour before they hear their subtle sounds or they may hear them immediately. If you are not familiar with meditation techniques, here are ideas to still your mind long enough to hear these subtle sounds. Not one method of meditating is better than the other, but people have decided preferences for one or another method.

Focusing on a single image in your mind's eye can produce a meditative stillness. For example, think of a rose and time how long you can keep this image without something else popping into your mind. Typically people can keep their mind steady for about ten seconds. Focus on only one feeling, such as peace, and extend this for as long as you can. Another meditation technique is to stare at a candle flame and concentrate only on what you see.

When a distracting thought enters your mind, pinpoint where the intruding thought is in your head. For example, the thought came from one inch above your right ear and about two inches inside the skull. Imagine a ghostly hand coming from above your head and plucking the thought from where it came …one inch above your right ear and two inches deep…and this imaginary hand throws the distracting thought away. When another interrupting thought enters your head, repeat the same process. After you do this four or five times you enter stillness, without distracting thoughts.

If none of these techniques are successful, try a guided meditation, in which someone speaks to you and simply follow along. After mastering this, proceed to other meditation techniques.

Focusing on the sounds that we hear internally produces a theta brainwave state.[379] In the book, <u>Beyond Biofeedback</u>, we learn benefits of experiencing theta brain waves. "Those who produce many theta brain waves are highly creative, less rigid and conforming, and healthy. They also experience life altering insights, improved relationships as well as greater tolerance, understanding and love of one's self and world."[380]While in the theta brain wave state our intentions and spoken words are more powerful. The theta state corresponds to feelings that resonate with this idea: "I am in perfect harmony."

Listening to "sounds of silence" triggers theta brain waves. Researchers link theta and delta brain waves to our body's production of chemicals, such as beta-endorphins, vasopressin, acetylcholine, catecholamines, DHEA, melatonin, serotonin and the reduction of cortisol. Below are some benefits from these neuro-chemicals:

- Acetylcholine[381] is linked to memory[382] and intelligence.[383]
- Endorphins improve mental focus[384] and create a sensation of pleasure.
- Vasopressin increases memory and stimulates the release of endorphins.[385]

---

[379]Trivieri, Larry Jr. <u>Health on the Edge,</u> Penguin: N.Y., 2003. pg. 230.

[380]Green, Elmer and Alyce. <u>Beyond Biofeedback,</u> Delacourt: New York, 1977.
"Research Behind Acoustic Brain Entrainment," pg. 7. www.neuroacoustic.org

[381] U.C. Berkeley researcher Rosenzweig

[382] Studies by a research team at the Veterans Administrations Hospital in Palo Alto, and studies at MIT, article by Douglas Starr,"Brain Drugs," *Omni*, Jan 1983.
Researcher Lester A. Henry. "The Response to Acetycholine," *Scientific American,* Feb. 1977.

[383] "Research Behind Acoustic Brain Entrainment," pg. 9. www.neuroacoustic.org

[384] "Research Behind Acoustic Brain Entrainment," pg. 9. www.neuroacoustic.org

[385] "Research Behind Acoustic Brain Entrainment," pg. 9. www.neuroacoustic.org

- Catecholamines are vital for memory and learning.[386]
- Melatonin helps us sleep. As people age, they f ail to get enough sleep, which the body needs to regenerate. Theta brain waves increase melatonin levels on average by 98%.[387]
- Cortisol speeds up the body's aging mechanisms. Cortisol levels drop during theta brain waves.[388]
- DHEA increases one's resistance to disease. DHEA buffers against cortisol that we produce in response to stress.[389]
- Serotonin plays an important role in the central nervous system as a neurotransmitter in the modulation of anger, aggression, body temperature, mood, sleep, human sexuality, appetite, and metabolism.[390]

Focusing on our signature sounds and entering "the silence," which facilitates healing theta brainwaves, is a great way to receive information, such as answers to prayer. Let's say we are nervous; we can use the "sounds of silence" technique to receive guidance. First, get calm, still and listen to our inner sounds. Now, whatever comes to mind is our message from the inner core of our body and soul. For example, one could say, "Do I need this vitamin?" The answer can come from within, through feelings or in symbolic pictures.

---

[386] Dr. Margaret Patterson in collaboration with biochemist Dr. Ifor Capel at the Marie Curie Cancer Memorial Foundation Research Dept. in Surrey, England. "Research Behind Acoustic Brain Entrainment," pg. 8. www.neuroacoustic.org
[387] "Research Behind Acoustic Brain Entrainment," Pg. 11. www.neuroacoustic.org
[388]" Research Behind Acoustic Brain Entrainment," Pg. 11. www.neuroacoustic.org
[389] Dr. Vincent Giampapa, MD. from Longevity Institute International and vice president of the American Society of Anti Aging Medicine. "Research Behind Acoustic Brain Entrainment," pgs.10, 11. www.neuroacoustic.org
[390] *Wikipedia*

This communication or enlightenment that we receive is called many things. In Christianity it is called the Holy Spirit, in other disciplines it is called the Higher Self and there are other names as well.

Our signature sounds, and the "sounds of silence" are frequency representations of ourselves. They come from everything that we think, feel, eat and do; from the clothes we wear, the person we sit beside, the ground we walk on, the chairs we sit in and everything that happens to us and within us. Perhaps Jesus understood this because in the <u>Bible</u>, He said that, "as a man thinketh, so is he."

Subtle energies affect us more than we are aware. For example, a guru insisted on cooking his own food and cleaning his own laundry, claiming that if the cook was disgruntled then the cook's negative energy would blend with his food and become part of him. Therefore, he cooked and washed, while feeling peace and love. Wearing clothes that were lovingly washed put the feeling of love next to his skin - an organ with the ability to take in much energy through its extensive pores. He also ate vegetarian food lest he incorporate the horror of a cruel execution of an animal into his flesh and blood while eating meat.

At one time I thought this was extreme; then, I reflected that Sharry could hear different sounds from a red shirt or a blue one, the Templar cross, and a good versus bad mood. These tones interact with us as we incorporate all things around us into our energy. The things that we surround ourselves with become a part of ourselves.

Listening to the "sounds of silence" triggers the production of brain waves that stimulate our greater health, awareness, consciousness and well-being. Improving our integrity and harmony improves our physical, mental, emotional and spiritual energies. Listening to our signature sounds will hasten this blessed journey, changing our lives.

# Chapter Six

# Changing your Voice

Sound profoundly interacts with and influences matter. Photographs capture sound forming intricate shapes with various physical materials.

As mentioned in Part Two, Swiss physicist Hans Jenny made videos of sound creating shapes in sand. Similarly, Masuro Emoto photographed water freezing while being exposed to various types of sound and music. The resulting crystalline structure of the frozen water varied depending on the sounds that the freezing water was subjected to. These phenomena reveal sound's potential to mold and alter the human body.

Finally, Sharry demonstrates the powerful relationships between our voice, brain waves and health. Sound profoundly interacts with and influences matter, emotions and energy.

Why not consciously change the sounds in our voices for targeted benefits?

### *Exercise: Identifying and Changing Voice Qualities*

We can make changes to our voice in terms of:
- Volume
- Speed
- Pitches
- Dynamics of changing pitches
- Emotions carried on sounds
- Rhythm of phrasing
- Tempo
- Amount of breath in our voice
- Swallowing or projecting our voice
- Posture
- Equalization *(EQ),* which increases/decreases either high or low harmonics in a given pitch

Experiment changing each one of these variables and notice how your new voice changes the way you feel. Exaggerating each effect enhances the degree of change. Also, others will also feel differently about you when you use these different sounds in your voice.

Different voices yield interesting results. What message does a person who speaks rapidly convey versus one who speaks slowly and deliberately? How might we change the rhythm in our voice to subtly change the energy of our words? People who want to be more assertive should speak louder. An increase in the volume of a voice creates a firmer impression. One can sense a lack of strength in a feeble voice.

Many have played with the EQ button on their stereos. Turning up the EQ button to increases the treble qualities of sound, making it appear high-pitched and thin. In contrast, turning up the bass creates low tones that feel slower, heavier and more grounded. Have fun with your voice by turning up the treble and contrasting that by adding more bass.

You can change the pitch of your voice at appropriate times. If you wish to be forceful, add bass to your voice, making it thick and full.

In an experiment, I shoved a friend with my fingers while she was speaking. When she spoke with lower tones it was harder to push her. She was more rooted, grounded and stronger simply by lowering her voice!

### *Exercise: Injecting Emotion into Words*

The voice links our conscious mind with unconscious emotions. We experience emotions every second, whether or not we are conscious of them. Sounds "strike a chord" and tap our emotions through sympathetic resonance. When we speak, we engage emotions through resonance. We may not be conscious of this, but we can increase our awareness of subtle emotions. In fact, we can consciously select them!

We feel subtle feelings all the time, although we are not conscious of them. Easily we act out of alignment with these subtleties, creating inner discord. Concentrated attention on our tiny feelings heightens our awareness of them, allowing us to act in greater harmony. The truth sets us free! We achieve inner power when we act in alignment with subtle feelings.

When people speak their deep truth their walls come down and they allow you access to them. People believe and respect those who communicate with transparency. We achieve an influential power among others when we master attunement with our words and feelings.

This mastery begins by directing our attention to little feelings all the time and recognizing these same feelings in our words. It is not difficult, but requires persistence and concentration to notice these small variations in our feelings.

This exercise improves your ability to increase your awareness of emotional meaning within your spoken words. Select a feeling from the following list; then say a nonsensical sentence while focusing intently to convey the selected feeling. For example, repeat "Jack be nimble, Jack be quick, Jack jump over the candlestick," while deeply emoting each feeling from the list below.

- I am important.
- What I am saying is significant.
- I think I am falling in love
- I am sick and tired of life.
- I've had it with you.
- No one likes me.
- I care about you.
- Don't mess with me.
- Help me.
- I understand.
- I have a secret.
- I like you.
- You are boring.

Hazrat Inayat Khan elaborates, "What one 'speaks' is louder than what one says."[391] Successfully completing the exercise above illustrates this! The nanoVoice can document your success in this exercise.

Another way to fine tune your emotional overtones is to envision different roles that you may assume, such as teacher, mother, father, lover or friend. How does your voice change when your role changes? Can you be more effective in these roles if you perfect a fitting voice for each role? Notice that your voice and power of your messages may change even when your perspective changes. Also observe that your voice varies with your thoughts and feelings. For example, a teacher who thinks and feels the words she speaks enables students to get the lesson quicker than one who uses words without feelings and thoughts.

Select a desirable personality trait and observe how a person with that trait speaks. How is their voice different? When we copy their voice quality, we also create the energy of this desired attribute.

Recall a person's voice that is full of confidence. A confident person has a balanced voiceprint. The feeling of confidence is subtly carried on the words. If you speak with confidence, you will also feel and project confidence. People will respond to you differently when you use this confident voice quality.

Next time you watch experts discussing a topic on TV, notice each speaker's voice. They fight over the limelight, each voicing their opinion louder than the next. Two or more talk

---

[391] Khan, Hazrat, Inayat, The Music of Life, Omega Publishing: New Lebanon, N.Y., 1983, pg. 43.

at the same time, hoping to "solo" their opinion. The loudest spoken person does not necessarily win, but the one with the strongest charisma or "power." When the speaker believes in his words and exudes a strong feeling, others listen. People will listen to what we have to say too, when we use power in our words.

### *Exercise: Reconnecting with the Energy of Past Voices*

Our voice has changed many times throughout our lives reflecting physical, mental and emotional metamorphoses. For example, our voice at two years old was different than the voice we possessed at ages 17, 40 or 80. Our voice is also much different when we are depressed, in love or after we land that big contract at work.

When in a meditative state, imagine a time in the past. How did your voice sound then? Now, say your name aloud, while still pretending that you are in the past. For example, I vividly imagine being at a picnic when I was eight years old and I say, "I am Jill." I listen and feel the innocent emotions in my words.

Now select another memory, recreating the situation in your imagination and say your name again. How does it feel? Does it sound differently than the earlier voice? Our various voices contain the energy that we experienced at different times.

Here are some advantageous applications of this simple process.
- What was the best moment of your life? What did your voice sound like? If you recreate the voice, then you

recreate the energy of that moment. When you express this voice, you experience the accompanying energy.

- When have you felt the closest to God? What did your voice sound like then? Recreate that voice and you will go to that space, feeling the same divine connection!

- Remember a scene from childhood and submerse yourself in it. Now you can speak and hear your child's voice. If you go back early enough you will hear innocence and purity in your voice. Bring back those beautiful qualities by speaking as you did then.

- Recall a painful time, when your voice radiated negative emotions. Imagine reliving this event, but talk in an uplifting voice. This can change your perception of your painful memory so you move away from it. This can also facilitate an emotional transformation or release of the stored negative energy associated with this situation.

### *Exercise: Elements in the Voice*

Another variation of consciously using our voice to create positive change is demonstrated in the next exercise. In this case we are going to incorporate sounds of the following fundamental elements into our voice:[392]

- Metal
- Air
- Water
- Wood
- Fire

---

[392] "Vibrations pass from five distinct phases while changing from fine to gross. Each element - ether, air, fire water, earth - has a savor, color and form peculiar to itself." Khan, Hazrat, Inayat, The Music of Life, Omega Publishing: New Lebanon, N.Y., 1983, pg. 78.

- Earth

Many systems from various civilizations use the elements for balancing energy. The number of the elements and the elements themselves vary. The energies do not vary, but how they are categorized changes among various healing systems.

The elements represent energy that can be detected in our voices:[393]

- **Metal** has the feel of clarity and resonance. Some good teachers have metallic voices that keep the class awake and command attention. In an unbalanced state people with this voice can be overly meticulous or overwhelming in crowded places.
- **Air** has the feel of uplifting energy, taking one away from the earthly plane. This voice does not feel grounded or weighted down.
- **Water** emulates kindness and understanding. It can be intoxicating, soothing, healing and uplifting. A person with this voice links words and ideas. In an unbalanced state this voice type can be draining and sad.
- **Wood** has the feel of a soft and vibrant nature. A person with this sensitive voice needs peace and quiet.
- **Fire** emits enthusiasm, loving vibrations and can transmit joy. This quality can convey impressive, exciting, arousing and awakening impressions. On the flip side fire can be horrifying. When a person with this voice is unbalanced he can be overwhelming, to the point of hysteria.

---

[393]Maman, Fabien. Sound and Acupuncture. Tama-Do Press: Boulder, CO., 1997. Khan, Hazrat, Inayat, The Music of Life, Omega Publishing: New Lebanon, N.Y., 1983, pg. 95.

- **Earth creates** stillness, security, quietude, slow movement, reflection and a calm low pitch. It can offer hope, inspiration, encouragement and temptation. In an unbalanced condition, this person is too slow and depressed.

Which of these elemental sounds are in your voice? Your sounds may change over time reflecting your mood. Practice using all of these elemental sounds. Enhance the feelings associated with your words by adding the appropriate elemental sound.

Fabien Maman sums up voice energies, "The voice expresses 'perfectly' inner fear, anger, sadness or joy, and reveals even more subtle nuances which are related not only to emotions, but to a person's level of consciousness."[394]

The chart below details some targeted actions that a deliberate voice creates.

## Vocal Feng Shui

| Benefit | Elemental Sounds |
|---|---|
| To be flexible | Put water sounds in your voice |
| To increase strength | Add an earthy sound |
| To let go of the past | Use an airy voice |
| To command immediate attention | Increase fiery sounds in your voice |
| To calm someone down | Express an earthy sound in your voice |
| To express compassion | Strengthen watery sounds |

---

[394]Maman, Fabien. <u>Sound and Acupuncture</u>. Tama-Do Press: Boulder, CO., 1997. pg. 22.

You can manipulate your voice to create more of what you want in life. Use the elemental sounds in your voice to become more powerful, just as a persuasive speaker sways his audience. Use the voice sounds to balance troublesome relationships.

Your voice subtly affects people; a fiery voice repels a metallic one, while it gives stability to the airy voice. A person with an earthy voice can make a water person feel stifled, while it soothes a fiery voice.

### *Exercise: Empowering Your Words*

In antiquity, some "mystery-school"[395] students pronounced each letter in the alphabet with as much love as they could convey. After hours of practice, they then said a single word with love. They continued saying many words until all that flowed out of their mouths reflected love. The practice of saying words from their hearts and not just their mouths changed the way others responded to them.

In a similar exercise, visualize each letter of a word surrounded in white light. Use your imagination, then slowly inhale the word and pretend to assimilate the light around each letter. Now say each letter and visualize its light going down your spine and radiating out to all parts of your body. After this exercise, does the word sound differently? How do you feel?

---

[395] In history mystery schools were guarded and hidden schools that taught higher spiritual knowledge to a select few, so that powerful secrets would not be available to unscrupulous people.

Throughout antiquity spiritual groups placed solemn emphasis on sacred words. The Sufi master, Hazrat Inyat Khan, said, "As we delve into the mysteries of life we discover the whole secret is hidden in what we call words. All occult science, all mystical practices are based upon the science of the word or sound."[396] Evolved beings are said to carry energy and intent on their voices. Jesus is well known for his healing miracles, many of which were triggered by his words and commands. The Sufi's understand this phenomenon. "The word will have power according to the illumination of the soul."[397] With practice, we can increase the power in our own words.

Down through the ages, many groups projected energy in words to increase their consciousness, their intellect, health, emotions and spirituality. The Indian yogis have long honored and worshipped the sound god.[398] Ancient meditations use extinct Sanskrit words are still used today because of the power of sound and vibration that they contain. The Hindus and seers of the Semantic races also assigned great importance to the "word." The sacred "word" was esteemed in the Jewish religion. Some words were so sacred that their usage was restricted. Islam contains a doctrine of the mystical "word." The Zoroastrians, who had their religion long before Buddha and the Christ, always

---

[396]Khan, Inayat, Hazrat. The Music of Life, Omega Publishing: New Lebanon, N.Y., 1983. pg. 228.
[397] Khan, Inayat, Hazrat. The Music of Life. Omega Publishing: New Lebanon, N.Y., 1983. pg. 234.
[398] Worship of Nada Brahman by T.S. Parthasarathy. "The real aim of Indian music has always been to attain self realization and through music ... this is achieved much sooner." http://svbf.org/journal/vol1no2/nada.pdf

preserved their sacred "words."[399] Many ancient traditions instructed disciples to chant the names of god and other powerful words for internal transformation and power.

Although the actual word changes in these different traditions, the idea of sacred and uplifting energy within the word remains the same. We can attach this energy to our words as well, creating inner transformation as well as affecting those who hear our sounds.

Creation stories from many ancient and modern religions give sound and the spoken word an important role in the creation of the universe:

- "In the beginning was the Word, and the Word was with God, and the Word was God." John 1:1 *(A spoken word is a sound.)*
- Hindu tradition states in the Vedas, "In the beginning was Brahman with whom was the Word. And the Word is Brahman."
- Thot, an Egyptian God, was believed to have created the world with his voice.
- According to Mayan tradition, in the Popul Vuh *(the book on creation),* humans are given life by the power of the Word.
- In the Hopi Indian tradition, "Spider Woman" sings songs of creation to produce animated life.
- The Satapatha Brahmana reads, "In the beginning was God with power through speech. God said, 'May I be many...may I be propagated through subtle speech,' he united himself with that speech and became pregnant."

---

[399]Khan, Inayat, Hazrat. The Music of Life, Omega Publishing: New Lebanon, N.Y., 1983. pg. 228.

- In Chinese Buddhism, the Divine Voice calls forth the form of the universe.

If God used sound or words to create heaven and earth, what are you creating with your voice?

## Perfecting the Energy of our Words

What energy accompanies your words? Let's improve the energy that you send when you project your own name. In this exercise you will increase your consciousness of the messages and energy that you send to others when you introduce yourself. Most people are not aware that they tell others how they want to be treated, as they introduce themselves.

What voice do you use when you say your name? Say your name several times and feel how it sounds. These questions will help analyze your unconscious messages:
- Do you love your name as it comes out of your mouth?
- What feeling do you project?
- What are the speed volume, pitch, and EQ when you say your name?
- What is your posture, which affects your voice? Does the sound vibrate in the spine? It sounds richer, fuller, softer, lower and yet confident when it does. This also increases the volume of harmonics in your voice. The voice sounds differently with the head tilted up or down. The pitch goes up when you lean your head up. When your scalp or forehead is tightened your voice rises in pitch and it slightly lowers as these muscles relax.
- Where does your name vibrate in your body? The head? The gut? The throat? Thoughts resonate in your head

when you are in a thinking mode. When you have an emotional message the sound comes from your gut. When the sound reverberates in your throat, you are projecting or reaching out to others.

- Say your name and notice changes in your pitch. Is there a change in the pitch at the end of your name? When the pitch goes up, you project a more positive feeling as if you are raising energy. When the pitch dips at the end of your name, you project a sad feeling. When it lowers a tiny bit and is slower paced, it projects self-assuredness. What kind of melody do you project when you say your name?

- Do you say your name like a question, expressing uncertainty about who you are and what you want?

- Do you swallow your breath? Do you swallow the sound in your mouth, mumbling? What is it that you are holding back?

- If you imagine your name as a ball of colored air coming out of your mouth, does it shoot across the room? Only go several inches from your face? Or stay in your mouth? The energy of your voice can be aggressive or reach out to others.

- Is air going through your nose? This sound is less clear and does not projected well. The muffled sound reflects lack of confidence and clarity.

- With which ear are you listening to your name? Try hearing your name only with your right ear. Now cover your right ear and hear your name from your left ear. The sound appears more immediate and clear when you "hear" from your right ear. Your dictation will also be clearer when you get in the habit of "hearing" from your right ear.

- When you breathe, how deep is your breath? Before you say your name do you take a shallow breath or a deep one? Try taking a deep breath so that the air goes to your lower belly and hear the subtle sounds of your name change, as it becomes more rooted, confident and self-assured. Finally, relax your lower gut, as if it were falling onto the floor, and then take a breath. Your words now reflect a deeper conviction.
- Ancient Hindi texts describe benefits of certain vowels: E denotes a feminine quality of grace, wisdom, beauty and receptivity. O and U have a masculine quality of power and expression. A has the perfection of both qualities. What vowels are in your name?
- The mystic Sufis have also studied the impact of vowel sounds. They suggest that Ah represents the feeling of unity, opens your heart energy and radiates energy. Ooo *(sounds like cool)* relaxes and draws energy inward. Eee relates to mental energy. Hmm vibrates the top of your head and connects you to your higher spirit. Oh *(as in go)* combines ah and oo, which effects the endocrine system. Are any of these sounds found in your name?

What does our voice tell others about how we want to be treated? We readily believe others are independent and autonomous; but subconsciously they are affected by our messages. People respond to the qualities of our voice. Sharry says, "People treat you the way you train them."[400] We exchange feelings and energies with words, making our voice a bridge.

---

[400] Edwards, Sharry. The Making of a Soul, Sound Health: Albany, OH., 1988. pg. 20.

People react to the subtle energy we send out on words…energy that we may not be aware of. We can become more aware of our deeper messages and control them.

### *Exercise: Voices We Like*

Another method to develop our voice is to study the voices of people we admire. Keep a list of voices that you find desirable. We benefit from simply copying voices that we like. Within our favorite voices are energy and qualities that we desire. There is a reason why we are attracted to certain music, sounds and voices. We are seeking energies that we need to maintain our inner harmony and balance. These attributes are within our grasp waiting to be discovered, developed and expressed in our own voice!

For example, I like Sean Connery's voice. It is solid and strong, yet gentle. I sense patience and understanding with his voice. It has a slower pace than mine, with more bass tones. I sense that it is not easily swayed. There are some qualities in that voice that I want. I desire a steady and gentle strength that comfortably stands its ground. I am too quick to please others. My personal adaptations to the sound of my voice would be to add more bass tones and slow down its pace. Mimicking the sounds of Sean Connery's voice enables me to harmonize my own energy, while developing desired attributes.

In summary, we can analyze voices for good qualities and practice these attributes by changing our voices. All change does not come from exerting our will power. Sometimes it comes from a change in energy, which can be readily achieved by changing our voice.

## *Exercise: Voices We Do Not Like*

A person's voice contains a wealth of information that we can instantly access. We can access the body's energies and messages, even ones that are subconscious. Hazrat Inayat Khan tells us, "There is a sense within us that can understand 'language' spoken without words."[401] We can quickly interpret information that is carried on their voices.

We receive warnings when we hear unpleasant qualities in people's voices. Here are a few voices that I do not like:

- **Demanding voices** have energy that projects out. It has a jabbing effect and it swirls to the right.
- **Whining** voices rotate counter clockwise and suck in energy.
- A **boring** voice never slips down to the solar plexus. It resonates only from the upper part of the body as if the person has no feeling in their words. They feel disconnected from their words.
- The **manipulative** voice has a sweetness that lacks fullness and deep tones. The rhythm is compelling.
- The **loud** voice attempts to control you.
- The **soft muffled** voice sucks your attention and energy in.

We can develop our ability to hear unspoken words. Just paying close attention to subtle inflections increases our understanding of what people do not say. Most of what people say is in between the words. Many conversations are

---

[401] Khan, Inayat, Hazrat. The Music of Life, Omega Publishing: New Lebanon, N.Y., 1983. pg. 146.

superficial; while the underlying emotional content is revealing.

With training you can hear when someone is not telling the truth and when he is not wholly committed to his words. When people are not in their truth:

- The flow of breath changes. They almost hold their breath through a lie.
- There is less distance between the pitches in different words. These words are planned, flat and calculated.
- People do not project their words freely, as if the words hide in the back of their mouths.

Each person has a distinctive "voice" when lying. Get someone to say a few lies in fun and notice the subtleties in his voice. When these subtleties surface again, expect less than the truth!

It is easier to notice a liar than to acknowledge our own lack of truthfulness. Unconsciously, we hang on to ideas that are not true for us. People tell us what is in our best interest and we mold ourselves into what other people expect. We assume other people's beliefs without being aware that their advice does not ring true for us.

We are taught to be polite, avoid confrontation and to be pleasing. Should's, ought-to's and politically correct behavior influence and define us. We censor our honest words, not admitting things we dislike. We unknowingly push uncomfortable feelings into our subconscious mind, which has an invisible hold on us. We do not want others to know our deep feelings. We are different on the inside, than what we show others. Think about revealing your secrets to your mother-in-law, priest, competitors, or boss.

People maintain appearances by using insincere words that are in opposition to what they are feeling. They change their words to fit in. By saying one thing and meaning another, they unconsciously create internal tension. When people are fully honest they release stored, negative emotional energy. The truth sets them free.

One of the difficulties of speaking words that reflect the depth of who we are is that it is difficult to "know ourselves!" We can use our own voice to investigate our hidden subconscious feelings by listening to its subtle qualities.

How does our voice change when we are not committed to our words? How is our voice different when are polite, but not honest? Try the short exercise below:

- Try saying "I don't care" when you do. Pay attention to your voice qualities. When you hear these qualities, your voice and gut feelings are out of alignment.
- Now say that you do not care about something, when you truly don't. Notice the difference between the two voices.
- Pretend you are a movie star and you are acting. Now say, "I do not care" when you do. While acting one can say things that are not true, with close to a normal speaking voice. When pretending to be someone else, you disconnect your words and personal subconscious messages.

Suppressed emotions can surprise us, revealing clues about what invisible, emotional baggage we store. By recognizing our truth on deeper levels we grow.

- **Sacral area.** Sound resonating in our gut *(three to five inches below our navel)* carries our passions and emotions. Sexual, emotional and balance issues are carried from this chakra.
- **Solar plexus.** Sounds filling the area of our solar plexus chakra *(three to five inches above our navel)* resound with confidence and an empowered sense of self worth. Personal power is employed in this chakra.
- **Heart.** Sounds from our heart radiate love. Love energy and feelings about relationships vibrate in this area. Compassion and forgiveness are rooted here.
- **Throat.** The tones from our throat project to accommodate a large audience, reflecting clarity and self-expression.
- **Third Eye.** The thoughts from this spot between our two eyebrows create a dreamy, intuitive feeling. Intuition and wisdom resonate here.
- **Crown of our Head.** The thoughts vibrating in the top of our head create a holy feeling. We can feel our voice resonate here by acting selflessly and spiritually.

### Change Yourself with Your Voice

It is difficult to make a personal change using will power alone. That is why so many New Year's resolutions fail. We *can* change our essence quickly and effectively by altering our voice. We can change the pitches and rhythms that the body hears every time we speak. Changing our voice enables us to transmute our negative feelings, learn emotional lessons and make personal changes easier.

Hazrat Inayat Khan reminds us, "Healing that comes through a change of mind or feeling, instigated by personal will,

simply does not have the sustaining power to be permanent or complete. True healing requires the transformational ability of sound." [403]

Few people realize that they can change their life force with sound! Khan gives us more insight, "One need not be a singer, but every person should give some part of his day, even the shortest time, five or ten or fifteen minutes, to the development of his voice."[404]

Hazrat Inayat Khan comments, "The fortunate person has a different voice than the one who is not so fortunate. If you gather five people who have proved to be very fortunate and listen to their voices, you will find how great the difference is between their voices and the ordinary. When you compare the voices of great people, regardless of their occupations, with the voices of others, you will find there is a difference."[405]

Khan concludes, "From the voice, you can determine the stage of a person's particular evolution. You do not need to see him; just his voice will tell you how far he has evolved. There is no doubt that the character of a person is evident in his voice. At every stage, infancy, childhood, young adult and more advanced aged, the pitch of the voice changes. Advanced age is a culmination of what a person has gained throughout a lifetime and the voice is indicative of this

[403]Sikh Guru Nanak, pg. 143.
[404] Khan, Inayat, Hazrat. The Music of Life, Omega Publishing: New Lebanon, N.Y., 1983. pg. 277.
[405] Khan, Hazrat, Inayat, The Music of Life. Omega Publishing: New Lebanon, N.Y., 1983, pg. 95.

# Appendix A
# The Healing Flower Symphonies

## "The Chicory Flower: The Motherliness Flower
### *From Demanding Love to Giving Love Freely"[410]*

The chicory flower song helps those who are overly cautious for children, relatives and friends. These people smugly correct what they consider wrong. They also require that those they love be near them.[411]

The chicory melody crescendos from a seductive and demanding beat, as if it was singing, "This is what I'll do for you, when you do what I want you to!" The chicory personality seeks to control someone, to insure he does what the chicory person perceives is right.

The unchanging seductive and rigid beat in this song endures while the melody frees itself from the chains of the control of the rhythm. The feeling of demanding energy is replaced by the feeling of enjoyment. The continual seductive beat surprises us, similar to the wonderful feeling one gets when one stops controlling people and loves them unconditionally. This new type of love produces a beautiful peace, not possible with the energy of control.

## "The Cerato Flower: The Intuition Flower
### *From Indecisiveness to Inner Certainty"[412]*

The cerato flower helps those who lack confidence in making decisions. Constantly seeking advice, these people are often misguided.[413]

The symphony builds to a peak that is never culminated…as the melodic line changes its direction and rethinks the melody line

---

[410] Mechthild and Scheffer. Encyclopedia of Bach Flower Remedies. Healing Arts Press: Rochester, Vermont, 2001. pg. 76.

[411] A quote from Edward Bach by Mechthild and Scheffer. Encyclopedia of Bach Flower Remedies. Healing Arts Press: Rochester, Vermont, 2001. pg. 76.

[412] Mechthild and Scheffer. Encyclopedia of Bach Flower Remedies. Healing Arts Press: Rochester, Vermont, 2001. pg. 62.

[413] A quote from Edward Bach by Mechthild and Scheffer. Encyclopedia of Bach Flower Remedies. Healing Arts Press: Rochester, Vermont, 2001. pg. 62.

again and again without any conclusions. This lack of "knowing what to do" or decisiveness builds pressure. Worry clouds the music until it discovers a simple and happy "knowing" of what to do.

## "Agrimony: The Honesty Flower
### *From Pretended Harmony to Inner Peace*[414]

The vibration of the agrimony flower uplifts people who love peace and are distressed by argument. To avoid confrontation, these people sacrifice too much. They feel tormented, compromised, restless and worried, while they hide their negative feelings.[415]

A beautiful harmony is presented in the agrimony music, but the after-vibes of the notes are bent out of tune. The lovely melody leaves a bad taste in the mouth, just as inner turmoil builds with lack of emotional integrity. The soul flower symphony then raises its vibration into pure and absolute harmony, creating the transparent and deep emotions of peace.

## "Centary: The Service Flower
### *From Passive Service to Active Service*"[416]

The centaury song blesses those who are kind, quiet and gentle, but anxious to serve others. People on this path overtax themselves, becoming more like servants than willing helpers. Due to their good nature they do more than their share of work, neglecting their own mission in life.[417]

The centaury melody sounds like a ballerina dancing on a music box. She twirls and delights people as she goes round and round in her prescribed path. She is beautiful, yet mechanical, repeating what movements are expected. The dance of the music box ballerina then unravels and freely flows, as if the chords ascend into light.

---

[414] Mechthild and Scheffer. Encyclopedia of Bach Flower Remedies. Healing Arts Press: Rochester, Vermont. 2001. pg. 44.
[415] A quote from Edward Bach by Mechthild and Scheffer. Encyclopedia of Bach Flower Remedies. Healing Arts Press: Rochester, Vermont, 2001. pg. 44.
[416] Mechthild and Scheffer. Encyclopedia of Bach Flower Remedies. Healing Arts Press: Rochester, Vermont, 2001. pg. 58.
[417] A quote from Edward Bach byMechthild and Scheffer. Encyclopedia of Bach Flower Remedies. Healing Arts Press: Rochester, Vermont. 2001. pg. 58.

life. These quiet people are dissatisfied, living more in the future than in the present.[427]

A breath becomes the percussion beat, combining with diffuse tones to create a state of dreaminess. Foggy tones and echoes muffle clarity. As the song continues, the warmth of the sun beckons the soul to awaken, to see more clearly and dance in the glory of the fully awakened light and with clear melodic tones.

## "Gentian: The Belief Flower
### From Doubt to Trust"[428]

The gentian flower has special gifts for easily discouraged people. Any small delay causes doubt and disheartens them. Doubt transforms into the energy of faith and overcomes obstacles.[429]

The frantic struggle and scurry of the music anticipates Murphy's Law: "Anything that can go wrong will!" While focusing on potential problems, the melody worries, as it is never satisfied with any answers. The steady frustration from struggles and the emotion of doubt are later replaced by a sense of "knowing" that things will work out for the best.

A steady "ah" sound underlines the conclusion of the Gentian melody. The "ah" sound is said to be associated with the heart, love and compassion. The "ah" sound is found in the words "Ma" and "Pa." The same sound is in the name of many gods and goddesses, such as Jesuah *(Jesus)*, Muhammad, Buddha and Krishna. An open heart easily allows the energy of trust to enter in.

## "Scleranthus: The Balance Flower
### From Inner Conflict to Inner Equilibrium"[430]

---

[427] A quote from Edward Bach by Mechthild and Scheffer. <u>Encyclopedia of Bach Flower Remedies</u>. Healing Arts Press: Rochester, Vermont, 2001. pg. 81.

[428] Mechthild and Scheffer. <u>Encyclopedia of Bach Flower Remedies</u>. Healing Arts Press: Rochester, Vermont, 2001. pg. 95.

[429] A quote from Edward Bach by Mechthild and Scheffer. <u>Encyclopedia of Bach Flower Remedies</u>. Healing Arts Press. Rochester, Vermont, 2001. pg. 95.

[430] Mechthild and Scheffer. <u>Encyclopedia of Bach Flower Remedies.</u> Healing Arts Press: Rochester, Vermont, 2001. pg. 161.

Those who can't make up their minds are relieved with the energetic power of the scleranthus flower. These indecisive people are usually quiet and bear their difficulties alone.[431]

The music goes this way and that, mulling over the negative sides of options. Despair and tension arise from the lack of confidence that any decision will not produce the desired results. The song eases into the feeling of confidence, like the feeling you get when you know you are doing the right thing. Repeated experiences of "knowing" create feelings of peace and inner balance, leaving the feelings of isolation and dread behind.

### "Rock Rose: The Liberation Flower
### *From Panic to Heroic Courage"*[432]

The rock rose soul type lives "mutely under intense pressure of fear."[433]

In the rock rose symphony gloom and fear drip onto the listener, as the sound of a heart beat struggles with terror. Eventually, a sobering resolve is birthed; one can overcome any obstacle. Determination and power increase as the momentum of energy builds and lifts the listener into emotional space of courage.

Sample "The Healing Flower Symphonies" at
www.jillswingsoflight.com.

---

[431] A quote from Edward Bach by Mechthild and Scheffer. Encyclopedia of Bach Flower Remedies. Healing Arts Press: Rochester, Vermont, 2001. pg. 161.

[432] Mechthild and Scheffer. Encyclopedia of Bach Flower Remedies. Healing Arts Press: Rochester, Vermont, 2001. pg. 152.

[433] Barnard, Julian. Bach Flower Remedies: Form and Function. Lindisfarne Books; Great Barrington, MA., 2004. pg. 132.

"Some say it was the Devil in music because the tritone is so close to the interval of a perfect 5th that two monks could too easily sing dissonantly as they tried to chant in pure parallel 5ths. But this cannot be the only reason because when they sang out of tune anywhere else, those wrong intervals weren't the Devil. They were just out of tune.

"An April 2006 article in BBC News Magazine quotes Bob Ezrin, a former business associate of mine and music producer of rock bands like Pink Floyd, KISS and Alice Cooper, as saying: 'It apparently was the sound used to call up the beast. There is something very sexual about the tritone'.

"While walking the streets of London some years back, Bob and I had discussed this subject and conjectured that the symmetric contraction of the tritone must have been taken as a symbol of symmetry in the human body and thereby sexuality and carnal knowledge. At the time, this was the only reason I could imagine for its exclusion from the Church and avoidance in music theory. There were no other psychological or physiological studies I knew that suggested the tritone was some kind of harmonic Viagra to enhance feelings of sexuality. But even if this were found to be the case, surely the procreative act should be considered a beautiful spiritual experience!

"Probably the most common reason given for the evil reputation of the tritone is its connection to the number '666', the Number of the Beast referenced in the Biblical Book of Revelation. The importance of this number appears to have originated in the ancient Hebrew practice of gematria, or number geometry known today as numerology, where the tritone's 3 wholetones *(the Devil's Trident perhaps)* spanning 6 semitones could have suggested three consecutive sixes.

"A more likely gematria theory correlates to the number 216 as the ancient Hebrew symbol for God. It was believed that finding the missing code for this number would bring about the return of the Hebrew Satan in a final showdown, thus triggering a Messianic Age of peace. Not coincidentally, the cube root of 216 is six, or 6×6×6. Perhaps the missing code for the Hebrew Satan was once associated with the tritone.

"Similarly, when 6 tritones, each composed of 6 semitones, are stacked over 3 octaves it surrounds the pentagonal cycle of perfect 5ths with a triple hexagonal cycle of tritones, or 666. In the end, it seems to make little difference which theory we choose to accept because alignments with the old Beast of Christianity pops up everywhere we look. As we shall see later, these sixes are neither coincidences nor silly mysterious numerological symbolisms, but are in fact numerical proportions related to the physics of highly resonant vibration. Still, the speculation surrounding the tritone continues because nowhere in the mountains of religious or scientific literature will you find it taken seriously and explained as a natural property of acoustics.

"In the final analysis, the most likely justification for the tritone's evil reputation arrives to us from the harmonically inspired mythology of the Greeks and the "error" Pythagoras found in the irreconcilable schisma at mid-octave. This error, intertwined with the pentagram, golden ratio and Devil's interval were nothing less than the Biblical forbidden fruit with the tritone itself an audible version of 'original sin.'

"Yet even when we disregard religious and numeric symbolism there remains a real sensation of tension in the tritone and an anticipated tendency for it to automatically spring closed. We don't really need religious symbolisms and stories to see how the priests could have concluded that something demonic was involved. At a time of deep mysticism and belief in satanic forces, the tritone was probably seen as some kind of daemonic planchette, sliding along a musical Quija board under its own supernatural power.

"Far more than just a musical concept, the tritone offers us a window into the collective psyche, touching on our concept of God and belief in good and evil. Like an anthropological microscope equipped with a musical lens, the tritone allows us to see inside a society shaped by the Roman Catholic Church. Indeed, it brings into focus a world still largely under the influence of its anti-pagan, anti-harmonic doctrine.

"As for me, I'm going to listen to a little Bach, enjoy the musical universe we live in and do my part to try and change things for the better. This is my new unapproved harmonic worldview."

# Jill Mattson:  Artist, Composer    and Author

Jill Mattson is an accomplished Artist, Musician and Author who brings her deep spiritualism and intense curiosity and wonder to the many creative passions that she pursues.  Jill seeks to help others achieve personal growth and healing through her paintings, music and writings.

Jill is a three-time author and widely recognized expert and composer in the emerging field of *Sound Healing*!   Jill lectures throughout the United States on **"Ancient Sounds ~ Modern Healing"** - taking followers on an exciting journey revealing the Healing Power of Sound.  She unveils secrets from ancient cultures as well as the latest findings of the modern scientific community showing the incredible power and healing capabilities of sound.

Jill Mattson is a prolific Healing Arts Musician & Composer, Author and Artist.  She draws on her extensive research of modern Sound Healing, and 17 year study of Antiquities and Secret Societies in her lectures, workshops and writings. Jill has produced and recorded numerous CD's utilizing her classical musical training and Sound Healing techniques.

**Music samples, art, videos, articles:**
www.jillswingsoflight.com,

**Soundhealing** website:
www.soundspiritandmatter.com

**Art**:
redbubble.com/jillmattson, artist rising.com/JillMattson

**Soundhealing newsletter** and **free soundhealing mp3's**:
www.jillshealingmusic.com and www.jillswingsoflight.com
www.paintyoursoul.com

**Social Networks**:
myspace.com/jillswingsoflight. and YouTUBE jillswingsoflight.

**Contact**
jillimattson@yahoo.com